REGULATORY POLITICS IN TRANSITION

INTERPRETING AMERICAN POLITICS
Michael Nelson, Series Editor

Regulatory Politics in

TRANSITION

MARC ALLEN EISNER

The Johns Hopkins University Press   Baltimore and London

© 1993 The Johns Hopkins University Press
All rights reserved
Printed in the United States of America on acid-free paper

The Johns Hopkins University Press
2715 North Charles Street
Baltimore, Maryland 21218-4319
The Johns Hopkins Press Ltd., London

Library of Congress Cataloging-in-Publication Data

Eisner, Marc Allen.
    Regulatory politics in transition / by Marc Allen Eisner.
        p.   cm.—(Interpreting American politics)
    Includes bibliographical references and index.
    ISBN 0-8018-4557-2 (hc.: acid-free paper).—ISBN 0-8018-4558-0
(pbk.: acid-free paper)
    1. Industry and state—United States.   I. Title.   II. Series.
HD3616.U46E37   1993
338.973—dc20   92-40435

A catalog record for this book is available from the British Library

To My Parents

Contents

Foreword

ONE OF THE CRUDER EFFECTS OF BOTH THE "BEHAVIORAL revolution" and the more recent public-choice movement in modern political science was that the institutions of American government came to be regarded by many scholars as a kind of passive, neutral basketball court on which the great game of politics is played by a host of private and public participants. As a corrective, Theda Skocpol, Stephen Skowronek, and a number of other political scientists have recently created a "state-capacity" approach to the study of government and politics. They argue that the staff, autonomy, legislative mandate, and other resources of bureaucratic agencies have much to do with how the state affects and is affected by the society. To state-capacity theorists, government institutions are less like a basketball court than a golf course, where the idiosyncratic mix of land, weather conditions, and hazards substantially shapes both how the game is played and how it turns out.

Marc Allen Eisner's *Regulatory Politics in Transition* is very much in the state-capacity tradition. Eisner skillfully traces the history of federal regulation through four successive regulatory regimes in the period from 1880 to the present. A regulatory regime, according to Eisner, is "a historically specific configuration of policies and institutions which structures the relationship between social interests, the state, and economic actors in multiple sectors of the economy." Each regime is sustained by "a unique synthesis of interests, political-economic ideas, and administrative reform doctrines."

The first regulatory regime, a child of the Progressive Era, was the *market regime*. Its main purpose was to restore, through government regulation, some semblance of market competition in the face of emerging national monopolies and oligopolies. The *associational regime,* which was created in response to the Great Depression of the 1930s, sought to use regulatory policies to promote industrial stability through the organization and integration of business groups into the governmental process. The regulatory reach of the *societal regime,* of the 1960s and 1970s, extended to internal business operations in an effort to protect citizens from the unpleasant health and environmental side-effects of large-scale industrial production. Finally, in the late 1970s and the 1980s, a largely deregulatory *efficiency regime* was created to remedy the nation's poor macroeconomic performance by reducing the government's role in the economy.

Continuities as well as contrasts mark this succession of regimes. In particular, Eisner finds, each of the four regimes included an effort to enhance the natural- and social-scientific expertise of federal regulatory agencies. Such enhancements occur through both the hiring of more experts and their retention in office, so that the expertise they bring to the agencies has cumulative force over an extended period of time. Thus, Eisner concludes, state capacity has grown in recent years because of the trend toward replacing lawyers, many of them policy generalists who remained in the public sector only for a short time, with specialized, long-staying economists and research scientists. This transformation in staff expertise has reduced most agencies' need to rely on interest groups for the data on which to base their decisions; it has also made it harder for members of Congress and their staffs (mostly lawyers) and for all but a few citizens and groups (mostly nonspecialists) to monitor, much less influence, agency behavior.

Eisner argues that the autonomy from public (and even statutory) influence that accompanies the recent growth in state capacity is disturbing. "Professionalization insulates both policies and agencies' decisionmaking from popular politics," he concludes. "It also enhances agencies' responsiveness to debates within the [academic] disciplines and within the specialized policy communities surrounding most policy areas. The consensus within these communities regarding the justification for certain policies and enforcement priorities may have little relation to an agency's mandate or to the political consensus."

MICHAEL NELSON

Acknowledgments

I INTRODUCED EARLIER VERSIONS OF THE FOLLOWING ARGU-ments to audiences at the New England Political Science Association meeting in 1991 and 1992, at the Midwest Political Science Association meeting in 1991, and at the American Political Science Association meeting in 1992. Discussants and participants at these meetings provided useful comments and forced me to sharpen my arguments. Michael Nelson, Jeff Worsham, and a reader for the Johns Hopkins University Press provided careful comments on the manuscript. Over the past two years, I have presented the central arguments in various contexts at Wesleyan University. My colleagues in Wesleyan's Department of Government and John E. Andrus Center for Public Affairs proved particularly willing to weather my discussions of regulatory policy change. My students had no choice. In addition to a supportive environment, Wesleyan provided a project grant to support some of the research.

I reserve the greatest thanks for my wife, Patricia. Without her love and friendship, my work would be hollow. Patricia and my sons, Jonathan and Benjamin, were often forced to function as a family of three as Papa worked on his book. I have dedicated this book to my parents, Dale and Sharon Eisner. Although the miles separate us, they continue to contribute to my work in many ways.

Introduction

THE TERM *REGULATION* ENCOMPASSES A BROAD ARRAY OF policies governing economic activity and its consequences. Regulatory policies address firms' entry into and exit from particular markets; prices; rates of return; and modes of competition; as well as the characteristics of the goods being produced, the quantities being produced, the means of production, and the negative externalities (such as pollution) arising from the production process. Such policies purposefully restrict the behavior of corporations and often impose large costs on the economy and the consuming public. They shape economic development by influencing investment and production decisions. By placing constraints on the production process and forcing corporations to internalize certain costs, regulatory policies affect the performance of American firms in domestic and international markets. Given the effects of regulation and the growing concerns with U.S. economic performance, it should not be surprising that much of the recent literature on regulation addresses its economic effects and the question of whether these costs are justified.

For many politicians and policy analysts, regulation has been the villain of choice for many years. Critics of regulation, seeking to ignite traditional American fears of big government, have decried the "regulatory timebomb" and "social engineering" based on the imposition "command and control" policies. This specter can easily be contrasted with "the market," a natural institution that promotes individual choice, entrepreneurial initiative, and business efficiency. Such simple contrasts are ideologically charged and can be politically convenient. Unfortunately, they obscure an important fact about regulatory policies. Rather than being the product of an oppressive elite or of a partnership between monopolies and the state, the major regulatory initiatives of the past hundred years originated in popular demands that were stimulated, in most cases, by the perceived threats of economic and social change. These demands were not simply translated into policy but have been linked to prevailing political-economic theories and administrative doctrines. Thus, regulatory change has often taken the form of a unique synthesis of policy change and institutional reform.

This book has three broad objectives. The first objective, and the primary one, is to explore the origins of regulatory policies and examine the factors that promoted significant shifts in regulation during the Progressive Era, the New Deal, and the contemporary period. This goal is novel because, in sharp contrast with many contemporary treatments of regulation, this study focuses on broad policy objectives and patterns of state-economy relations. The contemporary debates surrounding many regulatory policies focus almost exclusively on costs and benefits. The economic consequences of regulation are an important subject that deserves sustained scholarly attention. However, when seeking to understand regulatory policy it is useful to move beyond the narrow focus of many contemporary regulatory studies. Although the goals of each regulatory policy have definite economic implications, the purpose often extends beyond the technical features of the problems facing a particular sector of the economy. From the Interstate Commerce Act in 1887 to contemporary regulatory legislation, regulation has been one means of accommodating economic change and addressing its consequences. Thus, although the goal of the Clean Air Act of 1970 was to reduce air pollution to acceptable levels, the act's legislative supporters were also trying to force greater corporate accountability and protect the public from the more dangerous by-products of an advanced industrial economy. This broader purpose united the environmental legislation with other policy initiatives of the period which were designed to promote consumer protection and prevent workplace injury and disease.

This primary goal of this book is also unusual because it requires the consideration of multiple policies initiated during a given period. Regulatory studies usually focus on a single policy or a related set of policies. In light of the complex administrative and technical features of many regulatory policies, this focus is, in many ways, necessary. Despite the considerable merits of policy-specific studies, however, such an approach may be too narrow to situate regulatory initiatives within their historical and social setting, and may veil the purpose of public action, broadly construed. Examining multiple policies entails obvious costs: the depth of the analysis must be sacrificed to achieve greater coverage.

However, by examining a group of policies inaugurated during a given period, one can consider regulation in a more comprehensive fashion, exploring the political and economic dimensions of policies and the continuity across regulatory arenas.

The second goal of this book is to explore the interplay of institutional evolution and policy change. During the Progressive, New Deal, and contemporary periods, initiatives combined new regulatory policies and administrative reform programs. Elected officials actively designed and redesigned institutions to address a perceived lack of administrative capacities or to meet the specific political and technical demands of implementation. This dual focus on policy innovation and institutional change is crucial. Policy is purposeful *pattern of action* rather than a mere expression of intent or proclamation of goals.[1] Policy analysts must be concerned with the pattern of implementation actions directed toward a distinct set of objectives. Because regulatory legislation is often imprecise, policy is routinely defined through implementation. This being the case, one must examine the administrative tools and analytical models used in implementation. One must also examine the relationship between administrators and organized interest groups. These factors, when taken together, will determine what kinds of actions administrators are capable of executing, and whether these actions will bear any relationship to legislatively established goals.

Administrative capacities are not stagnant. They can change dramatically as a result of legislation, resource allocations, and staffing decisions; they are constantly evolving in response to the daily demands of policy implementation. Because implementation defines policy, changes in administrative capacities commonly drive parallel changes in policy. Access to new forms of expertise or the adoption of new planning and evaluation processes allows an agency to formulate new kinds of policies or improve on existing practices. The regulated groups or other social interests can be given a greater role in implementation or can be brought more fully into the policy process, thus lessening the demands on the agency's resources. Professionalization and a greater integration of interest groups into the policy process have been common in most regulatory agencies, particularly in the last several decades. As a consequence, the "pattern of action" has changed: new goals and priorities have been given concrete expression.

To explore the purposes of regulation, and the interplay of policy and institutions, this book focuses on regulatory regimes.[2] A regulatory regime is a historically specific configuration of policies and institutions which establishes certain broad goals that transcend the problems specific to particular industries. Institutions, because they provide certain interest groups with access to the making and implementation of policy, play a central role in structuring regulatory politics and the relationship between societal interests, the state, and economic actors (e.g., corporations, labor unions). Regulatory change often occurs in response to economic change and the uncertainty that such change creates. Grouops mobilize in hopes of preserviang or promoting certain values and interests. They demand an alteration in the relationship between the state and the economy to compensate for the changes in question. Officials link these demands with prevailing political-economic ideas and administrative reform doctrines, thus giving shape to a distinctive synthesis of new policy initiatives and institutional change.

Using a regime framework allows one to explore a wide range of policies and regulatory agencies throughout several historical periods. In the following chapters, I explore the policies, politics, and administrative routines of several agencies, including the Interstate Commerce Commission, the Federal Trade Commission, the Department of Agriculture, the National Labor Relations Board, the Securities and Exchange Commission, the Civil Aeronautics Board, the Environmental Protection Agency, and the Occupational Safety and Health Administration. Addressing a variety of agencies regulating everything from railroad rates to exposure to workplace carcinogens will make it possible to touch on several important themes in regulation, and adopting a historical focus will make it possible to consider how regulatory policy and administration have changed over time.

The third goal of this book is to explore the interrelationships between regulatory complexity, institutional design, and political accountability. Throughout the periods addressed in the following chapters, policy-makers have sought to address problems of ever-greater complexity. This change in regulatory focus, combined with efforts to reform agency administration, has promoted bureaucratic professionalization. Increasingly, regulatory policy is shaped by the interactions of attorneys, social scientists, and natural scientists working within the confines of the agencies. Quite naturally, in the process of designing and implementing policies, these experts bring their own disciplinary models and assumptions to bear.

Regulatory complexity can impede active participation in the policy process. Thus, recent decades have seen a series of administrative reforms designed to force agency action and promote greater opportunities for group participation. The regulatory legislation of the 1970s, for example, forced agencies to abide by strict implementation timetables and allowed citizens to sue to force agencies to perform nondiscretionary functions. An extended rule-making process provided greater access for groups interested in participating in the definition of regulatory policy. Although the attempts to ensure compliance and group access were laudable, they came into conflict with regulatory complexity in three ways.

First, the action-forcing provisions commonly required agencies to address highly complicated regulatory problems, such as pollution control, without providing adequate time for the underlying research and analysis to be done; and the entry of the courts into regulatory decision-making because of citizen suits sometimes forced agencies to abide by decisions that either had no basis in scientific evidence or conflicted with other policy objectives. In short, these politically expedient reforms were difficult to reconcile with the execution of complicated regulatory tasks. Second, democratic control can be made difficult by regulatory complexity. Because of the complexity of contemporary regulatory issues, elected officials commonly lack the expertise needed to engage in detailed regulatory design. Thus they delegate significant authority to regulatory agencies and try to structure the exercise of that authority through the imposition of timetables and administrative deadlines. This lack of expertise not only affects regulatory design but also affects the capacity of members of Congress to oversee and assess the decisions made at the agency level. Third, in spite of reforms, regulatory complexity can still create a significant barrier to participation. Although public-interest groups can hire professional staffs so as to be able to participate in regulatory policy debates, a given group's ability to adopt such a strategy depends on the resources available to it. Indeed, one of the great ironies of the contemporary period is that some of the interest groups that were instrumental in promoting the passage of new regulatory initiatives and designing institutions to maximize access have subsequently lacked the resources to participate effectively.

This book explores regulatory regime change in three broad periods: the Progressive Era, the New Deal, and the years since the late 1960s. Chapter 1 provides an overview of regulatory regime change and interplay of ideas, interests, and institutions. Chapters 2 and 3 address the regulatory regime that emerged during the period 1880–1920. Chapter 2 examines the economic transformation of the late nineteenth century, the demands for a new national regulatory presence, and the way in which these demands were transformed through the core themes of Progressivism into a set of policies and institutional reform measures. Chapter 3 presents a more detailed examination of the systems created for regulating the railroads and corporate conduct. In the first instance, because the structure of the railroad industry made it immune to market forces, the goal was to reproduce, by administrative means, rates roughly equivalent to those that would have been created in a market. Antitrust policy, in contrast, was created to revitalize markets, regulating forms of corporate behavior that threatened to create and extend monopoly power and thus undermine competition.

Chapters 4 and 5 examine the regulatory regime put into place during the New Deal. Chapter 4 focuses on the Great Depression and Roosevelt's recovery program. The model adopted in the National Industrial Recovery Act drew on the associationalism of the 1920s, albeit combining industrial self-regulation with a more explicit state role to produce a quasi-corporatist regulatory structure. This model was extended to the regulation of agriculture, industrial relations, and industrial finance, all of which are explored in Chapter 5.

Chapters 6 and 7 examine the regulatory regime created in the 1970s. Chapter 6 explores the roots of this regulatory regime, which include the prevailing critique of capitalism presented by New Left scholars, the related assessment of existing institutions and modes of regulation, and the demands for new regulations addressing the hazards that industrial society poses to health and environment. These elements, when taken together, shaped the basic principles of the new regulatory regime. Chapter 7 examines two of the principal regulatory agencies created during the 1970s: the Environmental Protection Agency and the Occupational Safety and Health Administration. In both cases, regulations addressed complex problems that could be regulated only through a heavy reliance on scientific research and the promulgation of standards that forced businesses to absorb unprecedented compliance costs.

Chapter 8 presents the regulatory reform and deregulation efforts of the 1970s and 80s. During this period, executive review processes were established to increase executive oversight of the regulatory agencies. The challenges posed by these review processes forced many agencies to create or expand their own internal review processes and economics staffs. Increasingly, economic criteria were being applied to determine whether policies were justified. The goals of the deregulatory and reform initiatives were to return to market mechanisms wherever possible, and to reject any policies that failed to meet specific cost-benefit or cost-effectiveness criteria. These goals forced significant changes in policy, many of which found an ultimate expression in the deregulatory initiatives of the period.

The regulatory initiatives of the 1960s and 70s and the regulatory reform and deregulatory efforts of the 1970s and 80s share a common feature, namely, a heightened reliance on social-scientific and scientific expertise in the policy process. This reliance translated into an acceleration of agency professionalization; the creation of staffs for the planning and evaluation of policy; and the integration of social-scientific and scientific theories into the policy process. Although agency professionalization can yield important gains, it is also a source of great concern because of its effects on political control, public participation, and the stability of policy goals. The introduction of new norms and new analytical frameworks creates a profound vulnerability to changes in the core assumptions in the chosen body of expertise. Such changes, if integrated into the policy process, may shape the development of policy in ways that may be unexpected or difficult to reconcile with the legislative mandate. Indeed, the contemporary period is interesting because it marks the rise of a new regime that, I will argue, lacks popular roots. Unlike its predecessors, it has its foundations in elite politics and in the regulatory agencies. It may be, in part, the unanticipated consequence of earlier agency professionalization.

List of Abbreviations

AAA	Agricultural Adjustment Administration
AFL	American Federation of Labor
AFL-CIO	American Federation of Labor–Congress of Industrial Organizations
CAA	Civil Aeronautics Authority
CAB	Civil Aeronautics Board
CEA	Council of Economic Advisers
CIO	Congress of Industrial Organizations
COWPS	Council on Wage and Price Stability
EIS	Environmental impact statement
EPA	Environmental Protection Agency
FDA	Food and Drug Administration
FTC	Federal Trade Commission
IBA	Investment Bankers Association
ICC	Interstate Commerce Commission
NAAQS	National ambient air quality standards
NIOSH	National Institute for Occupational Safety and Health
NLB	National Labor Board
NLRB	National Labor Relations Board
NRA	National Recovery Administration
OMB	Office of Management and Budget
OSHA	Occupational Safety and Health Administration
OSHRC	Occupational Safety and Health Review Commission

OTC	Over-the-counter
PAC	Political action committee
RARG	Regulatory Analysis Review Group
RFC	Reconstruction Finance Corporation
RIA	Regulatory impact analysis
SEC	Securities and Exchange Commission
USDA	United States Department of Agriculture
WIB	War Industries Board

REGULATORY POLITICS IN TRANSITION

1

A Regulatory-Regime Framework: Understanding Regulatory Change

CONTEMPORARY DISCUSSIONS OF REGULATION OFTEN charge that there is excessive state intervention in markets and in corporate affairs. The term *regulation,* it would seem, describes much of what the government does which it should not do. Such a characterization would have come as a surprise in decades past, when regulatory policies were held to provide instruments for protecting the citizenry from the exploitative advances of the trusts, promoting economic stability under precarious circumstances, or holding corporations responsible for environmental degradation and threats to public health. Each generation interprets regulatory policies and state-economy relations from its own historical position as part of a specific political-economic milieu. This book focuses on the dominant characteristics of the major regulatory regimes of the past hundred years and places the evolution of regulatory policies in a broader historical and social context.

We can best understand a regulatory regime as a historically specific configuration of policies and institutions which structures the relationship between social interests, the state, and economic actors in multiple sectors of the economy. Whenever there is a change of regime, it is possible to identify a unique synthesis of interests, political-economic ideas, and administrative reform doctrines that shaped the new regime. Likewise, it is possible to discover the broad goals established in the process. As the following chapters show, regulatory policies were created in pursuit of a wide variety of objectives. Policy-makers designed and redesigned institutions to facilitate effective administration, and officials addressed specific regulatory problems and the technical demands of implementation. However, the new policies and institutions, when taken together, resulted in an extensive redefinition of property rights, political authority, and group participation in regulatory politics. Before exploring the regimes inaugurated during the Progressive Era, the New Deal, and the contemporary period, I must expand upon the concept of "regulatory regimes" and address the question of regime change.

REGIMES AND REGIME CHANGE

Regimes are political-institutional arrangements that define the relationship between social interests, the state, and economic actors such as corporations, labor unions, and agricultural associations. In so doing, they structure the interplay of various economic organizations. Each of the regimes addressed in this book emerged in response to political demands roused by economic change. Economic change produces uncertainty, posing a challenge to established routines, property rights, and distributions of wealth and economic power. Producers, social groups, and elites who hope to preserve or further some values or interests endangered by the changes in question, and aspire to establish procedures to allow for the ordered management of economic activity, respond to this uncertainty by demanding a redefinition of the state's role in the economy.

Because of the electoral imperative, political officials are highly sensitive to group demands. However, the interests that mobilize for policy change are often diverse. Their demands are not monolithic and often lack clarity. During the last decades of the nineteenth century, for example, many groups felt threatened by the evolving corporate economy that was engulfing the local, decentralized markets that had characterized earlier decades. Farmers, agrarian radicals, shippers, commodity producer's associations, social reform groups, and railroads demanded regulation. Each group perceived the challenges and remedies in different terms. Under such chaotic circumstances, policy-makers can creatively link the diverse demands, and advance proposals that predate the expression of popular discontent. They commonly introduce order by appealing to the mental constructs at their disposal—the prevailing political-economic theories.[1]

Theory may be no easier to translate into policy than the demands of a diverse set of interests. The range of policy alternatives that receives serious consideration is limited by political, institutional, and administrative constraints. Although electoral pressures create incentives to respond to the demands of mobilized social groups, major economic organizations and local interests may have a stake in preserving the existing distribution of power and wealth. New policies may threaten to alter the structure of an industry or the commercial relationship between regions. Because new regulatory initiatives may threaten existing political-economic alliances, they must be designed, in part, with the goal of preserving coalitions. When demands are diverse and in conflict, or significant regional cleavages exist, it may be necessary to sacrifice legislative precision and state policy goals abstractly in order to forge a broad coalition. This vague legislation, in turn, results in a broad delegation of authority to administrators.

Existing institutions also limit the range of feasible policy options. A bureaucratic organization performs a limited set of related functions. Established bureaucratic routines, the availability of policy expertise, experience with a given set of policies, and well-entrenched relationships between the agency and interest groups shape the agency's administrative capacities.[2] These factors place constraints on the range of possible implementation actions. As a result, policy-makers must often accompany innovations in policy with experiments in institutional design. In each of the regulatory regimes explored in this book, new regulatory initiatives were coupled with administrative reforms chosen as a response to the failure of earlier implementation efforts and the demands of new policies.

A regime emerges when new regulatory policies are initiated in several regulatory issue areas (e.g., finance, agriculture, and industrial relations) and are combined with significant institutional changes. The policy initiatives commonly display set of a related goals which transcends the specific problems of a given industry. Moreover, the new administrative procedures often establish a common role for economic interests in the definition and implementation of policy. This continuity reflects the power of prevailing political-economic theories and administrative reform doctrines, and the common reference point provided by the larger economic changes. Rather than concentrating solely on the stated goals of securities regulations or agricultural regulations, for instance, one must ask, What were the regulatory policies initiated in a given period designed to accomplish, when taken together? How did the new policies change the role of the state in the economy? The answer to this question differs dramatically for each of the periods addressed in this book. The model of regime change is presented schematically in Figure 1.1.

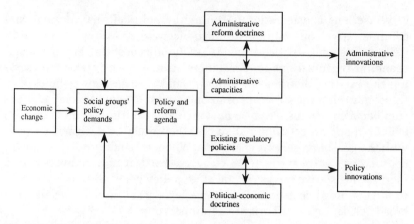

Fig. 1.1   A model of regulatory regime change.

AN OVERVIEW OF REGULATORY REGIMES

This study divides the history of regulation in the United States since 1880 into four regimes, each of which was created in response to economic changes that threatened the perceived self-interest of various groups. The market regime emerged in the decades surrounding the turn of the century. Through regulation, policy-makers tried to compensate for the tremendous economic-structural changes of the period. Corporations had expanded so as to internalize many functions previously accomplished through market transactions, and they adopted joint strategies to manage competition and expansion, albeit with mixed success. The emergence of a large-scale corporate economy forced the integration of formerly local economies and threatened the economic independence that many businesses and consumers had enjoyed in earlier decades. In response to popular demands, elected officials fashioned regulatory initiatives to do one of two things. First, as in the case of antitrust, policy-makers aspired to force a return to the market. They prohibited the forms of corporate conduct and organization that allowed for a circumvention of market forces. Second, where the structure of an industry prevented a return to the market, as was the case with electric power generation and the railroads, legislation created administrative agencies to set rates that roughly approximated those that would have existed under market conditions. The regulatory regime of the Progressive Era is best termed the "market regime" because of its use of the market as a benchmark.[3]

The market regime was a response to the rise of a new corporate economy. A second wave of regulation followed that economy's collapse in the Great Depression. The economic and social dislocations of the depression led Franklin Roosevelt and his advisers to focus on the question of recovery. The National Industrial Recovery Act was an important regulatory initiative that was central to the recovery effort. It was, in essence, an attempt to promote economic stability by means of an integrated regulatory framework governing production and pricing across multiple sectors of the economy. During the same period, moreover, Congress and the president created or expanded regulatory subsystems in industrial relations and a variety of other sectors, including commercial banking, industrial finance, civil aeronautics, trucking, communications, and agriculture. Many of the initiatives shared a common goal, patterned after the National Industrial Recovery Act. Policy-makers and administrators sought to use regulatory policies to promote industrial stability and to redistribute national income toward certain regulated groups. As part of this approach, the Roosevelt administration actively encouraged the organization of economic interests. Regulators gave economic associations a central role in defining and implementing regulatory policy. In so doing, they created a system of government-supervised self-regulation. By integrating interest groups into the regulatory process through the creation of quasi-corporatist arrangements, they promoted economic stability, allowed regulators to draw on the expertise and resources of the regulated, and minimized confrontations.[4] Although this new regime emerged during the New Deal, it had its origins in the associationalism of the 1920s. It is thus useful to refer to this regime as the "associational regime."

The regulatory regime of the New Deal was rooted in associationalism that was, in large part, a synthesis of Progressivism and the experience of economic planning during World War I. Whereas the dominant strand of Progressivism sought to revitalize markets or produce marketlike results, a second strand promoted a more active role for the state in managing and guiding economic change by means of structured interaction with economic associations. The Federal Reserve Board, a Progressive Era agency, embodied this second strand of Progressivism and foreshadowed the institutional arrangements enshrined in the New Deal. Other agencies, such as the Interstate Commerce Commission and the Federal Trade Commission, were clearly designed to execute market-corrective functions. However, by the 1920s both agencies were vesting greater authority in economic associations and implementing policy to promote industry stability rather than reasonable rates or strict reliance on market mechanisms. Whereas the continuity between the Progressive Era and the New Deal is clear, continuity is entirely absent as one moves to the third regulatory regime under examination.

The regulatory initiatives of the 1960s and 70s stand in contrast to those of the New Deal and the Progressive Era. Deep skepticism about the distribution of economic power in society and about the excesses of capitalist production contributed to a rejection of the earlier goals of regulation. The major initiatives of this period, rather than promoting economic stability or revitalizing markets, were designed to protect citizens from the health and environmental hazards that were an outgrowth of large-scale industrial production. The so-called "new social regulation" extended regulatory authority into the production process itself. Aspects of production that had formerly been under the control of corporate managers now became the objects of regulatory concern. Thus, environmental legislation authorized the Environmental Protection Agency to set standards regulating the contents and quantity of plant emissions and effluents, and to mandate the adoption of pollution control technologies. The Occupational Safety and Health Act of 1970 created the Occupational Safety and Health Administration to regulate workplace safety and occupational exposure to harmful substances. Because of this regime's concern with the societal implications of industrial production, I refer to it as the "societal regime."

During the 1970s and 80s, the political agenda was shaped by the nation's poor macroeconomic performance. The combination of high inflation rates, sluggish growth, and mounting foreign economic competition forced policy-makers to reconsider the justification for many policies. Public officials and policy analysts identified regulation as one of the factors contributing to stagflation. A series of presidents initiated executive review processes to force agencies to consider the costs and benefits of their regulations. Increasingly, the economic analysis of regulation was conducted by economic staffs or policy offices within the agencies themselves. At the same time, a number of deregulatory initiatives were implemented. In each case, efficiency was identified as the key value to be promoted by policy. Throughout this book, I refer to the regime established during this period as the "efficiency regime." Table 1.1 presents important characteristics of each of the four regimes described above.

Thus far, the discussion has focused on qualitative changes in regulation. It is necessary to recognize, however, that the history of regulation reveals much continuity as well. The emergence of a new regulatory regime need not entail the elimination of an earlier regime. Many of the policy initiatives of the Progressive Era's market regime remained in place, little changed by the new regulatory regime that emerged during the New Deal. Policies and institutions created during the New Deal's associational regime continued to function during the wave of social regulatory initiatives in the late 1960s and the 1970s, later becoming the object of deregulatory initiatives in the 1970s and 80s. The existence of overlapping regulatory regimes reflects, in part, the fragmentation of American institutions. Rather than tampering with existing agencies, the president and Congress commonly create new agencies to administer new policies. Over time, owing to existing jurisdictional boundaries, relationships with organized interests and congressional subcommittees, and the specialized discourse that surrounds most policy subsystems, these agencies become insulated from external threats. As policies become embedded in institutions and shape political alliances and capital investment decisions, they become resistant to change.

Although the four regimes differ in focus, there is continuity of a sort among them. All involved attempts to enhance administrative agencies' scientific and social-scientific expertise. Progressive reformers sought to promote an expanded role for expert administrators as part of a broader program of fostering administrative neutrality and creating the capacity to address the complexities of regulatory policy. Greater professionalization was driven by the growing complexity of regulatory problems, the analytic demands of enforcement, and the recognition granted to specialized knowledge during the Progressive Era. During the New Deal, the role of expertise was once again enlarged as policymakers began to take a more comprehensive approach to regulation, economic management, and industrial planning. By the contemporary period, because of the sheer complexity of the new social regulation, virtually all regulatory agencies relied on staffs of scientific or social-scientific experts. As noted above, concerns about the economic ramifications of regulation introduced an additional layer of expert analysis, as economists and economic criteria were integrated into the policy process.

There is also some continuity in the ongoing attempts to find an appropriate means of integrating interest groups into the regulatory process. Concerns about the potential for undue influence by industry and partisan groups stimulated Progressive attempts to promote independent regulatory commissions that could make policy free of external pressures. A much different response was clear in the New Deal efforts to integrate regulated interests into the policy process: as part of the associational regime, economic organizations were granted quasi-public status. Congress addressed the broad delegation of regulatory authority and the role of interest groups in the policy process by passing the Administrative Procedure Act of 1946, which established strict procedural norms for administrative policy-making. During the societal regime, ex-

Table 1 Characteristics of Regulatory Regimes

Regime	Market Regime	Associational Regime	Societal Regime	Efficiency Regime
Primary goal	Promotion of market governance; creation of marketlike results through administrative means	Promotion of industrial stability and redistribution of national income toward regulated interests	Prevention of hazards to health and environment that occur in advanced industrial production	Elimination of policies that interfere with market mechanisms or impose large compliance costs
Political-economic context	Emergence of large-scale corporate economy and national markets during period 1880–1920	Collapse of industrial and agricultural economies during the Great Depression	Postwar growth promoting the emergence of postmaterialist values and quality-of-life concerns	Economic stagflation and growing foreign competition in the 1970s and 80s
Institutional innovation	Broad reliance on independent commissions and boards	Interest associations as quasi-public entities defining and implementing policies	Limits on agencies' discretion imposed by means of action-forcing mandates and implementation timetables	Centralization of regulatory authority and formal review in the Office of Management and Budget, White House review offices, and agency evaluation offices

	Antitrust regulations and regulation of railroads, commercial banking, foods, and drugs	National Industrial Recovery Act and new regulatory systems in agriculture, commercial and industrial finance, and labor relations	New social regulations focusing on environmental quality, workers' safety and health, and consumer protection	Executive orders requiring formal economic analysis of regulation; deregulatory legislation addressing surface transportation, airlines, and finance
Policy initiatives	Antitrust regulations and regulation of railroads, commercial banking, foods, and drugs	National Industrial Recovery Act and new regulatory systems in agriculture, commercial and industrial finance, and labor relations	New social regulations focusing on environmental quality, workers' safety and health, and consumer protection	Executive orders requiring formal economic analysis of regulation; deregulatory legislation addressing surface transportation, airlines, and finance
Role of expertise	Progressive efforts to promote and foster neutral competence; some reliance on specialized expertise in commissions	Broad reliance on specialists within key agencies; efforts to tap private-sector expertise through close relations with the regulated interests	Expansive reliance on scientific and social-scientific expertise as a result of the complexity of new social regulations	Formal application of economic evaluation methodologies (e.g., cost-benefit and cost-effectiveness analysis) and risk assessment
Integration of interests into policy process	Interests integrated at legislative level; little regulation of interaction at administrative level	Interests integrated through the creation of quasi-corporatist arrangements and government-supervised self-regulation	Interests integrated into policy process by means of extended rule-making process, intervener funding, and expanded access to courts	No innovations in formal interest integration; informal access to White House review offices

tended rule-making, public funding for interveners, and expanded access to the courts were adopted as ways to enhance regulators' accountability and ensure opportunities for participation by groups that might otherwise be excluded from the regulatory process.

POLICIES AND INSTITUTIONS, IDEAS, AND INTERESTS

Ideas and interest groups shape the politics and policies within a regime; they define the terms of regime change. They shape popular expectations and convictions about appropriate behavior and legitimate state action. Once embedded in new policies and institutions, ideas and interests gain a certain permanence. It is thus critical to examine them in greater detail. First, however, the role of institutions must be explored with some care. In the broadest sense, institutions are the formal and informal rules that structure human interaction. For the purposes of this book, however, I am concerned with institutions in a more restricted sense. When speaking of institutions, I am referring chiefly to the set of roles, rules, and decision-making procedures that define the internal workings of public organizations and the relationships among public and private organizations in the policy process. In particular, I focus on the institutional governing arrangements that shape the pattern of regulatory policy actions.

Institutions

Do institutions shape policies, or do policies shape institutions? This question has been at the center of debates in political science for several decades. There is a growing consensus that causality runs in both directions. Institutions provide the context for the formulation and implementation of policy. They are central to politics and the policy process because they define the tasks of organization members, determine the way in which and the extent to which specialized knowledge will be brought to bear on policy problems, and shape the relationships among agencies, private associations, and organized constituencies. Thus they play a central role in shaping policy. But policies shape institutions as well. By virtue of their specialization, bureaucratic organizations tend toward policy specificity. As Dietrich Rueschemeyer and Peter Evans note, such organizations "are geared to do certain things relatively well and, as organizations, cannot easily switch to or expand into other fields of action. Organizational structures tend to work with specific sets of policy instruments and form a fairly stable amalgam."[5] Institutional evolution and policy change are inevitably linked. Because bureaucracies are relatively rigid, significant changes in policy often occur as the accumulation of a series of incremental adjustments to existing policies.

Many contemporary regulatory studies focus on the interplay between organized interests and "regulators." Economic critiques of regulation, and much of the work done in the public-choice tradition in economics and political science, adopt the simplifying assumption that regulators behave as rational utility-maximizers who are willing and able to trade policies for political and financial resources. For the utility-maximizing regulator, policy becomes a tool used in the pursuit of narrow self-interest. According to this logic, one who seeks to understand the failure of regulatory policy (i.e., the tendency of regulations to benefit the regulated and harm the consumer) need only understand the incentive structure facing the regulators. One of the great problems with much of the economic literature on regulation is the failure to place regulation in a sufficiently rich institutional context. George Stigler's "regulator," who is part legislator and part entrepreneur in charge of a compliant regulatory agency, stands as a case in point. If regulators are seen as free of institutional or organizational influences and cast as rational utility-maximizers, it only makes sense that they will use their policy authority to realize self-interested ends.[6]

James G. March and Johan P. Olsen challenge this position by contrasting a "logic of consequentiality" (which holds that public authority is used as a means to self-interested ends) with a "logic of appropriateness" which prevails within institutions. They suggest that individuals aspire to work within the institutional roles, rules, and routines that specify what actions are appropriate in response to various situations: "In a logic of appropriateness . . . behaviors (beliefs as well as actions) are intentional but not willful. They involve fulfilling the obligations of a role in a situation, and so of trying to determine the imperatives of holding a position. Action stems from a conception of necessity, rather than preference. Within a logic of appropriateness, a sane person is one who is 'in touch with identity' in the sense of maintaining consistency between behavior and a conception of self in a social role. Ambiguity or conflict in rules is typically resolved not by shifting to a logic of consequentiality and rational calculation, but by trying to clarify the rules, make distinctions, determine what the situation is and what definition 'fits.'"[7] Rule systems are central to most bureaucratic organizations. They define organizational roles and routines even if they allow for a good deal of discretionary authority. Although bureaucrats may fail to divorce self-interest from their official duties, their ability to function within an organization will be determined, in large part, by their willingness to conform to existing rules, roles, and routines.

The President, the Courts, and Congress

It is useful to consider institutions at two levels of the political system. At the highest level of the system are Congress, the presidency, and the judiciary, while at a lower level, individual agencies define and implement policies. At the highest level, power is highly fragmented, as intended by the framers of the Constitution. The system of separate institutions sharing powers has provided the foundation for ongoing conflicts that have affected policy in general, and regulatory policies in particular. Over the course of the past hundred years, the power of the presidency has increased relative to that of Congress. The growth of the executive branch and an expansion of regulatory authority have accompanied and strengthened the movement from congressional to presidential government. During this period, each president has contributed to regulatory legislation. Several have played decisive roles in defining the basic principles of new regulatory regimes. Moreover, presidents can shape regulatory policy through the power of appointment, selecting political executives who are sympathetic to their broader policy agendas. During the past two decades, presidents have tried to shape regulation on a policy-by-policy basis by implementing review processes centralized in the Executive Office of the President. They have justified executive review as part of an attempt to increase the net benefits of regulation and eliminate the more burdensome costs of compliance.[8]

The judiciary is also critical in the definition of regulatory authority. Throughout the nineteenth century, the courts played the primary role in defending private property and free markets, and maintaining the boundaries of federal authority. The courts limited the success of many early regulatory initiatives at the state and national levels. They routinely dismissed regulatory actions by invoking conservative interpretations of the interstate commerce clause of the Constitution and ruling that corporations subject to regulation were entitled to Fourteenth Amendment protections against the deprivation of "life, liberty, and property without due process of law." During the 1920s, the Supreme Court held unconstitutional more than 130 regulatory statutes.[9] Although the regulatory initiatives of the early decades of the century forced a gradual redefinition of property rights—one that the courts only belatedly acknowledged—the cataclysm of the Great Depression, Roosevelt's attempt to pack the Supreme Court with sympathetic judges, and a number of strategic judicial appointments during the latter years of the New Deal eroded the Court's opposition to the expansion of the federal government's regulatory authority. As a consequence, the interstate commerce clause lost much of its relevance in regulatory politics.[10]

Despite the change in the Court's position, the judiciary is still crucial to regulatory politics. Indeed, it has become more important as of late. Much contemporary regulatory legislation provides expanded standing allowing citizens to sue the regulatory agencies to force them to fulfill their legislatively mandated duties. All regulatory decisions can be appealed before the courts, and major rules are routinely challenged. Advocacy groups have been particularly active in their use of litigation-based strategies. The courts have freely used these opportunities to identify the limitations of agencies' decision-making authority and to question the role and relevance of economic and scientific data in the definition of standards. This "reformation of American administrative law" has had distinct effects on the policy process at the agency level, and on the role of interest groups in the definition of policy.[11]

Although the president and the courts are quite important in shaping regulatory authority, Congress bears the primary responsibility. It passes regulatory legislation, oversees agencies' activities, and tries to shape implementation actions. Reflecting its composition, the frequency of elections, and the existing system of campaign finance, Congress is exceptionally sensitive to interest group's demands and local constituencies' concerns. It commonly passes skeletal legislation with broad mandates (e.g., to regulate "in the public interest") and then delegates to administrators the authority to define policy. Resource constraints and regulatory complexity contribute to the need for delegation. However, as argued earlier, delegation commonly is a result of the logic of coalition-building. Because it is difficult to reconcile the demands of diverse local and state constituencies and interest groups, and because legislative specificity would alienate some constituencies and reduce the size of a potential coalition, vague legislation is a political necessity. However, this delegation of authority has an important effect on the definition of regulatory authority. Administrators become, in effect, policy-makers. As Congress transfers authority to administrators, it loses its own capacity to control the exercise of this authority.

Localism and the electoral vulnerability of Congress also shape the relationship between Congress and the agencies on a day-to-day basis. In its regulatory legislation, Congress may establish broad and expansive goals and delegate authority to a specific regulatory agency. This provides benefits without political responsibility, for legislators can claim credit for legislation without accepting responsibility for individual implementation decisions and the ultimate success of policy.[12] However, if an agency's enforcement actions promote the mobilization of disaffected interests, Congress may seek to limit the agency's authority, redirect the agency's future efforts, or force a reversal of the enforcement actions. The history of the past several decades is replete with examples of regulatory authority that was delegated by Congress only to be withdrawn forcibly in response to the complaints of local constituents and affected interest groups.[13]

The Constitution created a federal system that assigned certain powers to the national government and reserved others for the states. Particularly as expressed in the composition of Congress, the federal system gives local concerns and regional disputes national significance. As Elizabeth Sanders has shown, regional voting blocs in Congress may pass regulatory legislation to impede economic changes that could affect patterns of economic development. Take the example of early national regulatory legislation. The growing corporate economy of the North and the East threatened the autonomy of formerly independent regional economies. The representatives of districts in the West, the Midwest, and portions of the South met this challenge with regulatory legislation. Legislators representing the nation's commercial core opposed the economic restraints this legislation imposed. In the end, the regulatory legislation was an expression of economic changes that pitted one region against another.[14]

National legislation is often necessary to compensate for the inadequacy and inconsistency of state-level regulations. At times, this has created a dual regulatory system in which different policies regulate the same industry at the state and national levels. For example, financial institutions may choose to carry state or federal charters. The decision will affect their capitalization requirements and deposit insurance. In the decades following the passage of the National Banking Act of 1863, state and national regulators competed to attract new banks. This competition resulted in a regulatory race to the bottom, as state and national regulators relaxed standards to entice banks to adopt national or state charters.[15] A much different state of affairs has characterized recent decades. A deregulatory posture at the national level has met with the opposition of state regulators.

Finally, the national government commonly relies on state and local governments to implement national policies through an extensive grants-in-aid system. The Environmental Protection Agency administers national air pollution regulations through state implementation plans. Although Congress authorized the EPA to establish programs where state efforts are insufficient, the resource demands would be prohibitive if such programs were undertaken on a wide scale. Similarly, the Occupational Safety and Health Administration authorizes and funds state worker safety programs, and allows states to make regulations in areas where OSHA has decided not to promulgate rules. This proxy administration allows the federal government to initiate policies without bearing all of the costs. However, policy becomes highly vulnerable to differences in the administrative and budgetary resources available to regulators in fifty states. Some state agencies have adopted more stringent regulations than their national counterparts, but the competition among the states for investment creates a bias against strong state-level regulation.[16]

Regulatory Agencies: Expertise, Interests, and Autonomy

The most relevant level of analysis for regulatory studies is the individual agency. Regulatory policies commonly originate in legislation that defines policy goals in the broadest possible terms. Administrators must give ambiguous expressions such as "the public interest" substantive content. In the late 1960s and the 1970s, Congress passed highly detailed legislation with strict implementation timetables and action-forcing provisions. However, this did not mean that delegation was eliminated. On the contrary, Congress failed to specify the precise policy goals, the assumptions underlying the standards, and the means of meeting the timetables. Thus, agencies such as OSHA and the EPA continued to exercise what amounted to unlimited discretion in these important areas.[17]

Public policy is a goal-oriented pattern of action.[18] Here I am concerned with the pattern of action which is rarely specified by regulatory legislation. Thus, I must focus on the factors that shape agencies' decision-making and implementation. Because administrators must determine how to pursue statutory goals, one cannot easily divorce policy and administration. In addressing administrative capacities, three factors are particularly worthy of discussion: bureaucratic expertise, the integration of interests into the policy process, and agencies' autonomy from other governmental institutions.

A bureaucracy is a highly specialized organization designed to execute a relatively limited set of tasks. This specialization and the requisite competence of administrators foster a unique synthesis of technical knowledge and extensive experience. The level of bureaucratic expertise depends on many factors, including the length of time that an agency has been executing its mandate, and the agency's past staffing practices. The importance of experience is clear: the accumulated experience of administrators provides a stock of expertise that can be useful in evaluating policies and searching for solutions to policy problems. The question of staffing, however, is worth exploring in greater detail.

Some agencies are highly professionalized, with large staffs of scientists or social scientists engaged in research, planning, and evaluation.

In such agencies, the professional norms and analytic assumptions of these expert administrators may eventually come to dominate the agency. Professional administrators introduce esoteric decision variables into the policy process. They apply discipline-specific criteria to evaluate the need for, and the performance of, policy. When one professional group is dominant, the agency's ethos may mirror the professional ethos. However, when multiple professional staffs exist, conflicts between their norms and methodologies may create problems of management and coordination.[19]

Unlike agencies with highly specialized professional staffs, some regulatory agencies are dominated by attorneys, who tend to be generalists by training. Attorneys often approach government service as a sort of apprenticeship, for it can give them experience and specialized knowledge that may enhance their value in subsequent private-service employment. One may celebrate the prosecutorial zeal of agencies that function as large litigation shops. However, high rates of staff turnover impede the accumulation of practical expertise. Moreover, when scientific or social-scientific analysis is available, attorneys may use it merely to bolster cases that are based on legal precedents and existing evidence. In essence, expert analysis serves a support function.

As noted earlier, a common feature of the regulatory regimes under consideration is support for bureaucratic expertise. The New Deal marked a continuation of the Progressive belief in the separation of politics and administration, and the consequent faith in neutral competence. Although the advocates of the new social regulations of the 1960s and 70s were more discerning in their support for expertise, the policies they promoted required an ever-greater reliance on scientific and social-scientific knowledge. As a result, the new regulatory agencies had large technical staffs charged with providing the scientific foundations for regulatory standards. During the past several decades, all major regulatory agencies have created policy-planning and policy-evaluation units staffed by economists. This growing reliance on economists was a product of both popular concern about the cost of regulation in an environment of economic stagflation, and the imposition of executive review processes that forced agencies to justify their actions by cost-benefit analysis. The growing role of economists and research scientists in the policy process has partially eroded the dominance of lawyers.

A listing of professional administrators would include accountants, attorneys, biologists, chemists, economists, engineers, environmental scientists, epidemiologists, industrial hygienists, nuclear physicists, physicians, and statisticians, with multiple subdivisions within each professional grouping. Professionals—and commonly, competing professional groupings—are important participants in all aspects of regulatory policy-making. The inclusion of natural and social scientists has improved the quality of regulatory policy and provided a basis for more comprehensive planning and management. However, it has also introduced new professional norms and disciplinary debates into agencies. This is of critical importance when one is attempting to understand bureaucratic behavior. As William Gormley explains: "Each profession brings with it a peculiar world view, a set of predispositions, and certain blind spots . . . Thus, if the level of resources determines a bureaucracy's ability to cope with different kinds of problems, the mix of professionals determines how it copes with such problems."[20] Many of the new ideas, theories, and professional norms integrated into the policy process have proven difficult to reconcile with the original missions of the agencies in question, creating conflicts and unanticipated changes in policy priorities.[21]

Another factor to examine when considering institutions at the agency level is the role of interest groups in the regulatory process. Before World War II, interest groups' access to the administrative process was neither consistently assured nor regulated in any consistent fashion. Certain agencies became highly responsive to the demands of the regulated. The regulated interests successfully secured policies that excluded potential competitors by creating regulatory barriers and protected profitability by approving rates that exceeded costs.[22] Of course, the devolution of authority to the regulated was often part of a deliberate strategy, particularly during the New Deal, when policy-makers organized economic interests and gave them quasi-public authority.

During the postwar period, interest groups' access to the administrative process has come under greater scrutiny. The Administrative Procedure Act of 1946 and later changes in the rule-making process gave organized interests greater opportunities to present proposals and supporting evidence during the public-comment period before the promulgation of final standards. During the 1970s, policy-makers combined extended rule-making with programs that provided limited public funding for groups that might otherwise lack the resources to present testimony and evidence at administrative hearings.[23] Many of the new social regulatory initiatives also gave citizens expanded access to the courts. Because many contemporary regulations force corporations to absorb significant compliance costs, proceedings can become lengthy and highly adversarial. The demands of the regulatory process can make a significant claim on an agency's resources and can place many consumer advocacy groups at a disadvantage relative to their better-funded industrial counterparts. Moreover, court challenges have become routine following the promulgation of major rules. For some agencies, such as OSHA and the EPA, court appeals are a regular part of the policy-making process.

In the past, many regulatory agencies relied almost exclusively on interest groups for data and analyses. The regulated interests and their organized opponents commonly possessed superior information on industry practices and performance. Although one might question the reliability of this information given the stakes involved, many agencies simply lacked the financial and human resources to assemble their own data bases and conduct comprehensive analyses. In addition, many agencies relied exclusively on the complaints of interest groups and individual firms as a basis for regulatory enforcement actions. The professionalization of the agencies and the development of planning and evaluation staffs have reduced this dependence on interest groups. Regulators have gained a greater capacity to assess interest groups' contributions and integrate independent analysis into the definition of standards.

The final factor to consider is the extent of regulators' autonomy from other governmental actors—in particular, Congress. As noted above, regulatory policies often have their origins in broad legislative mandates. Although such legislation may be politically expedient because it promotes coalition building, it entails a significant loss of control. Once Congress delegates authority, it can be impossible to assure that policy as implemented will reflect the goals expressed in the legislative debates. Congress can never be certain that its bureaucratic agents are not shirking their duties or interpreting their mandates opportunistically.[24] A lack of political control raises significant normative concerns as well. As Richard Stewart notes, "Insofar as statutes do not effectively dictate agency actions, individual autonomy is vulnerable to the imposition of sanctions at the unruled will of executive officials [and] major questions of social and economic policy are determined by officials who are not formally accountable to the electorate."[25]

Traditionally, political scientists have understood the relationship between elected officials and the bureaucracy as to be what Emmette Redford described as "overhead democracy."[26] Although bureaucratic agents may interpret their mandates liberally, elected officials possess an array of political and financial mechanisms by which to force bureaucratic compliance with congressional will. Congressional committees can reduce agencies' budgets, redefine jurisdictions, threaten appointments, and involve agency officials in prolonged and contentious oversight hearings. Congress can give legislative mandates far greater specificity, thus limiting bureaucratic discretion and forcing regulators to incorporate new criteria into the internal policy process. In extreme cases, Congress can even force the elimination of the agency in question. Some scholars suggest that congressional control of the bureaucracy is highly effective.[27] However, such a conclusion can be sustained only by adopting a highly simplified representation of regulators, one that portrays them as unitary actors functioning as rational optimizers. With this caricature in place, the existing mechanisms of control may appear deceptively powerful. As suggested above, a fuller understanding of bureaucratic organizations leads one to question the simplifying assumptions underlying the political control thesis.

Political control theses become difficult to sustain once the inadequacy of oversight is appreciated. Without adequate information on agencies' performance, Congress cannot use the existing mechanisms effectively. For many years there was a consensus that congressional incentives limited the efficacy of oversight. Following David Mayhew, most analyses of oversight began with the assumption that members of Congress emphasize reelection above all other goals.[28] Other goals (e.g., making good policy, gaining a reputation in Washington) are at all times contingent on reelection. Given the power of the electoral incentive, the primary limitation of oversight becomes clear. The goal of reelection conditions the allocation of resources and the attention paid to competing tasks. By comparison with competing duties such as legislation and constituent service, careful bureaucratic oversight does not yield returns for members of Congress seeking reelection. Thus, they rarely grant it significance.[29]

Oversight underwent a resurgence in the 1970s and 80s owing to growing budgetary constraints, the emergence of subcommittee government, and increasing conflicts between the executive and legislative branches. Between 1961 and 1983, the days devoted by Congress to oversight increased by more than 300 percent. Moreover, the average length of statutes more than tripled, suggesting that Congress was limiting delegation by passing more specific legislation. In keeping with the argument presented above, Joel Aberbach's study of oversight reveals that 55 percent of top staffers cited the increasing size and complexity of government as the chief reason that oversight activities had increased.[30] However, even if Congress members emphasize oversight, they still face the knowledge problems that force delegation in the first place. As Aberbach notes, "Members are predominantly professional political-lawyers, trained specialists in the form but not in the substance of legislation."[31] Although committee specialization and staff support promote more meaningful oversight, top congressional staffers, like the members they serve, tend to be generalists trained in law. The backgrounds of legislators and their staffs stand in contrast to the backgrounds of the top career bureaucrats, a majority of whom (52 percent) took degrees in a scientific or technical field.[32]

It is important to note that much oversight takes place outside of formal oversight hearings. Indeed, there is much to suggest that oversight most often occurs in response to pressures from interest groups. Matthew McCubbins and Thomas Schwartz have contrasted formal "police patrol" oversight with what they call "fire alarm" oversight. In designing legislation, Congress may create a number of opportunities for interested parties to gain access to administrative decisions and to seek relief from Congress, the courts, or other administrative agencies. The benefit of such mechanisms is that interest groups bear much of the cost of monitoring agencies' activity. Even if formal oversight is ineffective, the informal mechanisms give those parties who have the greatest incentive to oversee agencies' actions the opportunity to sound an alarm when the agencies fail to fulfill their mandates or exceed the limits of their statutory authority.[33]

However, because of the limited scope of oversight and the routine delegation of authority, regulatory agencies function with a great deal of autonomy. Outside of those periods when regulatory action stimulates a widespread mobilization of interests and forces a congressional response, agencies are more or less free from congressional restraints. Although the courts and the White House may exert a degree of control, it is the agencies that define policy. Within the confines of the agencies, bureaucrats transform legislative mandates into a pattern of enforcement actions, selectively incorporating interest groups' demands and appealing to specialized expertise.

Ideas

It is difficult to separate the influence of ideas from that of interests. Individuals and groups often embrace ideas that justify the pursuit of self-interested goals. At the same time, however, political and economic doctrines provide a lens allowing individuals to decipher a complex reality. By emphasizing certain aspects of this reality, ideas may prove critical in shaping groups' perceptions of what is in their interests. Moreover, because they define the parameters of legitimate state action, ideas may shape public authority and political demands. Despite this close connection, however, it is useful to examine ideas and interests separately. Under the broad heading of ideas, one can include both the dominant political-economic ideas that structure expectations about the role of the state in the economy, and the administrative doctrines that define appropriate modes of administration. Let us address them in turn.

Historically, norms of market liberalism have shaped the popular understanding of the proper relationship between public policy and economic activity. Market liberalism rests upon the dual pillars of private property and the market. James Willard Hurst notes that in the United

States, private property was defined "in terms of a legally assured measure of autonomy for private decision makers as against the public power . . . property was primarily a bundle of legal limits on the intrusion of official power into unofficial decisionmaking."[34] Private property was secure only in the presence of checks on state authority. If left unguarded, it was assumed, the government would impinge on the expression of individual creativity and intervene in an autonomous and self-sufficient market system. Economic activity has always held a favored position in the United States. As Tocqueville wrote more than 150 years ago when describing the status of economic activity in the United States, "Nothing is more great or more brilliant than commerce: it attracts the attention of the public, and fills the imagination of the multitude; all energetic passions are directed to it."[35] As the chief organization involved in the production of wealth and the accumulation of private property, the corporation has been awarded special status. Attempts to regulate corporate activities have been attacked as "interventionist," a violation of market norms. Indeed, the adversarial relationship and the appeal to norms of noninterference continue to structure policy debates in the last years of the twentieth century.

Although market liberalism has continued to exert ideological force, its influence has varied with the concrete demands of the time. Its effects have been, at best, ambiguous. Throughout American economic history there have been strong and incessant demands for a direct state role in the economy. In the early decades of the nineteenth century, national and subnational governments created an infrastructure for economic exchange by defining contract rights and liability, and by providing protection through bankruptcy laws. Beyond simply furnishing a positive legal environment for growth, the federal government invested a good deal of capital. During the nineteenth century, supposedly the heyday of laissez-faire capitalism, the federal government became involved in a number of mixed enterprises in the area of transportation. Special franchises, land grants, direct funding, and in-kind support were critical in promoting the construction of turnpikes, canals, steamboats, and a transcontinental railroad system. The resulting reduction in transportation costs was essential in stimulating economic demand and development.[36]

Rhetorical support for a laissez-faire political economy weakened dramatically during the late nineteenth and early twentieth centuries, the period that saw the creation of the market regime. Rapid changes in the nation's economic structure challenged the decentralized system that had existed in earlier decades. The integration of formerly local markets, waves of corporate consolidation and expansion, and the emergence of industrial giants stimulated a revision of norms for government's relations with the economy. Popular demands for a positive governmental role resulted in regulatory initiatives at the state and national levels. Ironically, market norms were invoked by those seeking to extend public authority over the market and place new and unprecedented regulatory restraints on corporations. During the 1930s, the Great Depression stimulated attempts to define the parameters of a new political-economic order based on the organization of economic interests and the active role of the government in macroeconomic management. By the 1960s and 70s, the New Left critique of capitalism politicized many quality-of-life issues and legitimized government's playing a broader role in corporate investment and production decisions. Even if periods of crisis have altered dominant conceptions of the political economy and created new expectations, opponents of regulation continue to appeal to the market. Thus, in the 1970s and 80s, conservative critics of regulation subjected policy to formal economic analysis in hopes of determining whether the results of policy were preferable to those of the market. At the same time, consumer advocates, responding to policies that allowed a few major corporations to extract excess profits and impose supra-competitive prices, promoted market competition. The market remains a potent, if ambiguous, symbol representing both individual autonomy and the primacy of property rights.

Each of the century's major waves of regulation has provided an opportunity to experiment with new approaches to administration.[37] Policy-makers combined new regulatory initiatives with administrative reform efforts designed to meet the technical demands of the new policies, to accommodate interest groups, or to correct for past failures. These reform initiatives were, in many cases, based on contemporary theories of administration and the proper organization of public authority. Thus, during the Progressive Era, policy-makers linked demands for national regulation with debates about the need for neutral administrative competence. The result was the creation of a number of independent commissions intended to allow for the application of expertise to regulatory problems without the excessive interference of political officials. During the 1930s, associationalist theories of cooperative administration provided a model on which to base the New Deal system of government-supervised self-regulation. The new social regulatory initiatives of the 1970s also embodied new approaches to administration. Concerns over excessive delegation, and agency capture by the regulated interests, stimulated debates over institutional design, the optimal level of legislative specificity, and various means of enhancing the participation of previously excluded groups. Those involved in designing policy placed action-forcing provisions in the legislation to compel agencies to execute their duties. In the 1970s and 80s, reform doctrines promoting an expanded role for economics in regulatory review caused a centralization of regulatory authority in the Office of Management and Budget. In each case, policy-makers integrated a new vision of state-economy relations into new administrative reform doctrines, thus giving the main initiatives economic and institutional significance.

Although the broad political-economic and administrative philosophies function at a systemic level, ideas also play a critical role on a policy-specific basis. Evidence of policy failure and new potential policy problems commonly give rise to intensive debates on the nature of the problems and on alternative regulatory approaches. In Congress, the bureaucracy, interest groups, think tanks, and universities, policy analysts and experts engage in a continuing dialogue over the design and administration of policy. Officials make and administer policies within the intellectual environment created by these issue networks or policy communities. Intellectual innovations are translated into policy and administration through formal and informal channels, particularly if these innovations can be effectively linked to the demands of mobilized interests or used in problem-solving.[38]

Regulators also gain access to ideas through the activities of professional administrators within the agencies. The professional staffs of administrative agencies serve in many ways as a transmission belt linking the academic disciplines and policy implementation.[39] Although staffing practices have differed dramatically over time, all major regulatory agencies have staffs of scientific and social-scientific experts (e.g., economists, engineers, and environmental scientists) who play a role in analyzing problems, designing standards, selecting enforcement actions, and assessing the impact of regulations. Economists have been particularly influential, because economic debates about the effects of regulations on economic efficiency have cut across all regulatory issue areas.

The theories and assumptions that professionals bring to bear in their work shape policy. Likewise, this specialized knowledge plays an important role in structuring political participation in regulatory politics. As Douglas Yates explains: "Professional specialization . . . makes it increasingly difficult for laymen and for specialists from different areas of expertise to speak one another's language. Inability to communicate creates a barrier to entry into policy discourse and thus has an inherently fragmenting effect."[40] The "barrier to entry into policy discourse" created by specialists both within the agency and in the larger policy community limits the access and influence of groups incapable of mustering the necessary resources. The power of ideas thus affects the influence of interest groups and their ability to participate in the policy process.

Interests

All individuals and social groups have interests that are affected by economic change; they seek to execute certain economic functions within the constraints imposed by existing institutions and regulations. To protect or advance their interests more effectively, they commonly form organizations or associations. The importance of organization varies from group to group. Corporations, for example, exist both as unitary actors and as members of organizations. Although social movements are important in the history of some new regulatory initiatives, organized interests tend to have the greatest effect on regulatory politics. Indeed, broad social movements are often reducible to collections of political and economic interest associations which are part of larger political coalitions.

The American interest-group system, when compared with those of other industrialized democracies, can be characterized as large, disaggregated, and diverse. Some seven thousand organizations have representatives in Washington, D.C. The system is remarkably decentralized. There are some active business peak associations, which represent firms from a wide range of industries. However, these groups, which include the National Association of Manufacturers and the U.S. Chamber of Commerce, are weak by comparison with trade associations organized on an industry-specific basis. Reflecting the limited role of peak associations in the United States, there are almost twelve hundred trade associations functioning at the national level. More than four hundred additional groups represent foreign commerce and corporations. Moreover, individual corporations are political actors in their own right: more than three thousand corporations have Washington representatives. There are, in addition, almost five hundred professional associations and more than one hundred labor organizations.[41]

The figures presented above represent the composition of the contemporary interest-group system. That system itself has evolved over the course of the past hundred years. From the early decades of the century, when the national system consisted of a small number of business peak associations, labor unions, and agricultural commodity groups, the interest-group system has grown both in size and in diversity. The heightened influence of public policy and budgetary decisions on corporate profitability and the welfare of a host of nonbusiness-related interests has stimulated this growth. However, the interest-group system continues to overrepresent certain groups, particularly business. Although individuals occupying managerial and administrative positions make up 7 percent of the population, business associations and corporations with Washington representatives account for 71 percent of the interest groups. In contrast, nonfarm workers comprise 41 percent of the population but are represented by 4 percent of the interest groups.[42] Moreover, one must note that corporations are represented at different levels of aggregation. Large corporations commonly have their own Washington representatives and are also represented both by multiple trade associations and by peak associations. In contrast, industrial workers find representation—assuming they are unionized—in their union locals, which are seldom involved in national politics, and in labor peak associations such as the AFL-CIO.[43]

A number of factors can be cited to explain why peak associations have remained relatively weak in the United States. For example, it might be suggested that peak associations have been weak precisely because business has been so strong. Historically, the lack of a credible political threat to business interests, the broad ideological support for capitalism, and a comfortable relationship with elected officials have made the formation of strong peak associations unnecessary. In other nations, in contrast, class-based programmatic parties and strong labor movements force businesses to rely more heavily on peak associations.[44] Although ideological or cultural explanations are attractive, one can gain much by focusing once again on the role of governmental institutions. As noted above, the United States has an institutional structure characterized by high levels of horizontal and vertical fragmentation. This fragmentation contributes to a decentralized interest-group system. When legislation is written at the subcommittee level and regulatory standards are drafted by agencies that regulate on an industry-specific basis, political organization at the industry level is efficient and sufficient for participation in regulatory politics. In short, the specialization of interest groups closely parallels the specialization that characterizes governmental structures.

Institutions are crucial for another reason. As noted earlier, during the past several decades the regulatory state has become professionalized. Virtually all regulatory agencies place a great reliance on expert administrators in the definition of standards and the assessment of the economic effects of various regulations. As regulatory policy addresses problems of ever-greater complexity, policy will be administered and discourse dominated by specialists. Interest groups lacking the resources necessary to employ professional staffs may encounter difficulties when attempting to participate in policy debates. The greater opportunities for group access provided in much contemporary regulatory legislation may, in the end, be of little compensatory value.

Institutional evolution is of paramount importance to those who seek to understand the development of regulatory policy. It strongly affects the content and implementation of policy by determining which forms of expertise and which policy tools will be available to administrators; it determines how societal interests will be integrated into the policy process. As Stephen Krasner explains: "It is necessary to understand both how institutions reproduce themselves through time and what historical conditions give rise to them in the first place . . . once an historical choice is made, it both precludes and facilitates alternative future choices."[45] The evolution of regulatory regimes—combinations of institutions and policies—structures the interaction of economic interests and the pattern of state-economy relations over time. Each of the periods examined in this book combined significant regulatory initiatives with administrative reform efforts. Over the course of the past hundred years, there has been a trend toward greater professionalization and greater control over interest groups' participation in the policy-making process. Professionalization has been promoted as a means of limiting corruption and addressing the complexities of the implementation of regulatory policy. Control over group access has been justified as a means of promoting agencies' independence and assuring that the interactions between regulators and the regulated are open to the public. These dual themes, administrative professionalism and bureaucratic independence, have their origins in the Progressive Era, the same period that saw the emergence of the first coherent regulatory regime. In the next chapter I examine this period.

2

Progressivism and the Creation of National Regulatory Authority

THE FIRST SIGNIFICANT SURGE OF NATIONAL REGULATORY legislation and the first coherent regulatory regime emerged during the decades surrounding the turn of the century. The tremendous economic changes of the latter half of the nineteenth century forced the mobilization of diverse interests demanding a policy response to the growing concentration of economic and political power and the elimination of decentralized local market systems. The regulatory legislation of the period addressed corporate organization and practices and a number of industries including rail transportation, finance, meat-packing, and pharmaceuticals. The regulatory regime took form only after the turn of the century, when the demands were linked with Progressive arguments regarding state-economy relations and administrative reform doctrines.

When taken together, the policies of the period can be seen to have in common the use of the market as a benchmark. Take the example of antitrust policy. Congress passed the Sherman Act, the Clayton Act, and the Federal Trade Commission Act to eliminate or prevent those forms of industrial organization and corporate behavior which threatened to undermine market mechanisms. Policy-makers were committed to preserving the markets and a decentralized industrial structure. However, in some instances the structural features of an industry (e.g., large capital investment, economies of scale) precluded a return to the market. Thus, in the case of railroads and public utilities, policies were created to compensate for the lack of markets by producing marketlike results through administrative means. The new regulatory regime was, in es-

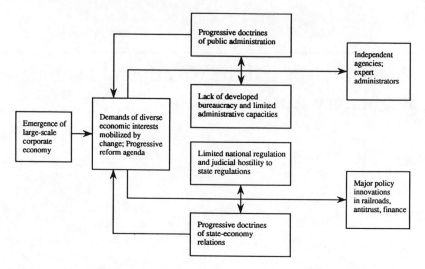

Fig. 2.1   The market regime.

sence, market-corrective. Markets were emphasized because of their economic function as decentralized systems of exchange. However, they also symbolized personal independence and local autonomy. The market was as much a political entity as it was an economic one. A return to the market was an affirmation of the economic structure that was being eroded by the changes of the period. The forces that shaped the market regime are presented schematically in Figure 2.1. The remainder of this chapter is devoted to exploring the origins of the market regime in greater detail.

THE RISE OF A NEW CORPORATE ORDER

In the decades following the Civil War, the American economy experienced a dramatic structural transformation. From the late 1860s to the 1890s, the real per capita gross national product grew at an average annual rate of 2 percent. Higher incomes translated into higher levels of savings and investment. The growth of tangible capital stock greatly outpaced the growth of the population: in three decades, the capital stock per worker increased by 80 percent. The growing capital intensity of production promoted tremendous gains in efficiency. While the percentage of the labor force engaged in manufacturing remained relatively constant at 19 percent, manufacturing output increased from 33 percent of all commodities in 1869 to 53 percent twenty-five years later.[1]

Economic growth was accompanied by significant changes in the organization of production and the structure of industry. The refinement and dissemination of critical mass-production technologies (i.e., standardized large-batch and continuous-batch production) allowed firms to increase production to meet a far greater demand. Corporations followed the example of the railroads and increasingly adopted hierarchical multidivisional organizations to coordinate, direct, and monitor their activities. Moreover, corporations vigorously merged into larger units to realize greater economies of scale. They integrated vertically, incorporating suppliers of raw materials, wholesalers, and retailers and thus internalizing transactions that had formerly taken place in markets. Advances in the railroads and the telegraph system provided access to new markets and facilitated ever-greater growth and coordination. The multidivisional, fully integrated firm placed a premium on managerial skills. Increasingly, large corporations used these skills to dominate industries and manage expansion and competition, threatening the highly decentralized, locally based economies that had prevailed in earlier decades.[2]

The rapid economic growth during the latter half of the nineteenth century was disrupted by troughs in the business cycle in 1887–88 and 1899–1900, and by a fairly deep depression that lasted from 1893 to 1896. Moreover, persistent problems of overproduction accompanied the expansion into new markets. Corporations had to discover some means of coordinating expansion and managing competition to exploit growing economies of scale while maintaining stability. The response they chose was the formation of the trust. During the period 1882–87, the Standard Oil Trust, the American Cotton Oil Trust, the National Linseed Oil Trust, and the Distillers and Cattle Feeders Trust were created. By 1904, some 300 trusts were alleged to exist. Moreover, between 1897 and 1904 the nation experienced a giant wave of mergers in which 4,227 firms merged to create 257 combinations, including such industrial giants as United States Steel and International Harvester. During this period of industrial consolidation, 1 percent of the nation's companies came to control the production of some 45 percent of manufactured goods.[3]

The economic changes of the period were combined with equally significant societal changes caused by immigration and urbanization. Reductions in the cost of ocean transportation and the growth of the American economy during the latter half of the nineteenth century facilitated high rates of immigration. Between 1865 and 1890, 9.5 million European immigrants came to the United States, and by 1915 an additional 20 million had arrived. New immigrants naturally settled in the cities to join ethnic communities and find work. The waves of immigration accelerated the urbanization of American society. Between 1860 and 1910, the rural population grew from 25 million to 50 million,

while the urban population grew from 6 million to 42 million. Like the
great manufacturing trusts, immigration and urbanization were salient
symbols of the changing circumstances that threatened the traditional
organization of American society.[4]

The combination of immigration and urbanization had three important effects. First, the rapid increase in urban populations stressed the
infrastructure and greatly outpaced municipal and social institutions'
capacity to address urban poverty. Much of the urban population lived
in poor conditions, particularly during the depression of the 1890s,
when the unemployment rate exceeded 18 percent, reaching 30 percent
in the nonagricultural work force.[5] Social reformers running urban settlement houses, such as Jane Addams's celebrated Hull House in Chicago, relieved some of the poverty.[6] However, given the dimensions of
the crisis, the community response was both piecemeal and insufficient. Second, the influx of immigrants contributed a dramatic expansion of the largely unskilled industrial labor force. The surplus labor in
the nation's cities placed downward pressures on wages, thus exacerbat-
ing the urban squalor and threatening labor organizers' efforts to make
employers recognize workers' right to union representation. Third, the
swelling electorate, and the demand for new services and capital investments in the cities, created a situation ripe for political corruption.
Growing populations required an expanded urban infrastructure and an
extension of social services. The power to assign construction contracts
fueled the urban political machines.[7]

THE ORGANIZATIONAL RESPONSE TO ECONOMIC CHANGE

Increases in capital investment, technological and managerial innovations within the corporation, and an expansion of the transportation
and communications infrastructure drove the economic changes of the
late nineteenth century. Core corporations (i.e., corporations engaging
in capital-intensive, continuous-process production) in the same line of
business commonly attempted to manage expansion by forming trusts
and holding companies or by making informal price-fixing agreements.
They resorted to mergers when the "loose combinations" proved difficult to manage or ran afoul of the law. Railroads managed expansion by
forming pools to distribute traffic and set rates. Because of the railroads'
capital requirements, large investment houses such as J. P. Morgan and
Company played an important role: they engineered combinations, reorganized unprofitable lines, and directed growth.[8] Effective organization was critical for corporations seeking to avoid overexpansion and
cutthroat competition. Organization was not, however, limited to the
dynamic core industries.

Peripheral firms adopted organization as well, albeit in a somewhat different form. The major corporations' expansion and their absorption of markets, small competitors, distributors, and retailers forced smaller businesses to form numerous trade associations. This was largely a defensive maneuver. These associations allowed decentralized industries to formulate policies and common strategies to promote stability. They also provided a defense against larger corporations, and became active proponents of state-level regulation. When organized by national business associations such as the U.S. Chamber of Commerce and the National Board of Trade, trade associations promoted national legislation to regulate railroads and restrain the increase in shipping costs.[9]

Workers also responded to the changes in the economy by creating organizations. During the decades following the Civil War, workers found representation in a number of labor organizations, including the ill-fated National Labor Union; many industry-specific unions; and the Knights of Labor, an organization that by 1886 could claim to represent more than 700,000 crafts and industrial workers. The Knights' spectacular history was short. The political response to the 1886 Haymarket Square riot in Chicago, tactical errors on the part of Terence Powderly, the Knights' Grand Master Workman, and a concerted effort on the part of employers to reject strikers' demands all took a toll, and after 1886 the Knights quickly fell into decline. In that year, however, the American Federation of Labor was founded to unite union locals in a national organization. The AFL represented skilled and semiskilled craft workers rather than the industrial workers who were of increasing importance in the emerging mass-production economy. Under the leadership of Samuel Gompers, the AFL pursued a program of business unionism, rejecting class-based politics to focus on the bread-and-butter issues of wages and working conditions. This pragmatic approach was initially successful: the AFL's membership increased from 250,000 in 1897 to 1,562,000 in 1910, and doubled again in size by the eve of World War I.[10]

Despite the rapid growth of organized labor, several factors limited the success of union efforts. As noted above, the constant influx of new immigrants militated against any concerted attempt to elevate wage levels. Moreover, corporations effectively resisted the unions' demands by using yellow-dog contracts to limit unionization and by resorting to violence in response to strikes. Business associations such as the National Association of Manufacturers orchestrated the attack on organized labor, particularly after 1903, when they began their efforts to promote the "open shop." The courts commonly sided with corporations in industrial disputes, freely issuing injunctions and interpreting strikes and boycotts as conspiracies in restraint of trade, subject to prosecution under the antitrust laws. The craft organization of the AFL, which incorporated skilled members of the trades, created another distinct problem. The AFL's largely white, Anglo-Saxon membership strongly opposed any sustained efforts to include the immigrant industrial workers in their organization. (The AFL officially abandoned the principle of craft autonomy in 1911, largely in response to the growing importance of mass manufacturing.) Although the federal government adopted a more conciliatory position toward labor during the Wilson administration and World War I, effective union organization would not be possible until the regulatory initiatives of the New Deal.[11]

Organization swept the countryside as well, particularly during the early 1870s and the 1890s, when depressed farm prices gave the larger economic-structural changes a new significance.[12] The Granger movement of the 1870s promoted the creation of local cooperative organizations that brought farmers together for purposes of purchasing and marketing and provided a basis for political mobilization. Farm groups, often working together with small merchants, focused on the clearest symbol of the new economic order, successfully demanding laws regulating the railroads. In the 1890s the Populists continued the activities of the Grangers, calling for the nationalization of the railroads and banks, and the coinage of silver in order to increase farm commodity prices. The Grangers and the Populists also entered partisan politics, forming political parties. Although these parties functioned primarily at the local level, the populist People's party ran a presidential candidate, James B. Weaver, in 1892. After joining forces with the Democrats behind William Jennings Bryan in 1896, the Populists suffered a resounding defeat. Their influence in partisan politics quickly declined as this realigning election placed the Republicans in firm control of the federal government.[13]

The political activism of the agricultural organizations was, at best, episodic. However, the local cooperatives evolved into more sophisticated enterprises. Beginning in the latter half of the 1890s, farmers began to organize into commodity groups. Functioning largely as cooperatives, they began operating their own warehouses and grain elevators. They employed business managers and functioned in many ways as small corporations. More developed commodity groups tried to exercise control over the prices charged or the quantities shipped to market, in hopes of increasing farm incomes. These commodity groups, organized on a state or a national basis, entered politics with far greater sophistication than their populist predecessors.[14]

The combination of dramatic changes in the structure of the economy and the organization and mobilization of new interests had a striking effect on the policy agenda and the nature of politics. Although many groups supported reform, their specific goals differed greatly. All groups interpreted the decline of the local market system and the growing power of large corporations as significant threats to prevailing property rights and to the existing distribution of wealth and economic power. The demands for reform stemmed from a common cause; but owing to the diversity of interests involved, these demands lacked coherence. This created an ample opportunity for elites to impose their own agendas. The Progressives provided broad goals that attracted many of these groups, promoted coalition-building, and gave direction to the uncoordinated demands for change.

THE PROGRESSIVE MOVEMENT

As explained in chapter 1, different groups interpret economic change in terms of vastly different sets of political and economic concerns, they demand governmental actions that may not be compatible with each other, or reasonably connected to the events in question. Because demands are often irreconcilable, overly vague, or locally oriented, elected officials have ample opportunities to shape the resulting policies. They reformulate the demands and give them greater coherence by linking them to prevailing political-economic and administrative doctrines and concrete policy proposals. The market regime has its roots in the economic transformation of the late nineteenth century. However, the demands for change were translated into policy only after they were coupled to the Progressive reform agenda.

The Progressives inherited much of their program from the reform movements of the last quarter of the nineteenth century. During this period, the problems of economic change, urban poverty, and political corruption stimulated a response from members of every class. The Mugwumps, drawn largely from the upper class, promoted reforms in partisan politics and the civil service to purge corruption from government and promote efficiency. They advocated tougher vice laws in hopes of bringing about a moral regeneration of the nation, and they strongly supported civil service reform. Muckraking exposés revealed the dark side of industrialism and urban corruption to a large middle-class population that expected a policy response. In the rural sections of the country, the Populists demanded reforms to limit the power of the large corporations, railroads, and financiers who were allegedly using their position in the new order to eliminate individual opportunity and exploit farm workers. The Populists called for numerous measures to protect farm incomes, as well as reforms to limit the influence of the railroads. In the cities, the Social Gospel movement united middle-class Protestant reformers to champion social change as an extension of their Christian faith. They established missions in the slums and provided a host of services for the new immigrants and the poor. This reform legacy—particularly that of the Social Gospel movement—gave the Progressives an agenda that had distinct political and moral dimensions.[15]

What differentiated the Progressive Era from earlier decades filled with demands for reform? The first major difference involved the political context. Although there had been ongoing calls for reform during the last quarter of the nineteenth century, highly competitive partisan politics had impeded any attempt to introduce initiatives that could threaten existing coalitions, and had increased the risk of any dramatic departure from existing policies and administrative practices. After the realignment of 1896, Republican hegemony outside of the South provided greater opportunities for reform. However, these opportunities were not in themselves sufficient.[16] This brings us to the second major difference. Progressivism was distinguished from earlier reform-based movements by its unique coupling of a reform agenda with a faith that scientific and social-scientific knowledge could be applied constructively to address numerous social problems. The Progressives believed that institutions could be rationally designed to restrain, control, or redirect the social and economic changes that the nation was encountering, and thus improve the human condition.

This faith in scientific and social-scientific knowledge was largely a product of the times. The period saw a great expansion of the nation's system of higher education. In 1900 the nation's college professors and instructors numbered seven thousand; by the end of the Progressive Era they numbered more than thirty-three thousand.[17] The expansion of higher education was combined with an organization of the disciplines which was similar to the organization that had taken place in other parts of society: the American Historical Association was founded in 1884, followed by the American Economic Association in 1885 and the American Political Science Association and the American Sociological Society in 1903. As the disciplines sought to professionalize and to carve out separate identities, many intellectuals contemplated their professional mission and the relationship between the disciplines and social change. Take the example of economics. Prominent founders and early members of the American Economic Association (e.g., Richard T. Ely, John R. Commons, John B. Clark, and Edward Bemis) had close ties to the Social Gospel movement and participated in church conferences on a regular basis. They saw the fusion of social science and societal reform as both natural and necessary.[18] Thus, when the American Economic Association was founded, its platform proclaimed: "We regard the state as an educational and ethical agency whose positive aid is an indispensable condition of human progress." Rejecting the laissez-faire doctrines of classical economics, the platform stated, "The conflict of labor and capital has brought to the front a vast number of social problems whose solution is impossible without the united efforts of church, state, and science."[19]

The Progressive social scientists presented their reformist ideals in the classroom and in the influential writings of the day. They trained a new generation to see the natural linkages between the responsibilities of the university and those of the government. Progressive academics formulated theories that they quickly translated into policy. They entered government service in an advisory role to assist in writing legislation, or they served in various capacities in government at the state or national level. Thus they brought new social-scientific research and a familiarity with European public policies and administrative doctrines to bear on many of the central policy debates. They transmitted their practical experience back into the universities, where it became the basis for further research.

The experimentation of the Progressive Era and Progressives' desire to bring new ideas and international experiences into the policy debates reflected both the pragmatism of the age and an obvious element of elite self-promotion. Although the enhanced role of intellectuals stimulated innovative policies and organizational reforms, it also introduced a distinct tension into the core of Progressivism. As Stanley Caine explains: "This heavy reliance on highly trained scholars worked at cross-purposes with the principle of expanding popular participation in government. Although some intellectuals showed a deep and abiding faith in the people and worked for popular reforms, others emphasized such elitist ideals as the restoration of efficiency and order in economic and political life. The reunion of intellectuals and politicians gave progressivism great innovative strength. At times, however, it proved to be a mixed blessing."[20] Most supporters of Progressivism were committed to limited reforms that would restore balance and protect the political and economic opportunities of the individual. Some Progressive intellectuals, however, envisioned the creation of a new institutional order that would serve a transformative, rather than a protective, purpose. As Herbert Croly wrote in *The Promise of American Life:* "Democracy must stand or fall on a platform of possible human perfectibility. If human nature cannot be improved by institutions, democracy is at best a more than usually safe form of political organization . . . if it is to work better as well as merely longer, it must have some leavening effect on human nature; and the sincere democrat is obliged to assume the power of the leaven. For him the practical questions are: How can the improvement be brought about? and, How much may it amount to?"[21]

The Progressives' View of the New Economic Order

The breadth of the Progressives' reform vision depended, in large part, on their underlying interpretation of the recent changes in the political economy. Were the current problems the unfortunate byproducts of an unavoidable but largely positive evolutionary process of economic change? Or, in contrast, were they but a manifestation of the age-old conflict between individual liberty and the concentrated powers that sought to usurp it? Accepting the existence of a broader evolutionary process meant recognizing the need to reconfigure public institutions to accommodate and direct the transformation. Believing that the current problems were long-standing ones in a new guise, however, meant that one could address monopoly and corruption by passing new laws to force a decentralization of capital and establish prohibitions on various forms of behavior. One would seek to redistribute power so as to approximate the situation that would exist under market conditions. This reaction, most common among the agrarians of the late nineteenth century, continued to play a significant role in the Progressive Era.

The radical agrarians attributed their changing circumstances to exploitation rather than to broader economic trends or to the inherent qualities of agriculture which created persistent surpluses. As the People's Platform of 1892 proclaimed: "The fruits of the toils of millions are boldly stolen to build up colossal fortunes for a few, unprecedented in the history of mankind; and the possessors of these, in turn despise the Republic and endanger liberty. From the same prolific womb of governmental injustice we breed the two great classes—tramps and millionaires." As the Grangers and the Populists searched for explanations for the changing circumstances, they focused on the most immediate targets. They attacked the railroads, which allegedly imposed a rate structure that made farm incomes impossible to maintain at traditional levels. They vilified the bankers who refused to make loans on the value of the land. They decried the merchants who charged too much for basic goods. And they denounced politicians who would "destroy the multitudes in order to secure corruption funds from millionaires."[22]

The demands for railroad regulation forced the passage of the so-called Granger laws, which fixed maximum rates or, in the case of Minnesota and Illinois, actually assigned regulatory duties to state railroad commissions. Although these laws reflected the demands of diverse interests, they encountered a common difficulty: attempts to establish state regulations came into conflict with the division of regulatory authority prescribed in the interstate commerce clause of the Constitution, and thus would prove vulnerable to challenges in the federal courts.[23] However, by the time the Supreme Court challenged the validity of the Granger laws, debates about national railroad regulation had already moved to Congress (see chapter 3, below). Similarly, with the passage of the Sherman Antitrust Act in 1890 antitrust laws in 17 states were supplanted by national legislation.

The extension of regulatory authority mandated a new role for the federal government, a new relationship between the national state and corporations. Although such a response could have been difficult to reconcile with the ideological adherence to a limited state and to market governance, it was justified in two ways. First, because of what Thurman Arnold referred to as the "trick of personification," public policy represented corporations as individuals.[24] Thus, regulation could be construed as a form of law enforcement. Because law enforcement was considered a legitimate function even in the most limited of states, "personification" made the extension of regulatory authority seem less problematic.

Second, because concentrated power was considered a threat to individual autonomy and democratic rule, the extension of regulatory authority could be interpreted as the creation of a counterweight, a means of forcing corporate accountability. Take, for example, the rhetoric surrounding the passage of the Sherman Antitrust Act. Legislators framed the trust problem in terms that reflected the nation's political heritage. As one senator proclaimed: "If the concentrated powers of this combination are entrusted to a single man, it is a kingly prerogative, inconsistent with our form of government, and should be subject to the strong resistance of the State and national authorities. If anything is wrong this is wrong. If we will not endure a king as a political power we should not endure a king over the production, transportation, and sale of any of the necessaries of life. If we would not submit to an emperor we should not submit to an autocrat of trade, with the power to prevent competition and to fix the price of any commodity."[25]

The main current of Progressivism did not depart markedly from the vision of the agrarian radicals. The Progressives recognized that the emergence of large corporations was a part of the evolution of the economy and that many corporations were highly efficient and contributed to social welfare by making goods available at lower cost. However, the scale of the large corporations' economic activity and the concentration of power in the hands of corporate chieftains created remarkable opportunities for abuse. As Louis Brandeis explained: "The displacement of the small independent business man by the huge corporation with its myriad of employees, its absentee ownership and its financier control presents a grave danger to our democracy. The social loss is great; and there is no economic gain. But the process of capitalizing free Americans is not an inevitable one. It is not even in accord with the natural law of business. It is largely the result of unwise, man-made, privilege-creating law, which has stimulated existing tendencies to inequality instead of discouraging them."[26] The laws that promoted corporate expansion could be modified to restrict the forms of behavior deemed unacceptable, thus revitalizing market mechanisms. Many Progressives, including Louis Brandeis, Robert La Follette, and Woodrow Wilson, believed that regulatory policies such as antitrust policy could be used to prevent or eliminate the industrial giantism that impinged on the freedoms of consumers, workers, and small businesses.

Theirs was not, however, the only vision of the role of the state in a new regulatory order. It could be contrasted with a second vision, a vision of a new political-economic order in which the state would not demand a forcible return to the market but would facilitate changes in the economic structure by means of a close working relationship with corporations and the representatives of leading economic interests. Theodore Roosevelt and Herbert Croly were two of the most influential proponents of this statist version of Progressivism. In 1910 Roosevelt began in earnest to articulate a program that he labeled the "New Nationalism," a reference to the need to vest greater authority in the national government and overcome sectional conflicts. Although the New Nationalism encompassed many economic and social policy proposals that prefigured some central features of the welfare state, I am concerned primarily with its regulatory implications. Roosevelt saw the large corporations as a natural and in many ways beneficial product of economic evolution. He thus had little sympathy for "the foolish radicals who desire to break up all big business, with the impossible ideal of returning to mid-nineteenth century industrial conditions."[27] As he noted: "Combinations in industry are the result of an imperative economic law which cannot be repealed by political legislation. The effort at prohibiting all combination has substantially failed. *The way out lies, not in attempting to prevent such combinations, but in completely controlling them in the interest of the public welfare.*"[28]

Rather than extending the antitrust tradition, Roosevelt called for the creation of a regulatory commission resembling the Interstate Commerce Commission or the Bureau of Corporations (in the Department of Commerce and Labor) to collect data on corporate activity, supervise capitalization, and regulate the terms and conditions of labor. The commission would use the Sherman Act selectively, applying it on the basis not of size but of conduct. As Roosevelt explained: "Such a Commission would have complete power to examine into every big corporation engaged or proposing to engage in business between the states . . . Where a company is found seeking its profits through serving the community by stimulating production, lowering prices or improving service, while scrupulously respecting the rights of others (including its rivals, its employees, its customers, and the general public), and strictly obeying the law, then no matter how large its capital, or how great the volume of business it would be encouraged to still more abundant production, or better services, by the fullest protection that the Government could afford it . . . Such a commission, with the power I advocate, would put a stop to abuses of big corporations and small corporations alike; it would draw the line on conduct and not on size."[29]

Roosevelt's vision found its most complete expression in the presidential campaign of 1912. He presented the state as a dynamic force in society which could join with business to promote ever greater efficiencies. This "system of constructive regulation" would allow businesses to develop "freed from confusion, uncertainty, and fruitless litigation."[30]

During the 1912 campaign, Wilson countered Roosevelt's New Nationalism with a more traditional program, which he called the New Freedom. Despite some semantic disagreements, both men accepted the distinction between corporations that profited from honest expansion and efficient practices and those that exploited the population through attempts to monopolize commerce and destroy competitors. The basic disagreement centered on the state's role in the economy. Wilson saw Roosevelt's plan as one in which the trusts would be "recognized as a permanent part of our economic order" and made "the ministers, the instruments, through which the life of this country shall be justly and happily developed on its industrial side."[31] This raised two concerns for Wilson. First, he charged that under such an arrangement the large corporations would have to "capture the government, in order not to be restrained too much by it."[32] Second, unlike the free-market system, in which individuals realize the fruits of their labors, Roosevelt's New Nationalism would make citizens dependent on the benevolence of the government or the large corporations. On these grounds, Wilson called for a continuation and expansion of the antitrust tradition. An elimination of monopolies and the methods they use was presented as "the restoration of freedom."[33]

After Wilson's election to the presidency, his vision of an order based on markets and market-corrective regulation would prove more influential than Roosevelt's plan, at least until the nation's entry into the war in Europe. Indeed, most of the regulatory initiatives of the Progressive Era can be placed within the Wilsonian vision of the proper role of the state in the economy. Roosevelt's New Nationalism and the role of the state it entailed were dismissed; but the dismissal was only temporary, for this understanding of the new industrial order played an important role in shaping the recovery efforts during the Great Depression.

Two points are of critical importance when one is addressing the political economy of Progressivism. The first is that, although the regulatory policies of the Progressive Era entailed a greater role for the federal government in the economy, they never seriously challenged the legitimacy of the corporation or the existing economic system. Even though the rhetoric of the times often suggested that such a challenge existed, the Progressive reforms did not have radical foundations. Second, the new regulations, in many cases, cannot be correctly interpreted simply as attempts to restrain corporations on behalf of consumers or small entrepreneurs. The rhetorical support for the "man on the make," to use Wilson's term, should not veil the fact that many of the regulatory initiatives of the period received the support of the regulated. Indeed, as revisionist histories of the Progressive Era suggest, representatives of the regulated industries commonly played a significant role in drafting the regulatory legislation. Thus the translation of popular demands into policy was influenced not only by Progressive ideas but also by a calculation of what kinds of policies would be possible without undermining the existing political coalitions—which, for the dominant Republicans, included many of the northern industries that would be subjected to federal regulations.[34]

This second point, namely that the regulated were commonly strong proponents of regulation, seems counterintuitive. As noted above, corporate expansion during the second half of the nineteenth century created problems, such as overproduction and intense competition which often hurt one or more of the businesses involved. Corporations had to find some means to manage corporate expansion and competition, to increase industrial stability, and to maintain profitability. They sought to address these problems, albeit with mixed success, through the creation of trusts and holding companies, and through mergers. The political reaction to these strategies was significant at the state level, particularly in those regions where agrarian radicals and small businesses exercised political power. Because state regulations were rarely coordinated and often reflected populist interests, the prospect of a single set of national regulations had a certain appeal. Moreover, federal regulations could rationalize production and guarantee profitability. Whether the policies would ultimately benefit the regulated was an open question, owing to the compromises necessary to forge broad coalitions, the excessive delegation of authority implicit in much of the legislation, and the associated reliance on new administrative agencies whose powers would be determined through interaction with the courts.

Institutional Design and the Organization of Public Authority

The state-building efforts of the Progressive Era were shaped, in large part, by the dominant ideas regarding institutional design. The Progressives saw institutional design as an important element of reform. Their reform agenda went well beyond economic regulation to address various forms of political corruption. Thus, the Progressives promoted nonpartisan municipal ballots and city managers to undermine the urban political machines. Reformers believed that the elimination of the machines would reduce corruption and improve the delivery of social services. They also promoted direct voter referenda and party primaries at the state level, the former to limit the influence of business in the state legislatures, the latter to lessen the role of party bosses in partisan politics. Primaries, although they allowed for a broad democratization of the electoral system, simultaneously weakened the parties by limiting their capacity to control their own labels. The parties could no longer determine who would run as a Democrat or a Republican. As Leon Epstein has argued, the Progressive reforms transformed parties into public utilities.[35]

For present purposes, however, I am concerned with the new administrative doctrines presented by some of the representatives of Progressivism. These doctrines played a central role in institutional design, shaping the definition of policy at the agency level. Essential to these doctrines was the belief in the separation of politics and administration advocated by a number of Progressives, including Frank Goodnow and Woodrow Wilson. Goodnow recognized that politics and administration were "two distinct functions": *politics* refers to "policies or expressions of the state will," whereas *administration* is "the execution of these policies."[36] No better expression of this sentiment exists than Wilson's article "The Study of Administration." According to Wilson, "the field of administration is a field of business." Drawing an analogy to the production process, he explained that administration is part of the political process "only as machinery is part of the manufactured product." The distinction between politics and administration was clear: "Administration lies outside the proper sphere of politics. Administrative questions are not political questions, Although politics sets the task for administration, it should not be suffered to manipulate its offices."[37]

Wilson and other Progressives believed that one could extract principles of administration from the practices of bureaucracies in other nations. As Wilson explained: "If I see a monarchist dyed in the wool managing a public bureau well, I can learn his business methods without changing one of my republican spots . . . I should like to serve my sovereign as well as he serves his."[38] Of course, Europe did not provide the only examples of efficient management. The "scientific management" of Frederick Winslow Taylor appeared equally applicable. Taylor, the chief proponent of reorganizing the production process to promote efficiency, argued that one could break the production process into its constituent parts and then reintegrate them scientifically. Public officials could accomplish the same thing in the public sector. By studying administration systematically, one could derive principles that would allow for more effective and efficient production.[39]

The administrative principles that the Progressives adopted were relatively simple, even naïve. But they were also revolutionary in light of the underdevelopment of the American bureaucracy. These principles guided the institutional changes of the Progressive Era and quickly became the orthodoxy with respect to public administration. First, positions in government agencies had to be filled on the basis of competence. Merit had to replace patronage in the making of staffing and promotion decisions. Second, hiring specialists was to be preferred to building a core of generalists. Each agency must be organized to reflect task specification and the division of labor; officials must be specialists possessing the expertise appropriate to their assigned duties. Third, personal discretion must be reduced through strict adherence to detailed rules within the organization: a government of rules would be more efficient than a government of men. Fourth, a government agency must be organized hierarchically to allow the executive to direct the activities of the staff toward a common set of goals. Moreover, hierarchy would facilitate bureaucrats' accountability to the head of the agency, who, in turn, would be accountable to Congress and the President. Fifth, and lastly, to facilitate oversight and enhance performance each agency must be given clearcut responsibilities. Progressive intellectuals believed that these principles, when taken together, would allow for more effective and efficient administration, a neutral competence that could be relied on to pursue politically determined goals.[40]

Although the Progressives sought to foster administrative neutrality and efficiency at all levels of government, their greatest legacy with respect to regulation was the independent regulatory commission. The independent commission was not itself a Progressive innovation. Commissions had been created before the turn of the century at the state level, and one had been created at the national level with the passage of the Interstate Commerce Act in 1887. However, the Progressives provided strong support and theoretical justification for the organizational form based on the principles presented above. To understand the appeal of the independent commission, it is useful to consider its major features.

Independent regulatory commissions are unique institutions for three reasons. First, they are formally independent from the executive branch. Commissioners are appointed by the president, subject to Senate confirmation. The commission must be bipartisan in composition, with no more than a simple majority belonging to the same political party. Moreover, to limit the influence of a single president, commissioners serve for staggered terms of five or seven years. The president's ability to remove sitting commissioners is limited by statutory restrictions—restrictions that were ultimately affirmed by the Supreme Court after Franklin Roosevelt dismissed a chairman without cause.[41] Members of Congress and advocates of regulation hoped that this political independence would insulate administration from the partisan agendas of presidents and elected officials who might have too close a relationship to the regulated industries.

Second, the independent regulatory commission constituted a significant departure from existing tenets of institutional design. Despite the continued allegiance to the constitutional principle of separation of powers, the commissions combined legislative, executive, and judicial functions within the confines of a single agency. An agency exercised quasi-legislative functions by promulgating administrative rules that had the force of law. Thus, the Interstate Commerce Commission established railroad rates to correct rates deemed unreasonable or unjust; the Federal Trade Commission promulgated rules prohibiting unfair trade practices in a given sector of the economy. These rules carried the force of law. Once rules were promulgated, the commissions exercised an executive function by filing complaints to enforce the rules. The independent commissions internalized the judicial function as well: violations were adjudicated by hearing examiners (later renamed administrative law judges) working within the agencies, the final decision being voted on by the commissioners. The decisions of a commission could be challenged in a U.S. court of appeals.

Third, and perhaps most significant from the perspective of the Progressive Era, the independent regulatory commissions were staffed by expert administrators with the appropriate technical competence. The Progressives recognized that many regulatory problems required the application of specialized expertise. The valuation of railroad capital, the definition of adequate rates of return, and the determination of what constituted an "unfair method of competition" were complicated tasks that were best executed by those with training in economics and accounting. Attempts to address complex regulatory problems within the confines of a legislature would open the debates to numerous political forces that could threaten established policy goals and undermine the technical coherence of the proposed solutions. It was believed that professionals within a commission would act in a nonpartisan fashion and resolve disputes on a scientific basis. Moreover the concentration of expertise within the commissions would allow these bodies to serve as investigative arms of Congress.

These unique features of the independent commission made it a superior organizational form, at least in theory. It was envisioned as an institution capable of compensating for the shortcomings of the "political" institutions of American government. As a Progressive Era writer, Samuel O. Dunn, explained: "The disqualifications of legislatures, courts, and ordinary executive officials for the regulation of business suggests some of the qualifications that ought to be possessed by the members of regulating commissions. Ability, expert knowledge, fairness in utterance and act, moral courage to resist public opinion when it is wrong, as well as to enforce their duty on refractory public utility managements when they are wrong—these are the prime essentials."[42] Such qualifications were necessary because many important decisions regarding the goals of regulation were left to be determined by administrators. Unfortunately, the independent commission's promise was often belied by its performance.

REGULATORY INITIATIVES VERSUS
ADMINISTRATIVE CAPACITIES

The Progressive Era saw the creation of many new regulatory initiatives, and in most cases these involved the creation of new administrative agencies. The list of regulatory initiatives is impressive. During the period, Congress passed the Interstate Commerce Act (1887), creating the Interstate Commerce Commission; the Sherman Antitrust Act (1890), establishing the foundation of U.S. competition policy; the Hepburn Act (1906), dramatically enhancing the powers of the ICC; the Meat Inspection Act and the Pure Food and Drug Act (1906), regulating the quality of meat and foodstuffs; the Federal Reserve Act (1913), creating the Federal Reserve Board and expanding national regulation of finance; and the Federal Trade Commission and Clayton acts (1914), strengthening antitrust enforcement. Moreover, the Department of Commerce and Labor was created in 1903. It contained the Bureau of Corporations, which was responsible for collecting and disseminating information on corporations. Advances were made in conservation as well, with the creation of the National Forest Service in 1905 and the attempts to regulate resource depletion through a system of sustained-yield forestry.

Despite the strong rhetoric and the moralistic undertones of the regulatory debates of the period, the early regulatory initiatives were limited in impact. Looking at these initiatives in general terms (a more detailed examination will be presented in chapter 3), one can identify at least three factors that shaped their performance. The first is the extraordinary vagueness of the legislative mandates. Congress defined policy goals in the most general manner, creating uncertainty about the ultimate aims of the legislation and the limits of agencies' discretion.

Congress considered legislative imprecision a necessity given the complexity of the regulatory issues. However, such vagueness was also politically expedient. At times, the mobilized interests expressed demands that were simply irreconcilable. The legislative initiatives in railroad regulation, for example, mobilized agrarian radicals seeking to restrain the emerging corporate order; large railroads hoping to escape the confusion of state-level regulations and the extreme demands of various agrarian groups; and shippers trying to obtain lower rates and deter the discriminatory practices that were affecting their ability to compete. Relatively vague legislation vesting authority in an independent commission simply displaced the conflicts from the legislative arena to the administrative arena.

The second factor shaping the initiatives' performance was that, although the Progressive faith in expert administration drew attention away from the significance of delegation and the loss of control it entailed, delegation made the success of regulatory policy contingent on the agencies' financial and human resources. Congress routinely failed to match the ambitious mandates with sufficient resources. In one extreme case, that of the Sherman Act, Congress neglected to appropriate any funds at all. Newly appointed regulators were thus left with limited budgets at their disposal. Moreover, because of the nation's limited regulatory experience, it was difficult to create staffs with the necessary expertise. One must place the early regulatory legislation in historical perspective. At the turn of the century, the American government was, in the words of Stephen Skowronek, "a state of courts and parties."[43] There was nothing resembling a strong regulatory tradition that could inform the implementation of the new statutes. The new regulatory authority was simply out of proportion to the existing administrative capacities. Indeed, when compared with the corporations they regulated, the Interstate Commerce Commission and the Department of Justice simply lacked the resources, the expertise, and the administrative capacities to offer anything resembling a credible challenge.[44] This lack of resources, when combined with the vague mandates, leads one to question whether some of the early initiatives were anything more than symbolic efforts designed to assuage the demands of mobilized constituents.[45]

Lastly, the third factor affecting performance was the resistance of other institutions to any substantial extension of regulatory authority. As will be shown in chapter 3, judicial decisions placed distinct limits on agencies' authority by extending constitutional protections to corporations and by questioning both the jurisdiction afforded by the interstate commerce clause, and the powers that regulators could derive from the vague legislative mandates. On the occasions when the agencies were successful in implementing the policies, the resulting mobilization of regulated interests was, at times, sufficient to create strong opposition within Congress. This, of course, is one of the problems with any expansive delegation of authority. Because legislative mandates were imprecise, there were few means of determining with accuracy how regulators would implement the legislation or how Congress would respond to the grievances of the regulated. Because of its own electoral vulnerability and the broad and persistent adherence to norms of market governance, Congress was willing to rein in agencies that were executing their mandates in good faith. However, this occurred primarily when the agencies' actions provoked a political reaction from the regulated interests. These points and the defining dimensions of the market regime are best examined in context. That is the subject of chapter 3.

3

Regulating Railroads and Corporate Conduct: The Political Economy of the Market Regime

THE LAST QUARTER OF THE NINETEENTH CENTURY WAS A PEriod of rapid economic change. A revolution in corporate organization and the progressive integration of a formerly decentralized, local market system stimulated a variety of demands for new policies at the state and national levels. Whether the railroads and trusts were actually a great threat to the public was largely irrelevant. Because they stood as the most salient symbols of economic transformation, they became convenient targets for citizens searching for some explanation of the changes they were experiencing. Moreover, despite the appeal of many legislators to the general welfare, interests were defined by economic sector and region. Groups in those sectors and regions threatened by the changes in question joined in the call for regulation largely as a defensive maneuver. In the end, railroad regulation and antitrust policies became two central components of the Progressive Era's market regime.

The major initiatives of the market regime shared a set of common characteristics, principles that addressed both the dominant goals of policy and the nature of implementation. Thus, antitrust policy was instituted, at least theoretically, to revitalize markets by breaking up monopolies and regulating corporate conduct. Where the structural features of an industry precluded this approach, Congress and the president initiated policies to compensate for the lack of effective market mechanisms by extending regulatory authority to include rate-making and other activities. In many ways, mainstream Progressivism was but an attempt to reclaim the market-based sphere of individual liberty and opportunity that had been threatened by the rise of a new corporate order. Fearing the uncertainty of economic change and the potential consequences of unregulated competition in a period of rapid economic expansion, many corporations joined in the call for regulation.

Progressivism was also characterized by a faith in the effectiveness of independent expertise functioning within the confines of administrative agencies. Agencies such as the Interstate Commerce Commission and the Federal Trade Commission were granted independence because those engaged in institutional design appreciated the complexity of the regulatory problems at hand and recognized the heightened potential for political corruption. As explained in chapter 2, the independent regulatory commission had many organizational characteristics that made it attractive to Progressive policy-makers. However, the independent commission as an organizational form did not emerge full-blown with the passage of the Interstate Commerce Act. Rather, it evolved over the course of several decades, coming to maturity late in the Progressive Era.

Consider the example of the Interstate Commerce Commission. The Interstate Commerce Act assigned a bipartisan commission of five, appointed by the president and confirmed by the Senate, to manage the agency. However, the ICC was not independent, nor had Congress intended to give it complete independence. Indeed, in the legislative debates there was no discussion of the commission's independence.[1] Congress placed the ICC under the direct supervision of the secretary of the interior, who was responsible for overseeing the commission's budget and administration and conveyed the commission's annual report to Congress. The ICC was granted complete independence from the Department of the Interior in 1889 at the request of the secretary. This willingness to sanction political independence was largely a historical accident. Congressman John Reagan, one of the authors of the Interstate Commerce Act, feared that President Benjamin Harrison, a former railroad attorney, would use his control of the Department of the Interior to undermine railroad regulation.[2] The independence of the commission received theoretical justification during the Progressive Era as public discourse affirmed the virtues of independent expertise.

Likewise, the mixture of legislative, executive, and judicial powers that makes the independent commission so novel was a product of institutional evolution driven by conflict. The debates surrounding the passage of the Interstate Commerce Act revealed little concern with the precise nature of the delegated powers, although there was some speculation as to whether the ICC would be given legislative and judicial powers. Following court challenges and remedial legislation, the nature of the commission's powers was eventually clarified. The late–Progressive Era debates surrounding the Federal Trade Commission, in contrast, showed a clear recognition that the new agency would be exercising executive, legislative, and judicial powers. Although this combination of powers was a source of some disagreement, the resulting legislation created, at least in form, a strong agency with economy-wide jurisdiction.

REGULATING RAILROADS:
THE INTERSTATE COMMERCE COMMISSION

The Interstate Commerce Act of 1887 was the first in a long series of national regulatory statutes. The act emerged after two decades of congressional debates—a period during which legislators introduced more than 150 bills to extend federal control over the railroads.[3] Prior to the passage of national legislation, the states bore the responsibility for railroad regulation. Beginning in 1871, the idea of creating a federal commission to regulate the railroads began to gain support in Congress. Although the legislative debates of the period revealed a diverse set of proposals, the most important were those presented by John Reagan, Democratic congressman from Texas, and Shelby Cullom, junior Republican senator from Illinois.

Beginning in 1878, John Reagan introduced successive versions of a bill to regulate the railroads. The Reagan proposal had four basic elements. There were strict prohibitions of discriminatory rates and rebates; and pooling—the creation of voluntary agreements to divide the market for rail transportation and to coordinate pricing—was prohibited in hopes of stimulating greater competition. In addition there was a strict "long- and short-haul" clause, which prohibited railroads from charging proportionally less for a long haul than for a short haul on the same line. Lastly, there was a requirement that railroad rate schedules be posted. Reagan's bills imposed large penalties for noncompliance and were intended to be administered by the courts. The proposals reflected shippers' interests and made few concessions to the railroads. Moreover, Reagan strongly opposed the idea of a regulatory commission because of concerns about Congress's excessive delegation of authority and the potential capture of such a commission by the railroads.

A second major participant in the regulatory debates was Senator Shelby Cullom of Illinois. In 1883 he introduced a bill to establish a commission to regulate the railroads. The bill passed the Senate in 1885 but was defeated in the House. Cullom quickly formed a select committee to study the railroad question. The committee report detailed the abuses of the railroads, including pooling, price discrimination, rebates, prohibitively expensive rates, and significant long- and short-haul differentials that placed certain shippers and regions at a disadvantage. On the basis of these findings, Cullom introduced revised legislation that was passed in 1886. The Cullom bill differed from the earlier Reagan bill both in the practices it prohibited and in the means of administration it mandated. Rather than presenting a long list of absolute prohibitions, the Cullom bill furthered the general principle that "every variety of personal favoritism or unjust discrimination between persons" was illegal. The bill had no antipooling provision (although it called for an investigation of pooling), and it had a long- and short-haul clause that could be interpreted with great latitude. The railroads were relatively supportive of Cullom's proposal because it would have allowed them to manage competition, albeit with the support and oversight of the federal government.[4]

Cullom's support for a regulatory commission anticipated the main themes of Progressivism. He justified the commission by citing the need for specialized expertise and flexibility. As the Cullom committee report explained: "Congress is entering upon a new and untried field. Its legislation must be based upon theory instead of experience, and human wisdom is incapable of accurately forecasting its effect upon the vast and varied interests to be affected. The magnitude of these interests and every consideration of prudence and justice demand that provision should be made for an intelligent investigation of the operation of the regulations prescribed . . . Without such a precaution experimental legislation of this character would hardly be justified."[5] Once the Cullom bill had been sent for consideration to the House Committee on Interstate and Foreign Commerce, Reagan removed the commission provisions and included the strict prohibitions he had proposed earlier. The revised bill quickly passed the House, albeit with a sizable minority dissent. The legislative impasse was broken by the Supreme Court.

At the time of the debates over national legislation, the regulation of the railroads was the responsibility of the states. In 1877 the Court had recognized the legitimacy of state regulation of the railroads, asserting that the railroads were "businesses affected with the public interest."[6] In the 1886 *Wabash* decision,[7] however, the Court reversed its position and rejected on constitutional grounds the states' authority to regulate the railroads. The Court suggested that the "right of continuous transportation" was essential to free commerce and that the interstate commerce clause would be "a very feeble and almost useless provision" if states were allowed to regulate and interfere with commerce at each and every stage as it passed through the country. In response to this regulatory vacuum, the House and Senate versions of the railroad legislation were combined in conference committee to produce the Interstate Commerce Act. In the end, the act contained many of the Reagan provisions—including an antipooling provision and a less flexible long- and short-haul clause—and provided for Cullom's commission.

Although some historians have attributed the movement for national regulation to one interest or another (e.g., agrarians or the railroads), a more balanced examination reveals a multiplicity of interests at work.[8] Each major provision of the Interstate Commerce Act represented the concerns of a particular constituency, defined in economic and regional terms. Thus, the antipooling provision represented the demands of agrarian radicals and New York merchants, the latter fearing the competition with other eastern port cities which would result from an equalization of rates with other terminal port cities on the eastern seaboard. Eastern farmers and shippers, whose advantages in regional markets were eroded by the rate differentials, were strong supporters of the long- and short-haul clause. Independent oil producers and refiners in Pennsylvania promoted the prohibition of various forms of discrimination (e.g., rebates and drawbacks). Although the various components of the legislative proposals could each be justified individually, the act as a whole had serious internal contradictions. This was particularly the case with the antipooling and long- and short-haul provisions. Pooling was justified, in part, by the large fixed investments that made underutilization costly, but although railroads could use pools to rationalize competition, they were commonly used for monopolistic purposes. To end pooling would dramatically increase competition, at least in the short run.[9] However, the long- and short-haul clause addressed rate differentials that were themselves the products of competition: the rates that railroads charged for travel along various segments were influenced by market forces. Although eliminating one provision or another might have given the act greater internal consistency, it would have reduced the size of the potential legislative coalition.[10]

Section 1 of the Interstate Commerce Act proclaimed, "All charges made for any service rendered . . . shall be *reasonable and just.*" It went on to prohibit various forms of unjust discrimination, including special rates, rebates, and drawbacks. It also prohibited charging or receiving more "for a shorter than for a longer distance over the same line, in the same direction" when the transportation is "under substantially similar circumstances and conditions." This section of the act declared it unlawful for common carriers "to enter into any contract, agreement, or combination with any other common carrier or carriers for the pooling of freights . . . or to divide between them the aggregate or net proceeds of the earnings of such railroads." To facilitate monitoring of the railroads' compliance, Congress required that railroads publish rate and fare schedules for the transportation of freight and passengers. Railroads were allowed to increase their rates provided they gave notice at least ten days in advance, but they could make reductions immediately so long as they published the new rates. The act prohibited charging or accepting fees that differed from those published. Railroads had to provide the ICC with copies of their rate schedules and of any agreements and contracts made with other common carriers. Section 7 established that railroads were financially liable for damages resulting from violations of the act.

The combination of provisions suggests Congress's need to accommodate multiple interests. Stephen Skowronek correctly characterizes the final result of the lengthy legislative debates when he wrote: "Congress . . . finally opted for the largest possible coalition of support with the most ambiguous of measures. Unable to agree on its own distinct purposes in regulation, Congress capitulated to all concerned. In the end, this first national regulatory policy partook of the old distributive principle that the best measure was the one that every legislator could take back to his district with some evidence of dutiful service."[11] Indeed, rather than resolving the conflicting demands, Congress gave in to them by placing conflicting provisions in a single piece of legislation. In the end, the legislators hoped that the courts or the ICC would resolve the most critical inconsistencies.

The Interstate Commerce Act was peppered with expressions such as "unjust and unreasonable charges," "unjust discrimination," and "undue and unreasonable prejudice or disadvantage." However, Congress gave the newly created commission no guidance regarding what kinds of charges might be considered unjust or what kinds of activities put shippers at an unreasonable disadvantage. In short, Congress delegated significant authority to the ICC. The clauses that gave meaning to the Interstate Commerce Act were redefined and narrowed in scope through the conflictive interplay between the commission and the courts. The results of these conflicts created a need for more detailed legislation to provide the commission with specific powers.

The Commission and the Court

The Interstate Commerce Act gave the commission limited powers to gather data and conduct investigations. It required the railroads to file annual reports with the commission, which was, in turn, empowered to impose a uniform accounting system for the maintenance of records. Moreover, the act gave the ICC subpoena power so that it could use witnesses and corporate records in exploring the railroad's inner workings and their management, and investigating complaints. If, after investigation, it appeared that a complaint was substantiated, the commission could demand reparation and issue a cease and desist order. However, the ICC had to rely on the courts to enforce its orders. Once the cases entered the courts, the railroads strategically presented new evidence. As a result, the courts ended up making judgments about questions of fact as well as questions of law. The court's willingness to try each case de novo caused long delays and discredited the ICC. It was common for railroads to discount the importance of ICC investigations and reserve vital information for the courts.[12]

The ICC's limited powers were combined with limited resources. Its budget for fiscal year 1888 was $149,453. In addition to the five commissioners and a secretary, the commission had seventeen full-time and six part-time employees in the operating division; twenty-eight full-time employees in the rates and transportation division; and sixteen full-time employees in the statistical division. With this limited staff, the ICC held seventy-three formal hearings and investigations in Washington, D.C., and another thirty-eight in other parts of the country. In addition, it filed 180,000 railroad rate schedules, corresponded with carriers and shippers on thousands of occasions, and solicited information from the carriers for annual reports.[13] Railroads quickly discontinued most activities expressly prohibited by the Interstate Commerce Act (e.g., discriminatory rates and pooling). The immediate effect of the legislation was a general reduction in rates. However, the railroad's compliance was short-lived. If the ICC's resources were sufficient to monitor a generally compliant industry, they became woefully inadequate once the railroads began to engage in routine evasion.

Following early conflicts over immunized testimony in ICC hearings,[14] the Supreme Court turned its attention to the commission's rate-making powers. The Interstate Commerce Act required, without further elaboration, that rates be "reasonable and just." The ICC, soon after its creation, had established a procedure, based on the approach employed by state-level regulators, for addressing unreasonable rates. Carriers would set their own rates, and if there were complaints the ICC would investigate the reasonableness of these rates. If the rates were judged to be unreasonable, the ICC would fix a maximum reasonable rate and rely on the courts to force compliance. This procedure, established during the early months of the ICC's existence, was not challenged within the commission or by the railroads, which were more concerned with the rates prescribed than with the legal status of rate-making.[15]

The Supreme Court addressed the rate-making powers in the 1897 Maximum Rate Case.[16] The decision stated that "the grant of such a power is never to be implied. The power itself is so vast and comprehensive, so largely affecting the rights of carrier and shipper . . . the language by which the power is given had been so often used and was so familiar to the legislative mind and is capable of such definite and exact statement, that no just rule of construction would tolerate a grant of such power by mere implication." Moreover, rate-making involved legislating, a power that Congress had not assigned to the ICC: "The power given is the power to execute and enforce, not to legislate. The power is partly judicial, partly executive and administrative, but not legislative."[17] The limited judicial powers assigned to the commission allowed it only to judge whether a given rate was reasonable. Any broader definition of the ICC's authority, the Court argued, exceeded the commission's mandate. The ICC's annual report devoted almost thirty pages to the decision, referring to it as "perhaps the most important since the enactment of the act to regulate commerce."[18]

Rate-setting was not the only object of judicial concern. During the same period, the Court questioned the ICC's interpretation of the long- and short-haul clause. The act prohibited common carriers from charging more on a short segment of a line than on a longer segment of the same line "under similar circumstances and conditions." Whereas the ICC identified factors that would make two segments dissimilar, it did not consider competition sufficient grounds for suspending the prohibition, despite the fact that competition was often responsible for rate differences. The Court focused not on the technical justifications of the long- and short-haul clause but on the ICC's interpretation of what constituted "similar circumstances and conditions." In *Texas and Pacific Railway Company v. Interstate Commerce Commission* (1896), the Court decided that rail transportation that was part of a transportation package bringing foreign goods to domestic markets was sufficiently dissimilar from transportation on the domestic route alone to justify a difference in rates.[19]

The next year, a Supreme Court decision addressed the importance of competition in the pricing of domestic traffic. The defendant argued that the existence of competition from other railroads on certain segments of the rail system made transportation on these segments sufficiently dissimilar to justify lower rates. The Court agreed, noting, "Competition between rival routes is one of the matters which may justify common carriers in charging greater compensation for the transportation of like kinds of property for a shorter than for a longer distance over the same line."[20] Of course, the critical question was not whether competition promoted low rates but whether railroads were justified in extracting a monopoly profit in the absence of competition. As the commission correctly stated, "Competition is the only reason why a carrier would desire to charge less to the more distant point, and if competition justifies him in so doing, there is nothing left for the section to act upon."[21]

The series of Court decisions essentially reduced the ICC to an investigative agency. Both the power to establish maximum reasonable rates and the long- and short-haul clause had been rejected by the Court. In reference to the 1897 case discussed above, Justice John Harlan noted that the ICC had become "a useless body for all practical purposes," the Court having defeated "many of the important objects designed to be accomplished by the various enactments of Congress." In essence, he argued, the commission had been "shorn, by judicial interpretation, of authority to do anything of an effective character."[22] The ICC's frustration was evident in its 1897 annual report. After reviewing the commission's remaining powers, the report cautioned: "But by virtue of judicial decisions, [the ICC] has ceased to be a body for the regulation of interstate carriers. It is proper that Congress should understand this. The people should no longer look to this Commission for a protection which it is powerless to extend."[23]

Progressivism and the Revitalization of the Commission

Congress increased the powers of the ICC in response to a number of related factors. First, finding that antitrust measures effectively limited their ability to form traffic associations, railroads had begun to combine through merger.[24] Consolidation eliminated competition in many parts of the country and effectively concentrated the control of the railroads in the hands of financiers. Second, there was some evidence that systematic rate discrimination was promoting the creation of monopoly power in other sectors of the economy. Third, freight rates began to increase rapidly in step with the high costs of consolidation and the reduction of competition. Shippers forced to bear the immediate burden of higher rates demanded that Congress strengthen the regulatory system that the Court had dismantled.[25] A first step came in 1903, when Congress passed the Elkins Act. The act strengthened the Interstate Commerce Act in a number of ways: it established that a departure from published railroad tariffs was a misdemeanor; it allowed for the issuance of injunctions in response to departures from published rate schedules; and it established penalties for accepting or providing a rebate. This act bolstered the ICC without addressing the powers undermined by the court decisions of the 1890s. However, it constituted the first step in the reformation of the ICC.

Following the disclosures of the *Northern Securities* antitrust case,[26] Theodore Roosevelt called on Congress to pass legislation granting ICC new regulatory powers. Despite some unsuccessful efforts, Roosevelt continued to make railroad regulation an important element of his policy program. In his 1905 annual address he stated: "The immediate and most pressing need, so far as legislation is concerned, is the enactment into law of some scheme to secure to the agents of the government such supervision and regulation of the rates charged by the railroads . . . as shall summarily and effectively prevent the imposition of unjust and unreasonable rates. It must include putting a complete stop to rebates in every shape and form. This power to regulate rates, like all similar powers over the business world, should be exercised with moderation, caution, and self-restraint; but it should exist, so that it can be effectively exercised when the need arises."[27] Roosevelt's support for new legislation, together with continued public pressure and additional evidence of abuses, facilitated the passage of the Hepburn Act of 1906.

The Hepburn Act strengthened the ICC in many respects. In response to the demands placed on the agency, it expanded the commission from five members to seven and authorized commissioners to appoint examiners and agents. The ICC's jurisdiction was expanded to cover sleeping cars, express companies, and oil pipeline companies. In hopes of preventing the expansion of railroads' monopoly power, the Hepburn Act prohibited railroads from owning the goods they transported. The most important provisions of the act were those that empowered the ICC to respond to complaints by setting maximum rates. The commission's orders were effective upon promulgation and could be suspended only by court injunctions. With the passage of the Hepburn Act, Congress gave the ICC the explicit powers denied by the Court.[28]

The Hepburn Act resolved several problems that had plagued the ICC since its inception. However, Congress failed to address a number of critical issues, including the status of the long- and short-haul clause, the role of the commission in railroad capitalization and consolidation, and the question of whether the commission should have the power to make rates on its own initiative. Thus, the debates over railroad regulation continued. Beginning in 1904, proposed legislation addressed some of the above-mentioned issues, as well as the creation of a commerce court that could offer specialized expertise and increase the speed of litigation in appeals. The notion of such a court failed to attract much attention until 1910, when the Mann-Elkins Act was passed with the support of President Taft. The act created the Commerce Court, composed of five judges selected from the circuit courts, to review appeals involving ICC orders. The act also expanded the ICC's powers and jurisdiction. The ICC commission gained the power to initiate proceedings even when no complaint had been made, and the authority to suspend proposed rate increases. In such cases the railroads bore the burden of proof. The act also strengthened the long- and short-haul clause by eliminating the "substantially similar circumstances and conditions" clause that had been the basis for earlier Supreme Court decisions. Finally, the act extended the ICC's jurisdiction to telegraph, telephone, and cable companies.[29]

In 1913 Congress reassessed the newly created Commerce Court. The court had failed to expedite cases and had retried them de novo—a practice rejected by the ICC, which asserted that its own findings of fact should be accepted by the courts, which should focus, instead, on questions of law. The court's delays were combined with apparent attempts to reduce the scope of the commission's decisions; and the pattern of decisions raised questions as to whether the court was promoting the railroads' interests. Finally, the court's record before the Supreme Court forced many to question its expertise: ten of the twelve cases that reached the Court on appeal were reversed. Because the Commerce Court had never received strong support, the evidence of its failure was sufficient to lead to its abolition. In 1913 Congress eliminated the court through a rider on an appropriations bill.[30]

The logical expansion and clarification of the ICC's powers came to an abrupt halt with the nation's entry into World War I. In 1916 the Army Appropriations Act gave the president authority to take control of the transportation systems in wartime. In April 1917, when the United States entered the war, President Wilson exercised this power. The railroads made some initial attempts to coordinate their activities through the Railroads War Board, a voluntary conference of railroad officials, but although the board was relatively successful, the ICC recommended the unified management of the rail system under direct or indirect governmental control. On December 26, 1917, Wilson took control of the rail system and placed it under the directorship of William McAdoo. The "federalization" of the railroads was completed with the passage of the Federal Railroad Control Act of 1918, which gave the president the authority to set rates. The ICC continued to play a regulatory role during the war, reviewing rates on complaint.[31] The wartime experience revealed that the rail system had a tremendous capacity that simply had not been realized prior to unified control. The potential benefits of a new regulatory system and general dissatisfaction with the prewar system gave rise to a major legislative initiative that dramatically expanded the powers of the ICC. When Wilson announced that the rail system would return to private control on March 1, 1920, he created a deadline for legislative action. After lengthy hearings, Congress passed the Transportation Act.[32]

The Transportation Act once again expanded the ICC, and also established the Railway Labor Board to manage labor relations. The act dramatically enhanced the ICC's powers and its authority to shape the structure of the railroad industry. The commission was given the power to set *minimum* rates that would allow for a fair return on investment, as determined through the valuation of railroad assets. For the first two years after the passage of the act, the rate of return was to be limited to 5.5 percent, with an additional 0.5 percent allowable to fund improvements. The act had a recapture clause that required that a carrier earning returns in excess of 6 percent divide the excess returns equally between a reserve fund to protect its future financial status, and a general railroad contingency fund to make loans and lease equipment to weaker railroads. Most notably, the act authorized the ICC to intervene directly in the organization of the railroad system. It gave the commission the authority to approve railroads' acquisition of additional assets. Before railroads could build new lines or abandon existing ones, the ICC had to issue a certificate of public convenience and necessity. The act also granted the commission supervisory responsibilities over railroad securities issues as part of the overall effort to ensure that the railroads were financially secure. Finally, reflecting the positive experience of unified wartime control, the act directed the ICC to construct a plan for the consolidation of the railroads into a limited number of rail systems.[33]

For many reasons that are outside the scope of this study, the goal of creating a consolidated rail system was not realized. However, the major provisions of the Transportation Act remained in force. Conflicts between the commission and the courts had been followed by Progressive efforts to shore up the regulatory system, and in response Congress had expanded the limited authority conveyed in the ICC's organic mandate. The ICC was, at least during the period under consideration, a welcomed success.

REGULATING COMPETITION:
THE FEDERAL TRADE COMMISSION

Antitrust policy was another response to the centralization of economic power which occurred in the last quarter of the nineteenth century. Rather than creating an agency to administer prices and services, Congress created a new policy designed to decentralize economic decision-making and revitalize markets. In 1890, Congress passed the Sherman Antitrust Act, the foundation for a national policy on economic competition. Section 1 of the Sherman Act declared illegal "every contract, combination in the form of a trust, or otherwise, or conspiracy, in restraint of trade or commerce." Section 2 stated that "every person who shall monopolize, or attempt to monopolize, or combine or conspire with any other person or persons, to monopolize in any part of the trade or commerce among the several States, or with foreign nations, shall be deemed guilty of a misdemeanor." The attorney general was responsible for prosecuting violations of the act. The Sherman Act also encouraged private litigation by allowing private parties to sue for treble damages.[34]

A number of factors severely limited the effectiveness of the antitrust legislation. First, the Sherman Act, like the Interstate Commerce Act before it, was incredibly vague. Although a number of detailed regulatory proposals were discussed, Congress failed to address the critical questions of what kinds of restraints were harmful to competition and what forms of behavior were truly monopolistic. Second, corporations commonly reacted strategically to the legislation, adopting modes of organization and restraints that according to the courts' interpretation fell just outside the categories prohibited by the Sherman Act. Thus, a frontal attack on trusts stimulated a wave of mergers that effectively increased the concentration of the economy.[35] Third, rather than vesting authority in a specialized regulatory agency Congress assigned enforcement to the Department of Justice and failed to provide funding for antitrust enforcement or the creation of a special enforcement staff. The Justice Department, in turn, chose not to make antitrust enforcement a priority. By casting competition policy as law enforcement, Congress gave the courts a central role in defining policy. In the end, the restrictive judicial reading of the interstate commerce clause, and narrow determinations of what precisely constituted a restraint of trade, limited the applicability of the Sherman Act. Thus, some advocates of antitrust policy began discussing the merits of a regulatory commission similar in many ways to that created by the Interstate Commerce Act.

The Supreme Court, when it handed down its 1911 *Standard Oil* decisions,[36] enlivened the debates over the creation of an independent trade commission to facilitate antitrust enforcement. The Court expanded its role in antitrust decision-making by establishing the rule of reason, which stated that because most commercial transactions imposed restraints on trade, the critical question was whether a restraint was reasonable. In the *Standard Oil* decision, the Court presented its methodology for making this determination. This was a necessary application of judicial authority, given the vague provisions of the Sherman Act and the complexity of industrial organization. However, the extension of the Court's authority made legislators painfully aware of the limitations of the existing legislation.

Advocates of antitrust policy had long objected to the way in which the Court interpreted of the Sherman Act and seemed to have a strong interest in halting the expansion of regulatory authority at every turn. *Standard Oil* only provided additional evidence that regulation that depended fully and completely on law enforcement through the courts was problematic. A regulatory commission was seen as providing a partial solution because it could apply specialized expertise when exercising its authority to establish whether a given restraint of trade was reasonable. This same expertise could be used when designing and executing remedies. The notion of creating a new administrative agency and new antitrust laws also found support in the business community. Despite the Supreme Court's history of making decisions supportive of business, some business leaders feared that the Court's rule of reason would introduce greater uncertainty into the business environment. A regulatory commission, in contrast, could interpret the law and advise businesses as to the legality of a given form of activity. Some even suggested that a new commission could preapprove certain forms of corporate activity and relations before they were undertaken. The business position also reflected economic realities: the nation was in recession and "ruinous competition" was undermining corporations in a number of sectors. Congress could prohibit many of the more problematic trade practices by means of further legislation.[37]

The broad debates over the need for an administrative agency were central to the Roosevelt-Wilson debates during the 1912 presidential campaign. As explained in chapter 2, Roosevelt's vision of a new political-economic order led him to call for the creation of a federal commission like the ICC or an expanded Bureau of Corporations which would regulate several kinds of corporate activity to facilitate and direct the transformation of the economy. Roosevelt claimed that an order based on the Sherman Act tradition would be fundamentally regressive and would sacrifice the advances that had accompanied the rise of the new corporate economy. Wilson distanced himself from Roosevelt by calling for a continuation of the Sherman Act tradition and the passage of new legislation that would strengthen the antitrust prohibitions and make them more specific. Although Wilson won the election, the subsequent regulatory initiatives left the fundamental conflict between Roosevelt and Wilson unresolved.[38]

Congress had been considering new antitrust legislation and the creation of a new administrative agency prior to Wilson's election, and Senator Francis Newlands had advocated a commission for years. After the election, a 1913 Senate Interstate Commerce Committee report suggested that such an administrative agency would be essential to the effective administration and enforcement of new antitrust laws. However, Wilson accelerated the legislative process. He directed his commissioner of corporations, Joseph E. Davies, to draft a report recommending new antitrust legislation and an interstate trade commission.[39] This report provided the basis for a special message to Congress in January 1914, in which Wilson called for new antitrust legislation. He noted: "Nothing hampers business like uncertainty. Nothing daunts or discourages it like the necessity to take chances, to run the risk of falling under the condemnation of the law before it can make sure just what the law is. Surely we are sufficiently familiar with the actual process and methods of monopoly and of the many hurtful restraints of trade to make definition possible, at any rate up to the limits of what experience has disclosed. These practices, being now abundantly disclosed, can be explicitly and item by item forbidden by statute in such terms as will practically eliminate uncertainty, the law itself and the penalty being made equally plain."[40] Wilson went on to call for the creation of an interstate trade commission with the limited authority to collect information, conduct investigations, serve an advisory function, and assist in designing dissolution decrees.

The House and the Senate began working on the proposed legislation. The House actually passed a bill to create a commission much along the lines suggested by the president. However, rather than specifying "item by item" the practices that restrained trade or contributed to monopoly, Congress adopted a more general prohibition of unfair trade practices and strengthened the proposed commission. During the Senate debates, Senator Newlands explained the decision in the following manner: "It is impossible, of course, to define in the law every phase of what is termed 'unfair competition.' If we should in the law attempt to do so, practices covered by the definition might be discontinued tomorrow and other practices equally effective substituted in their place. It was therefore necessary to put in some general phrase that would cover the practices which in common parlance are covered by the term 'unfair competition.'" Because Congress provided a general prohibition of unfair practices, it "left it to a commission to determine what acts come within the general phrase."[41] Imprecision required a delegation of legislative powers.

As will be discussed below, some legislators expressed grave concerns about the delegation of authority to a new administrative body and the lack of mechanisms for structuring the exercise of this authority. Nevertheless, the Federal Trade Commission Act passed with little difficulty. The commission was to be formally independent and bipartisan, and was to consist of five members appointed by the president, and confirmed by the Senate, to serve staggered terms of seven years. Section 5 of the act declared "unfair methods of competition" to be unlawful. Furthermore, it empowered the commission to begin regulatory proceedings when any "person, partnership, or corporation has been or is using any *unfair method of competition in commerce*, and if it shall appear to the Commission that a proceeding by it in respect thereof would be in the *interest of the public*." In response to violations of the law, the commission was empowered to issue cease and desist orders that were subject to the courts' review. The Federal Trade Commission was also given the authority to gather information on business and to conduct formal investigations at the request of the president or Congress. Section 6 of the act gave the commission the investigative authority to demand that corporations file reports or answers to queries in writing and under oath. It also allowed for physical access to documentary evidence. The act required corporations to comply with FTC requests for information and authorized the commission to gather documentation and testimony under subpoena. The act also allowed the FTC to assist the courts in designing regulatory remedies.

The Federal Trade Commission Act was paired with a second piece of antitrust legislation, the Clayton Act of 1914. The latter act specified and prohibited many of the activities commonly employed to undermine competition and maintain monopoly power. It prohibited price discrimination, exclusive dealing, and certain forms of interlocking directorates. Addressing the consolidation wave of the previous decades, section 7 prohibited the acquisition of "any part of the stock or other share capital of another corporation" if the effect would be "to substantially lessen competition" or contribute to the creation of "monopoly in any line of commerce." The act also provided an exemption for labor, noting that labor was not considered a commodity under the antitrust laws.

The Commission Debated

The Senate debates surrounding the passage of the Federal Trade Commission Act addressed numerous issues, including the appropriate relationship between the state and the economy, the advantages and disadvantages of an independent commission and of an executive-branch agency, and the propriety of granting the commission quasi-judicial powers. These debates are worth examining. The basic issues were central to the administrative and political-economic foundations of the market regime.[42]

Senator Newlands, author and chief advocate of the legislation, envisioned the proposed trade commission as an agency directed to promote competition. He was careful to distance his commission from that espoused by Roosevelt, explaining: "Some would found such a commission upon the theory that monopolistic industry is the ultimate result of economic evolution and that it should be so recognized and declared to be vested with a public interest . . . Others hold that private monopoly is intolerable, unscientific, and abnormal, but recognize that a commission is a necessary adjunct to the preservation of competition and to the practical enforcement of the law."[43] Newlands went on to say that the proposed commission was founded on the latter principle. It was designed to address the monopolistic practices that threatened market competition and individual liberties: "Either you have to break up these great combinations of capital, perhaps forbid the organization of corporations at all, or you must adopt some social machinery which will protect the individual from oppression and wrong. This tribunal is simply for the purpose of economically giving to each individual, at the lowest cost of effort and money, the power of asserting his right."[44]

Although there was some discussion of establishing a system of national corporate charters as a means of giving the federal government greater authority to regulate corporate conduct, these debates did not influence the provisions of the legislation. While there were frequent references made to the Interstate Commerce Commission, there was little if any support for giving the new agency the power to set reasonable prices. Participants agreed that markets could effectively determine prices once freed from "the multitude of price-fixing associations in different branches of business, which, together with the great trusts, have been potent causes of the present high costs of living."[45]

One of the topics of debate was whether it was desirable to create a new independent regulatory commission. On several occasions in the legislative debates, senators attributed the failure of the Sherman Act to the fact that Congress had vested enforcement responsibilities in an executive-branch department. As one senator explained, "The Attorney General's Office is part of the political department of the Government, subject, as we know, in the past to political influences, so that prosecutions have been accelerated and prosecutions have been slowed down because of the exigencies of the hour." It was suggested that major consent decrees were impotent and the Justice Department's efforts to monitor compliance with these decrees were meager largely because of the potential political consequences of active enforcement. In contrast, one could take the example of the ICC, which has "moved on with dignity, precision, consecutiveness, and power, until it has covered the entire field of railroad administration and has declared principles that are known to all."[46] The proponents of the new legislation had to defend the decision to create a new commission, but their opponents' objections to the commission were based on weak assertions that existing policy was adequate (clearly a minority position) and on concerns about the costs of further bureaucratic expansion.

Although there was a strong consensus on the need for an independent commission, there were sharp disagreements regarding the authority this commission would exercise. As one might expect, there was considerable debate about the broad prohibition of unfair methods in section 5 of the act. Many agreed that such delegation was a practical necessity, giving the commission the flexibility needed to address the changing practices of business and the competitive effects of these practices. However, some, like Senator Thomas, expressed grave concerns about the lack of clear statutory standards. The commission, he argued, would have "the absolute power . . . of arbitrarily determining whether any act submitted to it is or is not unfair competition." This objection was addressed by Senator Cummins, who noted that the term *unfair competition* had a well-understood meaning, one established through prior judicial decisions. Moreover, reflecting the Progressive faith in administrative expertise, he explained: "The whole policy of our regulation of commerce is based upon our faith and confidence in the administrative tribunals. If we are not willing to entrust the commercial fortunes of the United States to the honor, learning, and integrity of administrative tribunals, we had better suspend and cease any attempted regulation of commerce. I look upon this application of power to the trade commission as no greater, as involving no graver consequences, no more danger to vested rights, than the discretion that we have necessarily reposed in the Interstate Commerce Commission and that we have reposed in the courts when we ask them to apply the rule announced in the antitrust law." Indeed, Cummins's faith in "the honor, learning, and integrity" of the proposed commission was so great that he proclaimed his willingness to "exclud[e] courts from the review of the discretion or judgment of a trade commission."[47]

The concerns about section 5 were part of a broader objection to the commission's combination of legislative, executive, and judicial functions. As Senator Shield stated: "The commission is given judicial power by the authority to call the offender before it, to hear proof, and determine his guilt or innocence. Executive power is conferred by the authority to bring suit in the district courts of the country to enforce such orders as it may make . . . The objection to the bill is that it, in effect, authorizes the commission created to make the laws to be administered and enforced by it."[48] Some found the combination of executive and judicial power particularly disturbing. Senator Lippit cautioned: "I think it is also a great source of danger that in addition to the commission being first charged with these detective duties it is also empowered to act in a judicial capacity, for the commissioners will come to the judgment seat in many cases with the case prejudged. As it is the evidence their own representatives have collected which is the basis for their decisions, they must have every disposition to uphold its integrity, and in this respect they are given a broader power than any court in the land."[49]

Despite these objections, the Federal Trade Commission Act became law. The recognized need for additional regulation, the Progressive faith in administrative expertise, and the positive experiences with the strengthened ICC were sufficient to limit the practical effects of the critiques. Thus, Congress created the Federal Trade Commission and armed it with the mandate to regulate competition throughout the national economy.

The Commission, Congress, and the Courts

Congress gave the Federal Trade Commission a broad grant of power without providing guidelines for interpreting the prohibition of "unfair methods of competition in commerce." Interestingly enough, the commission appeared untroubled by this fact. In 1916, its annual report noted: "The Commission has made no attempt to define in general terms what methods of competition are 'unfair' . . . Unfair competition . . . is incapable of exact definition, but its underlying principle is clear—a principle sufficiently elastic to cover all future unconscionable practices in whatever form they may appear, providing that they sufficiently affect the public interest."[50] The commission's optimism regarding the elasticity of section 5 mirrored that of the earlier congressional debates. However, it would not be shared by the courts once the FTC sought to translate its mandate into regulatory proceedings.

The legislative imprecision of the Federal Trade Commission Act and the variety of duties assigned to the FTC placed a premium on the young agency's administrative capacities. Although the commission inherited the staff of the Bureau of Corporations, the increases in the FTC's duties greatly outpaced the growth of its economic and human resources. During its first decade of operation, the number of complaints filed per year increased by 290 percent, from 108 in 1916 to 421 in 1926. The number of investigations per year increased by 550 percent, from 257 in 1916 to 1,671 in 1925. However, the commission's staff, which numbered 224 in 1916, had only increased to 314 one decade later. Likewise, the FTC's budget increased from a mere $430,964 during the commission's first full year of operation to $1,010,000 in 1925. Increasingly, the commission lacked the resources to execute its mandate.[51]

Internal problems of management and coordination also hampered the FTC. Personnel turnover rates impeded the rapid accumulation of experience. By 1922 the commission could report that it had employed at various times approximately 2,100 individuals, some seven times the number of authorized positions.[52] Moreover, commissioners were commonly at odds over the FTC's proper role—a conflict that reflected the differences between the New Nationalist and Wilsonian strands of Progressivism. This conflict at the executive level forced a number of premature resignations and a failure to pursue a coherent set of enforcement objectives. However, even a unified commission that adopted a common agenda would have encountered difficulties in translating its agenda into a pattern of enforcement actions. There were no mechanisms for planning enforcement actions and evaluating the case load. As a result, the FTC pursued cases even after the corporations involved had abandoned their questionable forms of conduct. This depleted the commission's already limited resource base and had little or no effect on the level of competition within the economy.[53]

In addition to having limited administrative capacities, the commission had a conflict-ridden relationship with Congress and the courts. Congress happily availed itself of the commission's investigations.[54] However, legislators' localism and their vulnerability to interest groups' demands shaped Congress's relationship with the commission, particularly when the FTC's actions stimulated group mobilization. The problematic relationship between Congress and the FTC found its first and clearest expression just a few years after the passage of the Federal Trade Commission Act. During the war, the commission was assigned the duty of monitoring wartime production and pricing practices in key sectors of the economy. As part of this responsibility, the FTC, funded by a special appropriation of $250,000, prepared a series of reports on practices in the food industries. Most controversial was a report on the meat-packing industry, submitted to President Wilson in July 1918.

The FTC's investigation, based in large part on documentary evidence and corporate records, revealed that the five largest meat-packers (members of the "beef trust") used their ownership of transportation and storage facilities to erect entry barriers that effectively prevented smaller firms and new competitors from thriving. Free from competitive forces, the large firms colluded to divide markets and fix prices for livestock and finished products. The FTC recommended that the federal government take control of and administer the rail cars, stockyards, warehouses, and cold storage facilities and operate them as a "government monopoly." Such control could guarantee "open, competitive markets, with uniform scale of charges for all services performed" and "afford an outlet for all manufacturers . . . on equal terms."[55] The FTC's allegations and recommendations mobilized the opposition. Congress responded with the Packers and Stockyards Act of 1921, which effectively eliminated the commission's jurisdiction over the meat-packing industry. Members of Congress vilified the FTC in hearings and charged it with producing a biased report designed solely to support its radical proposals. Subsequent budget cuts forced the agency to make a significant reduction in its staff and abandon a number of future investigations.[56]

The events surrounding the meat-packing investigation revealed that congressional support for the FTC's much-celebrated independence and expertise was contingent on the political reaction to the commission's activities. In this respect the FTC can be contrasted with the Interstate Commerce Commission. Two strong constituencies, shippers and farm associations, supported the ICC and promoted an expansion of its powers. This political support insulated the ICC from congressional challenges during the first two decades of this century. In contrast, the FTC's mandate was so broad that the agency was without the support of any strong constituencies; and Congress would tolerate FTC activism only to the extent that it had no serious political repercussions. The FTC's relationship with Congress, in short, created incentives for that commission to refrain from vigorous enforcement. These political impediments were eclipsed by those created by the courts. Here there is great similarity to the experiences of the ICC. The courts resisted the extension of regulatory authority to new areas of corporate conduct because this extension rested on a vague legislative mandate. The Supreme Court restricted the Federal Trade Commission Act's generous grant of authority, with respect both to enforcement actions and investigations.[57]

As noted earlier, the Clayton Act and the Federal Trade Commission Act were largely responses to the Court's rule of reason. It should not be surprising that at its first opportunity to rule on an FTC decision the Court reasserted itself.[58] In *Federal Trade Commission v. Gratz*, the Court condemned the restriction of unfair methods in the FTC's organic mandate and reasserted the authority claimed in the *Standard Oil* decision. As in the *Standard Oil* decision, the Court's position focused on vague statutory language: "The words 'unfair methods of competition' are not defined by the statute and their exact meaning is in dispute. It is for the courts, not the Commission, ultimately to determine as a matter of law what they include. They are clearly inapplicable to practices never heretofore regarded as opposed to good morals . . . The act was certainly not intended to fetter free and fair competition as commonly understood and practiced by honorable opponents in trade."[59] After *Gratz*, the FTC largely restricted its prosecutions to activities explicitly identified as questionable by the judiciary. In essence, the rule of reason retained its strength—this time, as a barrier to regulation by commission.

The Supreme Court further restricted the FTC's prosecutorial powers in two subsequent decisions. In *Federal Trade Commission v. Western Meat Company*, the Court determined that section 7 of the Clayton Act—the section addressing acquisitions that restricted competition— was inapplicable to the acquisition of assets through merger. The FTC could use section 7 only to prosecute holding companies. In *Federal Trade Commission v. Eastman Kodak Company*, the commission sought to attack an anticompetitive acquisition via the blanket prohibition of unfair methods in section 5 of the Federal Trade Commission Act. In keeping with the logic of the *Gratz* decision, the Court found that the Federal Trade Commission Act did not explicitly give the commission the authority to force divestiture. *Gratz, Western Meat*, and *Eastman Kodak* placed clear limitations on the FTC's ability to enforce the new antitrust laws. The decisions created great skepticism about the FTC's actual powers while simultaneously informing business that growth through acquisition was beyond the reach of existing law.[60]

The courts challenged the FTC's investigative authority as well. In *Claire Furnace Company v. Federal Trade Commission*,[61] the Circuit Court for the District of Columbia banned an FTC investigation on constitutional grounds. In a decision reminiscent of the court decisions a few decades earlier, the court determined that the primary activities of the Claire Furnace Company placed it firmly within the category of intrastate commerce and thus beyond the FTC's jurisdiction. The following year, the Supreme Court handed down its decision in *Federal Trade Commission v. American Tobacco Company*.[62] With this decision, the Court eliminated much of the commission's investigative authority by restricting its ability to open investigations when there was no initial presumption of illegality. The commission's investigative powers were deemed to be too broad to be compatible with the Fourth Amendment prohibition of illegal search and seizure. By drawing an analogy to the judiciary's limited powers of investigation, the Court limited the commission's rights of access to documents of evidential value.[63]

Although the Federal Trade Commission was a bold experiment in regulation, it quickly ran afoul of the courts, which stripped it of critical enforcement and investigative powers. The Court claimed the power to determine what constituted unfair methods under section 5 of the Federal Trade Commission Act. Likewise, the Court undermined the agency's authority to initiate investigations under section 6. The problem, however, was not specific to the Federal Trade Commission but reflected the conflict between the traditional role of the courts and the attempts of Congress to transfer authority to new administrative agencies. The commission represented the widely held view that an extension of the Sherman Act tradition would not be sufficient for regulating the complexities of the emerging corporate economy. New initiatives and new modes of regulation were the order of the day. Yet because regulation continued to be portrayed as law enforcement, regulatory authority remained contingent upon the courts' willingness to advocate a transfer of authority to administrative agencies.

THE LIMITS OF THE MARKET REGIME

The Interstate Commerce Commission and the Federal Trade Commission, two of the chief components of the market regime, executed mandates designed to address the failure of markets or compensate for their absence. Both agencies reflected the Progressive faith in expert administration. Another similarity is that both the ICC and the FTC became enmeshed in conflicts with the courts, which sought to limit the expansion of federal regulatory authority. Of the two agencies, the ICC was undoubtedly the more successful, at least within the period addressed in this chapter. The ICC's narrow jurisdiction provided two benefits. First, it allowed the commission to focus on activities within a single sector of the economy. Because of the levels of concentration within the industry, the number of railroads involved was relatively small. Moreover, the ICC's narrow mandate allowed that agency to enjoy the support of several well-defined constituencies (e.g., shippers and agricultural commodity producers) who claimed direct and significant benefits from rate reductions. Widespread public concerns regarding the potential for monopolistic practices in the absence of the ICC's regulations limited the power of the opposition. The FTC, by contrast, had an expansive mandate: to regulate corporate practices throughout the economy. The diffusion of its regulatory actions limited the intensity of potential support. Moreover, its broad mandate left the FTC open to challenges both by the firms it regulated and by the courts. Both the ICC and the FTC underwent a transformation during the 1920s. Because the changes in the two agencies presaged some of the central principles of the New Deal's regulatory regime, they are worth examining.

As shown above, during the first two decades of the ICC's history the agency met with resistance from the railroads and the courts. The courts progressively stripped away the ICC's regulatory powers, challenging its investigative authority and its mandate to establish maximum rates. Congress responded with the Hepburn Act of 1906, empowering the ICC to set maximum rates in response to complaints that existing rates were unreasonable. After the passage of the Hepburn Act, the ICC became a very effective regulator. From 1908 to 1915, the commission routinely rejected requests for rate increases. As a result, freight rates remained constant. During the years 1916–18, the ICC restrained rail rates despite the large increases in wholesale prices, thus causing a real reduction in rates. One can attribute the history of stable and declining rates to the ICC's constituency. Shippers benefited greatly from the rate-making decisions and strongly supported the commission. The ICC nurtured this support by limiting rate increases.[64]

During World War I, it became clear that the railroads needed additional capitalization. The reduction of real rates over the past decade, when combined with abnormally heavy usage under wartime mobilization, left many of the lines in need of new facilities. The period of federal control also revealed some of the potential benefits of pooling. This wartime experience contributed to the debates surrounding the Transportation Act of 1920. The act met the demands for greater capital by guaranteeing a specific rate of return (5.5 percent) and directing the

ICC to set minimum rates to limit competition. In the Senate debates that preceded the passage of the act, Senator Robert M. La Follette warned that "the bill was framed in exact compliance with the wishes of the railway officials, with the provisions added for a guaranteed return on the investment made to comply with the demands of the committee of railway-security holders."[65] Indeed, when the Transportation Act is compared with the Hepburn Act, the change in focus is evident. The commission's original goal—preventing exploitation at the hands of the railroads, and compensating for the lack of workable markets—was replaced with new objectives: preserving industry stability and guaranteeing a base level of profitability.

The change in focus should not be surprising. The ICC's successes in restraining rates and eliminating the most disturbing railroad practices had reduced the political salience of railroad regulation. The shippers did not effectively mobilize to shape the Transportation Act. The growing urbanization of the population reduced the importance of the farm bloc; high commodity prices during the war attenuated the concern with rail rates. As a result, the railroad executives were successful in defining the central elements of the new regulatory legislation. The changing political climate ultimately affected the ICC's regulatory posture. As Samuel Huntington explains: "These factors dictated not only the shift in public policy which was made in the Transportation Act of 1920 but also a shift by the Commission in the sources to which it looked for support. Continued reliance upon the old sources of support would have resulted in decreasing viability. Therefore the Commission turned more and more to the railway industry itself, particularly the railroad management group."[66]

Beginning in the 1920s, the ICC's regulatory stance increasingly supported the railroad industry. It approved larger rate increases, expanding the margin between increases in wholesale prices and increases in freight costs. Even during the Great Depression, when wholesale price levels fell considerably, it approved rate increases. The ICC also allowed reductions in minimum prices to allow the railroads to underprice motor carriers that threatened to infringe on the railroads' business, and it sheltered price-fixing arrangements within the industry. In return, the railroad industry became the ICC's greatest ally, regularly supporting the expansion of its jurisdiction to cover unregulated carriers, and opposing the creation of rival regulators. The commission, which during the Progressive Era had been the greatest threat to the railroad industry, was essentially transformed into the industry's greatest benefactor.[67]

The shift in the FTC's position was less dramatic because that agency had failed to establish itself as a vigorous regulator prior to this period. As detailed above, the FTC was effectively reined in early in its history.

A series of court decisions and the congressional response to the meat-packing investigation reduced the agency's authority to conduct investigations and enforce the new laws. During the war, the FTC was responsible for monitoring compliance with the War Industries Board guidelines—an activity that allowed it to cultivate its relationship with business. Within the narrow discretionary field carved out by Congress and the courts, the FTC embraced an advisory function.

President Calvin Coolidge appointed to the commission William E. Humphrey, a vociferous opponent of antitrust policy and of the oppressive posture of the Federal Trade Commission. Once placed in charge of the FTC, he sought to replace the commission's enforcement duties with trade-practice conferences. Corporate representatives were invited to meet with the FTC staff to assess practices within their industries in hopes of identifying those which threatened stability or undermined competition. Once identified and voted on, the practices were prohibited by resolutions. In a single year, the commission held conferences and approved standards for fifty-seven industries. In essence, the FTC created a forum for facilitating voluntary agreements among corporations as a means of developing trade standards.[68]

The trade-practice conferences were in many ways a necessity given the FTC's limited resources and the congressional and judicial resistance to active regulation. While the conferences provided a means of developing consensual standards, they simultaneously provided an opportunity for corporate representatives to exchange information on prices and production. By the end of the 1920s, the commission was regularly endorsing codes that allowed for restraints in violation of the antitrust laws. Indeed, the Justice Department intervened in the FTC's affairs to warn the agency that its standards were approving forms of corporate conduct that were per se violations of the Sherman Act, and thus subject to prosecution.[69] As a result of these conflicts, the FTC vacated or modified many questionable standards without the approval of the corporate officials who had participated in the conferences. This discredited the use of the trade-practice conference as a regulatory mechanism.

The changed regulatory stance of the Interstate Commerce Commission and the Federal Trade Commission can be interpreted as due simply to agency capture by regulated interests, facilitated by the changing political environment and the constraints imposed by Congress and the courts. However, a more complete interpretation must consider the new understanding of the political economy which rose to prominence in the wake of World War I. During the 1920s, Herbert Hoover, first as commerce secretary, later as president, promoted an associationalist vision of economic governance. He argued that policy-makers should eschew the adversarial relationships that characterized the Progressive Era and should seek to manage competition and growth by means of state-sponsored cooperative associations and councils.[70] Reflecting the New Nationalist strand of Progressivism, Hoover and other public officials sought to foster a strong and supportive relationship between the state and corporations, a partnership designed to promote stability, growth, and technological dynamism. This vision of the political economy found theoretical justification in the New Era economics of the 1920s. It found its fullest expression in the associational regime of the New Deal.

4

The New Deal: Relief, Recovery, and Regulatory Change

THE GREAT DEPRESSION DEFINED THE POLITICS AND POLICIES of the 1930s and beyond. The economic and social dislocations of the period were dramatic, as suggested by many indicators. Owing to the 1929 stock market crash and subsequent declines, the Standard and Poor's composite index of common stock prices fell from 26 in 1929 to less than 7 in 1932. The steep and rapid downturn in the stock market sent waves throughout the economy because of investors' extensive reliance on credit to finance stock purchases. The losses in the markets were translated into losses at the brokerage houses and the banks that had extended lines of credit. Between 1930 and the spring of 1933, when Roosevelt declared a bank holiday, some nine thousand banks suspended operations. Outside of finance, the effects of the depression were even more intolerable. Between 1929 and 1933, real output fell by more than 30 percent, to the level it had achieved some twenty-five years earlier. By 1933 the drop in production had resulted in a 25-percent unemployment rate. Of those who kept their jobs, approximately one-third were working less than full time. When one compares this to the 3.2-percent jobless rate in 1929, the magnitude of the crisis becomes evident.[1]

The Great Depression was one of the turning points in U.S. history. It was a crisis of such magnitude that it stimulated urgent political demands and fostered a spirit of experimentation. New policy initiatives extended the national government's authority to problems that had formerly been the province of states, communities, or private organizations. The Roosevelt administration adopted a form of Keynesian demand management, albeit only late in the New Deal after an initial

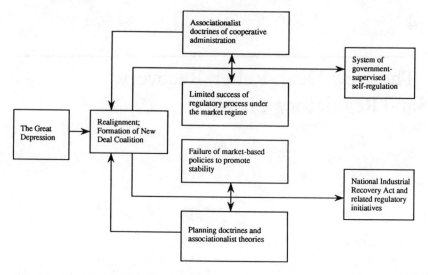

Fig. 4.1   The associational regime.

policy of fiscal restraint proved both counterproductive and impossible to sustain. The New Deal also gave rise to movements toward the creation of a national welfare state. These included first a variety of public works programs, and then the passage of the landmark Social Security Act of 1935. The new policy initiatives of the 1930s, when combined with the experiences of the national mobilization during World War II, completely transformed the American political economy. I am chiefly concerned, however, with the New Deal's effects on regulation. This brief period was responsible for more major regulatory initiatives than any other in U.S. history.

The New Deal saw the creation of a new regulatory regime based on a distinctive vision of state-economy relations, a new configuration of institutions, and a new position for economic interests in the definition and administration of policy. To be certain, elements of the Progressive Era's market regime remained in place, and many of the existing agencies continued to exhibit the organizing principles of that regime. Progressive attitudes toward the "curse of bigness" challenged some key initiatives of the period and provided the foundation for others, thus creating a certain inconsistency within the New Deal's associational regime. Likewise, the Progressive faith in the rule of expertise continued to be influential during the 1930s, resulting in broad new planning efforts and the continued delegation of authority to regulatory agencies.

However, the chain of delegation did not end at the agency. In a number of sectors of the economy, authority was formally extended to the interests being regulated, creating a system of government-supervised self-regulation. The basic components of the associationalist regime are shown in Figure 4.1. Before examining specific initiatives, we must place them in their proper context. That is the task of this chapter. Chapter 5 will review several of the new regulatory initiatives in greater detail.

THE SEARCH FOR A NEW ECONOMIC ORDER

Any account of the New Deal must begin with the experience of World War I and the 1920s. The Great Depression had its roots and the New Deal its intellectual origins in this earlier period. The 1920s was a time of steady economic growth and unbridled optimism. After a recession in 1921 that reduced prices by one-sixth, the economy grew at a steady pace, approximately 4.7 percent per year, for the remainder of the decade. Although farmers had difficulty sustaining prices and farm incomes during the period, corporations enjoyed a prolonged period of prosperity. Price stability and economic growth stimulated increased activity in the stock market and dramatic increases in the values of key stocks.[2] More important, for present purposes, was the new relationship forged between the federal government and the corporations during this crucial decade.

During World War I, the federal government attempted to direct and monitor wartime economic mobilization through the War Industries Board, under the direction of Bernard Baruch. The WIB was organized into fifty-seven commodity sections, allowing producer groups in virtually every line of business to work with the appropriate functional divisions in the WIB. These divisions sought to maintain price stability, establish production priorities, and promote the rapid clearance of orders placed by the armed services. Although the WIB had limited success—a point routinely overlooked in subsequent decades—the board was crucial for two reasons. First, it forged a closer relationship between industry and the state. Private economic associations—especially the U.S. Chamber of Commerce, which organized war service committees—played a critical role in facilitating mobilization. Second, the experiences of wartime mobilization introduced a generation to the benefits that could be derived from planning, albeit a form of planning that gave corporations a central role. By the end of the war many government and corporate officials had played some role in the WIB. This experience colored their interpretation of events a decade later.[3]

Herbert Hoover, among others, drew on the war experiences to promote a broad vision of intercorporate relations and the role of the state in the economy. He believed that a network of cooperative associations facilitated by the national government could serve to coordinate and rationalize production. Associational self-regulation as envisioned by Hoover would provide a means of directing economic development, eliminating damaging competition, and ensuring that firms producing comparable goods would agree to meet specific standards. Such self-regulation was not, at least in Hoover's estimate, a system of government-sanctioned price-fixing. As part of this associationalist plan, Hoover promoted the creation of trade agreements and industry-led standardization during his tenure as commerce secretary.[4] Some regulatory agencies adopted similar approaches, seeking to facilitate regulatory policy-making through the efforts of industrial associations. As noted in chapter 3, the Federal Trade Commission used trade-practice conferences to develop industry standards and codes of competition backed by the agency's sanctions.[5] The new role of the Department of Commerce in facilitating cooperative agreements among corporations, Hoover's faith in the progressive impulses of business executives, and the record of sustained economic growth and price stability enhanced business's support of Hoover when he assumed the presidency.

The stock market crash and the subsequent economic decline threatened to undermine Hoover's relationship with business. Hoover's response to this crash reflected his philosophy of economic governance. He began holding a series of conferences with the representatives of business, labor, and farm associations. As a result of these meetings, employers agreed to refrain from cutting wages. Hoover reasoned that wage reductions would undermine purchasing power, thus deepening the recession. However, the voluntary wage policy proved counterproductive. The combination of constant wages and deflationary forces meant that there was an actual increase in real wages. Employers responded by cutting their work force or imposing significant wage reductions.[6] In addition to trying to promote high wages, Hoover reacted to the recession by stepping up government spending: increasing the number of government-financed construction projects and creating the Reconstruction Finance Corporation. The RFC was created to shore up the financial system and ensure an adequate supply of credit. By the end of Hoover's presidency the agency had lent some $1.5 billion to banks, railroads, and state governments.[7]

In spite of the economic turmoil of the last years of his term, one might have expected continued business support for Hoover. His experiments with associationalism and his rhetorical support for corporations suggested that he would be a strong ally of business. Indeed, he consulted with the Chamber of Commerce when seeking a way of dealing with the economic downturn. However, that organization was less than sympathetic to Hoover. A number of large industrialists were concerned about the Republican tariff policy and Hoover's ongoing commitment to the gold standard. They sought greater protectionism and an inflation of the domestic economy as defensive measures.[8] Moreover, the Chamber of Commerce found the 1931 budget deficit—the first since the World War I—most disturbing. While accepting the possibility of increased taxes at a future date, the Chamber's president, Henry I. Harriman, called on the House Appropriations Committee to reduce government spending to 1925 levels to achieve a balanced budget. With a 16-percent unemployment rate and the Dow Jones resting at less than one-half the 1929 level, however, attention shifted from the budget to broader questions of industrial recovery.[9]

During the last years of Hoover's term, myriad recovery plans were offered by policy-makers, academics, and corporate executives. The most influential was the one devised by General Electric president Gerald Swope, a veteran of the WIB. The Swope plan would have required all firms with fifty or more employees to join trade associations, which would collect and transmit information and promote coordination. Corporations would engage in planning to manage production and prices and eliminate cutthroat competition. This would require both a suspension of the antitrust laws and a new regulatory agency to supervise the process and prevent firms from circumventing the decisions of their associations. For obvious reasons, the Swope plan received the support of the Chamber of Commerce and many former WIB officials.[10] Despite Hoover's earlier support for associationalism, he rejected the Swope plan, calling it "the most gigantic proposal of monopoly ever made in American history."[11]

Hoover's intransigence, the nation's worsening economic performance, and the Republicans' tariff and monetary policies were sufficient to force a change in allegiances. The Chamber of Commerce and officials of some of the largest corporations in the nation openly supported Franklin Roosevelt rather than Hoover. Even though many executives were cautious when considering an expanded government role in the supervision of trade agreements, most supported a relaxation of antitrust policy and a greater role for industry in administering prices and production. Indeed, during the early 1930s there were many variants of the Swope plan circulating in Washington. Although most of the plans allowed for industrial self-government through trade associations, the extent and nature of federal supervision remained an open question.[12]

THE NEW DEAL AND THE NEW ECONOMIC ORDER

Scholars commonly interpret the 1932 elections as being part of a pattern of changes in party dominance which led to a realignment in 1936. Periodically, U.S. history has seen party realignments entailing the disintegration and reformation of electoral coalitions and a shift in the balance of power between parties. Such realignments, which can be attributed to the emergence of new divisive issues or to crises that undermine existing allegiances, can be of particular importance in promoting significant changes in policy and institutions. The elections of 1932 brought significant Democratic victories in the House and Senate, and the election of Roosevelt as president. There can be no question that this electoral support for Democrats was a response to the economic dislocations of the Great Depression. Given voters' sensitivity to economic performance, it is difficult to envision a Hoover victory regardless of the program presented by the opposition. Although it may be convenient to assume that the public was voting for a significant change in public policy, the campaign of 1932 failed to reveal significant differences between the candidates of the two major parties. Roosevelt and the Democratic party did not try to offer the electorate a coherent alternative platform.[13]

The Democratic party platform of 1932 gave little indication of anything resembling a departure from existing political-economic relationships. The Democrats called for "an immediate and drastic reduction of governmental expenditures by abolishing useless commissions and offices, consolidating departments and bureaus, and eliminating extravagance to accomplish a savings of not less than twenty-five percent in the cost of the Federal Government." In response to the deficit run by the Hoover administration, it was the Democrats' policy to maintain "the national credit by a federal budget balanced annually." The Democrats called for "strengthening and impartial enforcement of the antitrust laws" and "the removal of government from all fields of private enterprise except where necessary to develop public works and natural resources." This conservative party platform stands in sharp opposition to what is normally interpreted as the legacy of the New Deal. There was no indication of some master plan that would provide the basis for a significant redefinition of the political economy.[14]

Although Roosevelt tried to distance himself from Hoover in the campaigns by making a number of provocative statements, he did not present voters with a theoretically intelligible vision of a new political-economic order. Some of his speeches, however, hinted at such a vision. For example, in a speech delivered in 1932 Roosevelt argued that the growing concentration of capital required "a reappraisal of values." He went on to say, "A mere builder of more industrial plants, a creator of more railroad systems, an organizer of more corporations, is as likely to be a danger as a help." The nation desperately needed an "enlightened administration" to engage in "the soberer, less dramatic business of administering resources and plants already in hand . . . of adjusting production to consumption, of distributing wealth and products more equitably, of adapting existing economic organizations to the service of the people." Roosevelt emphasized that corporations had to "work together to achieve the common end." However, he was quick to note that the federal government would have a role to play in restraining "the lone wolf, the unethical competitor, the reckless promoter" who "declines to join in achieving an end recognized as being for the public welfare, and threatens to drag the industry back to a state of anarchy."[15]

Roosevelt certainly expressed support for some form of industrial planning. In another 1932 speech, he addressed the "problem of controlling by adequate planning the creation and distribution of those products which our vast economic machine is capable of yielding."[16] Yet much to the displeasure of some members of his "Brains Trust" who inserted references to planning into his speeches, Roosevelt's vague discussions of planning were counterbalanced by his continued adherence to the older Progressivism of Woodrow Wilson. As Rexford Tugwell, a member of the Brains Trust, explained, Roosevelt moved freely from praising the planning model, to supporting an attack on monopolies, to restoring corporate profitability and business confidence because "he had a general indifference to systems of all sorts. He was determined to reach certain objectives but was not committed to any methods for their attainment. He was appealing first to one, then to another, group of voters."[17] With respect to the overall vision of a planned economy, Raymond Moley explained that Roosevelt "did not adopt [this] alternative ideology, perhaps never quite understood it; he was, in fact, inconsistent."[18]

Franklin Roosevelt's political skills were exceptional; his capacity to form coalitions became legendary. Indeed, many of the initiatives of the New Deal seem to be, if nothing else, instruments for building and maintaining political coalitions. However, there is little evidence that Roosevelt formulated anything approaching a comprehensive recovery plan. When addressing political-economic issues, he was essentially a Progressive reformer. Progressivism was "the furniture of his mind." As Tugwell recalled, "Roosevelt could be persuaded to depart from the old progressive line only in the direst of circumstances and then only temporarily."[19] Without a comprehensive plan of his own, he relied heavily on his key advisers. Many of Roosevelt's advisers had reputations as bright and energetic analysts. However, they disagreed among themselves about the proper role of the state in the economy. They did not have a shared understanding of what kinds of policies were necessary to restore growth and end the depression. Robert Higgs describes the members of the administration in very suggestive terms: "The New Deal, especially at its beginning, manifested no single coherent ideology . . . Within the ranks stood semi-socialist national planners like Rexford Tugwell; semi-fascist members of the pro-business Baruch gang like General Hugh Johnson; labor leaders like Sidney Hillman; consumerists like Leon Henderson; antitrust enthusiasts like Felix Frankfurter; avowed cartelizers like Donald Richberg; all stripes of agricultural reformers; spending fanatics as well as budget balancers; every species of inflationist and monetary crank; and assorted proponents of panaceas that ranged from spreading the work to building garden cities."[20] While this description captures the diversity of the New Dealers, there were distinct divisions that created relatively coherent blocs. Indeed, the major division among Roosevelt's advisers and within the administration was along the lines drawn two decades earlier, when Theodore Roosevelt's New Nationalism was presented as an alternative to the mainstream progressivism of Wilson's New Freedom.[21]

The administration proponents of the New Freedom position had not changed significantly in their thinking since the Progressive Era. Louis Brandeis continued to exert influence, both directly and through several of his disciples, including Felix Frankfurter, Thomas Corcoran, James Landis, and Benjamin Cohen. When writing a draft of the 1936 Democratic platform, Frankfurter expressed the old Progressive vision in terms that almost drew attention back to the Populists four decades before: "To destroy effective competition is to destroy capitalism. The trend toward concentration is a very real threat against our traditional competitive system. If that trend is not reversed there is a danger of a private socialism in this country as alien to traditional Americanism as state socialism." He went on to claim, "There is no practical way to regulate the economic oligarchy of autocratic, self-constituted and self-perpetuating groups . . . they are as dangerous a menace to political as they are to economic freedom."[22]

A number of New Dealers including Adolph Berle, Donald Richberg, and Rexford Tugwell, adopted a much different vision, one that reflected a synthesis of New Nationalism and the institutional economics of Thorstein Veblen and John R. Commons. This vision was very influential in designing the initiatives of the first Roosevelt administration. Although Raymond Moley, an original member of the Brains Trust, believed in a role for planning, his was a conservative, Hooverian vision of planning conducted by and for corporations. Rexford Guy Tugwell, in contrast, was the Roosevelt administration's most influential proponent of the statist variant of Progressivism. His influence was apparent in many of the early New Deal initiatives. Tugwell had little respect for mainstream economic thought. Economics as a discipline, he argued, was content with bathing in "the sterile dust of free-competition principles." In so doing, it created economists who were "handicapped," and "carr[ied] in their heads a formula of noninterference."[23] Tugwell believed that the economy had evolved along with the corporations, rendering the market irrelevant: "Industry has developed out of the face-to-face stage; huge factories exist; central-office organizations control many even of these organizations, great as they are in themselves; financial controls are superimposed on this; scientific management has come to stay—therefore the Government must legalize all these heretofore horrid developments so that it may shape them into social instruments."[24]

Tugwell's interpretation of the evolving economy was shared by many, including influential members of business peak associations such as the Chamber of Commerce and the National Association of Manufacturers who had supported various schemes of industrial self-governance. Tugwell, however, quickly departed from the business-based vision of economic planning. For instance, he called for a greater role for workers in the new order, referring to "a democratization of industry." While acknowledging that the nation would "have to sacrifice something of our industrial efficiency for the humanizing of the system," he viewed this as "one of the costs of progress."[25] Tugwell believed that "the voluntary linking up of the individual with the group through which he necessarily functions" would be the basis for a "voluntary socialism."[26] Whether this voluntary socialism would take place through a dispersion of ownership of corporate shares by unions or through a more corporatist arrangement of direct bargaining was unclear. What is clear, however, is that labor was to play a role in the new industrial order.

Another way in which Tugwell's vision departed from the Hooverian notions of industrial self-government was his belief in the need for the state to engage in economic planning. Drawing on the example of the Soviet Union, Tugwell believed that national planning was now possible. "The need for planning lies in the inability of a laissez-faire system to cope with the problems of modern industrialism. The technical difficulties can be removed. The chief handicap to overcome is our allegiance to ideals that belong to an earlier industrial setting."[27] Indeed, planning was not only possible but necessary, "because business is so huge and so interdependent that every action it takes is fraught with deep social implications."[28] Stalin's efforts in the Soviet Union had convinced Tugwell of the potential for planning. However, as a model for how the government could design and implement comprehensive planning Tugwell drew more heavily on the War Industries Board's mobilization of the economy.[29] The decade-long debates on planning—both in its statist and its corporatist guise—and the experiences of the wib were critical in justifying the major recovery initiative, the National Industrial Recovery Act of 1933. They also influenced the design of new regulatory initiatives and provided the core assumptions of the associational regime of the New Deal.

The New Deal's continuity with the New Nationalist strands of Progressivism was combined withh another legacy of the Progressive Era. The new initiatives combined an expanded role for interest groups with the Progressive promotion of efficiency and the faith in bureaucratic specialization and expert administration. James Landis, a key member of the Roosevelt administration, framed his advocacy of bureaucratic expansion in Progressive terms. He explained that "efficiency in the process of governmental regulation is best served by the creation of more rather than less agencies." The "continuity of interest" inherent in administrative specialization and the consistent devotion of administrators to a limited set of problems provided the basis for bureaucratic expertise. For Landis and other members of the New Deal, it was the application of specialized expertise that would provide the foundation for an effective administrative state.[30]

THE NATIONAL INDUSTRIAL RECOVERY ACT

Roosevelt's instincts were those of a coalition-building politician. His lack of a clear political-economic vision dramatically increased the influence of certain of his advisers, including Moley and Tugwell, who could provide theoretical justification for the major initiatives of the first New Deal. These initiatives, the National Industrial Recovery Act and the Agricultural Adjustment Act, were politically attractive, for they gave Roosevelt a means of forging a broad coalition that included business, labor, and agriculture. They departed from the central principles of the Progressive market regime by requiring an expanded role for the national government in the economy and a new role for interest associations in the regulatory process. They established a system of economic regulation in which the regulated would play a significant role in defining policy.

Roosevelt's advisors drafted the National Industrial Recovery Act in response to the Black-Connery bill, which would have established a thirty-hour work week in hopes of reducing unemployment. On behalf of the administration, Labor Secretary Frances Perkins recommended that the bill be amended to establish boards that could create exemptions to the thirty-hour week and set minimum wages. The administration feared that a reduction in the number of hours worked could seriously depress workers' incomes and reduce their purchasing power. However, business was strongly opposed to the addition of minimum-wage provisions. At the same time that the administration was attempting to modify Black-Connery, Roosevelt put his advisers in charge of drafting new, more comprehensive legislation. The administration's bill combined the minimum-wage provisions with a broad model of planning which in many ways resembled that presented in the Swope plan. Roosevelt stopped all attempts to modify Black-Connery and had the new legislation introduced in Congress, where it won overwhelming support.[31] The National Industrial Recovery Act became law in June 1933.

In essence, the National Industrial Recovery Act created a system of government-supervised industrial self-regulation. The act authorized trade associations or industrial groups to establish codes of fair conduct, subject to the approval of the president. A failure to write acceptable codes could result in the imposition of codes by the president, or direct regulation that involved the licensing of firms within a given industry. This threat was sufficient to force widespread compliance. The codes were exempt from the antitrust laws, and thus agreements that maintained artificially high prices in order to fight deflation were allowed. The Roosevelt administration erected a system of industrial planning in which power was vested in corporations and their representative organizations. Section 7(a) of the National Industrial Recovery Act addressed the role of labor and provided some important guarantees. It required that every code issued under the provisions of the act acknowledge that "employees shall have the right to organize and bargain collectively through representatives of their own choosing, and shall be free from the interference, restraint, or coercion of employers of labor, or their agents." It also prohibited business interference in labor organization, stipulating "that no employee and no one seeking employment shall be required as a condition of employment to join any company union or to refrain from joining, organizing, or assisting a labor organization of his own choosing." Finally, section 7(a) required employers to "comply with the maximum hours of labor, minimum rates of pay, and other conditions of employment, approved or prescribed by the President." This support for labor was combined with $3.3 billion for public works, to be dispensed at the discretion of the president.

The National Industrial Recovery Act, by its very design, deviated from the organizing principles of the Progressive market regime. The advocacy of markets and the decentralization of economic power was replaced by the active support of economic associations negotiating over the amounts to be produced and the prices to be charged. Roosevelt presented the system created under the new legislation as one in which "all employers in each trade" would join "modern guilds—without exception—and agree to act together and at once." Their challenge would be to "sink selfish interest and present a solid front against a common peril." In addressing the relaxation of the antitrust laws, Roosevelt explained that the "old principles of unchecked competition" were being replaced by "new Government controls" designed "to free business—not to shackle it."[32] In design and justification, the act was in many ways a direct expression of the New Nationalist strands of Progressive thought.

The act vested tremendous authority in the president and, in turn, in the regulated industries. With the exception of the concessions to labor in section 7(a), the act was vague with respect to the necessary features of the codes. It created an institutional mechanism to enable business to regulate itself via organizations that represented it, subject to the supervision of the yet-to-be created National Recovery Administration, and the constraints imposed by certain guarantees securing benefits for labor. As Ellis Hawley explains, with the National Industrial Recovery Act the Roosevelt administration "had appealed to the hopes of a number of conflicting pressure groups. Included were the hopes of labor for mass organization and collective bargaining, the hopes of businessmen for price and production controls, the hopes of competitive industries to imitate their more monopolistic brethren, the hopes of dying industries to save themselves from technological advances, and the hopes of small merchants to halt the inroads of mass distribution . . . the numerous conflicts had been glossed over by a resort to vagueness, ambiguity, and procrastination."[33]

The recovery act received the qualified support of business and labor, reflecting its ambiguity and its broad delegation of authority.[34] Section 7(a) virtually guaranteed the act the support of organized labor. By recognizing labor's right to bargain collectively through a chosen representative, the National Industrial Recovery Act had fulfilled one of the labor movement's long-sought-after goals. William Green, president of the American Federation of Labor proclaimed that with the passage of section 7(a) "millions of workers throughout the nation stood up for the first time in their lives to receive their charter of industrial freedom."[35] Indeed, Green claimed that between the passage of the act and the union's October 1933 convention the guarantees provided by the new law resulted in the addition of more than 1.5 million new union members, increasing the AFL's membership by more than one-third.[36]

Business, particularly the U.S. Chamber of Commerce, also welcomed the passage of the act. The act's relaxation of the antitrust laws and its reliance on the principle of self-regulation closely resembled the provisions of the Swope plan and appeared to show the influence of the Chamber's president Henry Harriman, who had been consulted by Roosevelt, Moley, and Tugwell in 1932 and 1933. Indeed, Harriman had sent a memo to Roosevelt in April 1933 to discuss "the vital necessity of establishing minimum wages, maximum hours of labor, and possibly minimum prices in order to stop the downward spiral of wages and prices and to check the ruthless competition from which we are suffering."[37] Before the National Industrial Recovery Act was passed the Chamber had, under Harriman's direction, drafted and disseminated model codes; after the passage of the act, the organization called for the trade associations that were its members to support the program.[38] Although the Chamber's support for the recovery legislation was significant, one cannot gloss over the sources of opposition. Many corporate leaders—particularly those in the more conservative National Association of Manufacturers—objected to the government's role in approving codes and licensing producers: these provisions conflicted with the high degree of corporate autonomy established in earlier business-led recovery proposals. Moreover, businesses were concerned about the section 7(a) concessions to labor, particularly the recognition of labor's right to organize and bargain collectively. They feared that labor would make permanent the gains it had realized as part of the recovery effort.

The prospect of economy-wide regulation could have constituted a threat to business, particularly given the vague language of the National Industrial Recovery Act. However, the act gave business a key role in shaping industrial codes. During the spring of 1933, Commerce Secretary Daniel Roper established the Business Advisory and Planning Council as an organ for regular consultation with business regarding the administration's recovery plans. The council, housed in the Department of Commerce, and chaired by Gerald Swope of General Electric, author of the Swope plan, included the executives of many of the nation's largest corporations, including U.S. Steel, Sears Roebuck, AT&T, General Motors, and Du Pont. The National Recovery Administration chose business executives from the council to serve as members of the Industrial Advisory Board. On this board, they assisted in the drafting of codes and the creation of code authorities, the bodies of business and trade association representatives which interpreted code provisions and granted exemptions.[39] In light of the strong presence of business in the administration of the recovery act, as well as the antitrust exemptions, the initial support of business for the act should not be surprising. However, this support would continue only as long as the NRA seemed to be necessary to promote profitability, and the interests of the firms within a given sector could be reconciled.

The NRA approved 557 basic and 189 supplementary codes in less than two years. Through these codes, it brought some 95 percent of all industrial workers under the provisions of section 7(a).[40] Despite this high level of activity, the codes caused many problems. In part, this was due to the complexity of the task and the NRA's lack of administrative capacities. Without the necessary expertise, the NRA delegated excessive authority to the business-dominated code authorities and lacked the time and resources to evaluate the potential competitive effects of the industry agreements. The codes that were the basis of the NRA's activities were essentially cartel agreements. Like any such agreements, they affected corporations in an industry unevenly and favored the larger firms. Corporations were able to use codes to increase prices and profits and to adopt standards that created difficulties for smaller businesses. Moreover, corporations that absorbed the inflated costs of critical inputs found it difficult to prevent further decline. Certain industry codes eliminated the cost advantages that certain firms had traditionally enjoyed. The production quotas thus threatened to redistribute economic power both among firms and among regions.[41]

Businesses that had been damaged by the NRA codes and production quotas increasingly made their dissatisfaction known to Congress, both individually and through their interest organizations. Roosevelt responded to the complaints and to growing congressional concern by appointing a National Recovery Review Board to examine the effects of the codes promulgated under the NRA. The review board's findings substantiated many of the complaints, concluding that the NRA created a system of "monopoly sustained by government" and functioned as "a regimented organization for exploitation."[42] Although the administration tried to reintroduce some modicum of competition, the NRA simply lacked the capacity to enforce its own rules.

Business support for the National Recovery Administration was relatively short-lived. By 1934, many large corporations, and even the members of a progressive business organization, the Business Advisory Council, rejected the NRA. Major firms in the steel, automobile, and chemical industries effectively ended their participation in the NRA, despite the potential gains associated with the codes and the elimination of competition. Gerald Swope and the Chamber of Commerce were calling for a further reduction of government supervision, despite the fact that businesses largely dominated the code authorities.[43] In the end, the objections seemed to hinge on the NRA's failure to promote rapid recovery; the codes' negative effects on production in a number of industries, deeply entrenched business opposition to government interference in the affairs of business, and fears that the role of the state would gradually increase, resulting in the realization of a policy agenda more farreaching than that unveiled in the spring of 1933.[44]

In September 1934, after the resignation of NRA administrator Hugh Johnson, Roosevelt placed the NRA under the leadership of a seven-person board that provided representation for labor, business, and consumers. The board was charged with reviewing the NRA's practices and revising the codes. However, its attentions were focused on the upcoming extension of the recovery legislation, which was meeting great resistance, particularly in the Senate. The Supreme Court ended the debate over the extension of the National Industrial Recovery Act in 1935, when in the *Schechter* decision it unanimously rejected the act on constitutional grounds.[45] The Court found that Congress had delegated to an executive-branch agency legislative authority that was not constrained by the provisions of the act. More importantly, the Court determined that the code's section 7(a) labor provisions violated the interstate commerce clause. The object of regulation (in this case, poultry) was not part of interstate commerce, nor did it affect this commerce. With the *Schechter* decision, the experiment of the NRA came to a close. Although some corporations tried to continue the code-making process without the NRA's supervision, these attempts were either largely ineffective or ran afoul of the Justice Department's Antitrust Division, which quickly resumed and expanded its activities following the *Schechter* decision.[46]

Under the New Deal the National Industrial Recovery Act was paired with a related effort, the Agricultural Adjustment Act, which established a comprehensive system of agricultural regulation. The latter act created a system of supervised self-regulation designed to increase farm incomes above the level that would have been possible under market conditions. A network of subsidies and a coordinated system of production controls that would impose supply constraints were designed to inflate farm incomes. Farmers' associations working with the Department of Agriculture's Agricultural Adjustment Administration set production guidelines and monitored compliance at the local level. The Agricultural Adjustment Act, like its industrial counterpart, became a victim of the Supreme Court. However, Congress retained and expanded upon its basic features in subsequent legislation. Because the New Deal legislation continues to provide the foundations for agricultural regulation, the Agricultural Adjustment Act will be addressed in the next chapter.

As these efforts suggest, the New Deal recovery program was essentially an attempt to use regulation on a sector-by-sector basis to promote macroeconomic stability and growth. The goal was not to recreate markets but to compensate for their destabilizing effects and to supplant the market-based distribution of income that depressed certain key sectors of the economy. The initiatives thus placed the state in a new position vis-à-vis the interest groups that were regulated. In addition, the initiatives required that organized economic actors—corporations, trade associations, labor unions, and agricultural commodity groups—play a central role in the definition and implementation of policy. In many cases, this meant that regulators would have to organize the interests in question in order to devolve authority onto their associations. Rather than imposing a detailed plan upon a universe of economic interests, the New Deal initiatives created a new structure within which industry actors could resolve their own conflicts and coordinate their own economic activities. The state would enforce the agreements of the regulated groups and would play a supervisory role. The Roosevelt administration and Congress established a quasi-corporatist system that was predicated on notions of industrial self-regulation more clearly linked to Theodore Roosevelt's New Nationalism than to the Wilsonian Progressivism that had played such an important role in defining the basic elements of the earlier market regime.[47] The administration applied this vision of state-economy relations and the new model of administration in a number of important regulatory initiatives. There are the subject of chapter 5.

5

Regulating Land, Labor, and Capital: the Political Economy of the Associational Regime

THE ROOSEVELT ADMINISTRATION ATTEMPTED TO PROMOTE industrial stability not by atomizing industry (as the writers of the Sherman Antitrust Act had envisioned) or by subjecting it to strict supervision (as the creators of the Interstate Commerce Commission had proposed) but rather, by implementing government-supervised industrial self-regulation. Organized industry actors (e.g., trade associations, labor unions, and agricultural commodity groups) formulated agreements designed to prevent deflation and maintain a base level of output without simultaneously stimulating competition. Thus there was, in essence, a government-sponsored system of cartelization on a sectoral basis. Although the National Recovery Administration was eliminated in 1935, its example continued to shape regulatory design and the political expectations of large economic groups.

The experiences of the NRA revealed the benefits of industry organization. The organizational imperative internalized in the National Industrial Recovery Act's code provisions forced corporations and workers to form associations, and these remained active after the NRA's demise. As Ellis Hawley explains, this had an immense effect on the nature of politics: "The programs of the early New Deal . . . had generated a new organization consciousness among previously weak and relatively unorganized groups. For [those] that lacked market power in an economic world where price and production control had become increasingly characteristic, the NRA and AAA had been eye openers. Public power, they learned, could be used to reinforce private power and control markets;

and the group that could develop sufficient political strength and a plausible ideological rationale could secure governmental intervention of this type."[1]

The model of industrial self-regulation that was at the core of the National Industrial Recovery Act found a permanent expression in the major regulatory initiatives of the New Deal. These initiatives vested authority in professionalized agencies, which sought, in turn, to define and implement policy through the organizational representatives of the regulated interests. In some instances, regulators could simply use pre-existing associations as implementing agents. When such associations did not exist, the regulators often organized the regulated interests, assigning the interest associations a central role in regulating their members, subject to supervision. In essence, many private economic associations became quasi-public in nature, for they were given public authority and an important role in making and implementing regulatory policy.

This chapter examines the New Deal policies and institutions established to regulate land, labor, and capital. Although the objects of regulation share few features, the design and implementation of the regulatory policies reveal remarkable continuity with the political-economic model adopted in the National Industrial Recovery Act. However, other efforts of the period had their roots in the Progressive Era. Thus, the chapter closes with a brief discussion of the inconsistencies within the New Deal's associational regime.

REGULATING AGRICULTURE

One of the pillars of the New Deal recovery program was the Agricultural Adjustment Act, passed in May 1933. The legislation was essentially a National Industrial Recovery Act for agriculture. Although the Agricultural Adjustment Act fell victim to the Supreme Court, it provided a model of agricultural self-regulation that is still influential today. Before exploring the principal features of the first and second Agricultural Adjustment Acts, I must briefly address the unique regulatory problems that characterize this sector of the economy. Agriculture is distinguished by both demand inelasticity (i.e., the demand for foodstuffs does not increase as consumers' income increases) and by phenomenal increases in farm productivity due to mechanization and numerous technological advances. Because the growth in supply dramatically outpaced the growth in demand, there was a constant downward pressure on the prices of agricultural goods and on farmers' incomes. Spurred on by the high levels of demand and record commodity prices during and immediately after World War I, many farmers expanded their acreage. However, in 1920 foreign demand and prices dropped dramatically. The expansion of the acreage under cultivation only placed additional pressures on farm incomes.[2]

Policy-makers searched unsuccessfully for a means of addressing the agricultural crisis of the 1920s. Under a plan developed by George Peek, president of the Moline Plow Company, farmers would sell commodities in the domestic market at prices that would provide the purchasing power the farmers had enjoyed before the war. Domestic prices would be inflated by a government corporation that would buy surpluses and sell them on international markets. Tariff duties would compensate for the difference between domestic prices and world prices. In 1927 and 1928, Congress passed the McNary-Haugen bill, which embodied this plan. On both occasions, President Coolidge vetoed the legislation. In the Agricultural Marketing Act of 1929, Congress adopted a far less ambitious approach. The act created a Federal Farm Board and made available a revolving fund of $500 million which would be dispersed in the form of farm loans. It was anticipated that these loans would allow farmers to maintain their incomes without placing surplus crops on the markets. However, the drop in foreign demand, the imposition of new import barriers abroad, and the decline in domestic incomes that accompanied the Great Depression made the Hoover administration's efforts insufficient.[3]

The depression was felt much more deeply in agriculture than in manufacturing. Between 1929 and 1933, agricultural commodity prices fell 63 percent, whereas there was only a 15-percent decline in industrial prices. The problem was once again one of supply. Industrial corporations were able partially to mitigate the effects of the depression by jointly cutting back on production. This strategy was not available in agriculture because the extreme levels of decentralization undermined effective coordination. Thus, industrial corporations reduced their production by 42 percent, but there was only a 6-percent reduction in agricultural output. By the beginning of 1933, agricultural commodities could purchase only one-half as much as they had been able to two decades earlier.[4] With some 30 percent of the work force engaged in agricultural production, the welfare of the farm economy affected the economy as a whole. Moreover, a strong farm bloc in Congress and a nationwide network of farming cooperatives gave the farm crisis great political importance. The agricultural depression and the advocacy of interest groups and members of Congress was sufficient to turn the Roosevelt administration's attention to agricultural regulation.

The Agricultural Adjustment Act

The Agricultural Adjustment Act was based on a model similar to that used in the National Industrial Recovery Act: voluntary cartelization backed by the authority of the federal government. The model for the agricultural legislation was the Voluntary Domestic Allotment Plan, developed by M. L. Wilson, an agricultural economist. The plan differed greatly from the McNary-Haugen bill in that it incorporated production controls. Rather than allowing farmers to produce as much as they desired only to dispose of it in international markets, the plan would provide government payments as an incentive to reduce production. The system would finance itself by taxing the processors of agricultural products, and administrators would distribute the revenues to participating farmers through a variety of programs. The Wilson plan had some powerful advocates, including Rexford Tugwell and future secretary of agriculture Henry Wallace. During the campaign and the formulation of recovery legislation, Roosevelt's advisers convinced him to support the plan.

Congress passed the Agricultural Adjustment Act in May 1933. The act committed the federal government to the goal of parity, that is, increasing prices so that the purchasing power of agricultural commodities would be equal to what it had been during the target period, 1909–14. The Agricultural Adjustment Administration (AAA) was to control the supply of agricultural goods by means of contracts restricting the number of acres planted or the quantities produced and brought to market. Although participation was voluntary, participants were given access to benefit payments, nonrecourse loans (i.e., loans using the commodity as collateral and establishing a minimum price for the commodity), marketing orders (i.e., agreements among producers establishing quotas and commodity prices), export subsidies, and government purchases of surpluses. The AAA would finance the agricultural recovery programs through a tax levied on the processors. On a commodity-by-commodity basis, the taxes were to reflect the difference between the actual prices and the parity prices. By 1934, controls covered numerous commodities, including barley, cattle, corn, cotton, flax, grain sorghum, hogs, milk, peanuts, rice, sugar beets, sugar cane, tobacco, and wheat.

This regulatory approach was similar to that adopted in industry in three respects. The first similarity, as noted above, was that there was a focus on cartelization and self-governance under the supervision of federal bureaucrats. Because of its commodity-specific focus, the AAA decentralized its administration and depended for implementation on farm associations. The AAA could rely, to some extent, on the farm bureaus organized some decades earlier by the USDA's Extension Service. Where preexisting farm organizations were not available, which (except in the dairy and cattle sectors) was often the case, the AAA organized farmers on a commodity-specific basis by creating advisory committees. The farm associations and advisory committees provided the technical expertise and information necessary to determine production levels and monitor compliance at the local level. The AAA succeeded in creating an administrative apparatus that allowed for the kind of planning that had long been vital to industrial production.[5]

The second similarity was that the Agricultural Adjustment Act, like the National Industrial Recovery Act, was the product of political compromise. Some of Roosevelt's major advisers—such as Rexford Tugwell, Henry Wallace, and Jerome Frank—convinced the president that the best way to limit supply and increase farm incomes was to impose production controls on certain important commodities. Some, including Tugwell, saw production controls as a first step toward creating a more comprehensive system of agricultural planning on a national basis. Others, including George Peek, architect of the McNary-Haugen bill, rejected production controls, arguing that the farm crisis could be solved by means of the vigorous marketing of surpluses abroad. Processors were concerned about the new tax and, with the distributors, were suspicious of production controls that could threaten the demand for their services. Whereas agricultural groups' support for the act fluctuated on a commodity-by-commodity basis, all such interests embraced a closer relationship with the administration and welcomed attempts to address the agricultural crisis, even if they did not uniformly endorse production controls as a central component of recovery.[6]

Roosevelt responded to the diversity of interest groups by combining a variety of elements in the recovery program. As noted above, the Voluntary Domestic Allotment Plan provided the core of the Agricultural Adjustment Act. However, the act also included provisions for selling surpluses abroad and allowing processors and distributors to formulate agreements regarding the prices they would pay to farmers.[7] Roosevelt named Henry Wallace, proponent of the allotment plan, as head of the Department of Agriculture, while placing George Peek in charge of the AAA. By stressing voluntary participation, incorporating farm organizations into implementation, and establishing a highly decentralized process, the administration hoped to limit farmers' resistance. Moreover, farmers' participation reinforced the politically useful impression that the farm program was an expression of farmers' demands.[8]

The third similarity between the agricultural and industrial recovery efforts was that both favored the larger participants. The AAA placed a disproportionate emphasis on large farmers, and correspondingly deemphasized small family farmers and tenant farmers, who were much more prevalent in some regions. When forming the advisory committees, the USDA Extension Service commonly called on the larger farmers who had been most active in adopting the new technologies that it disseminated. The large producers commonly ran their farms as businesses and were thus more sympathetic to production controls. The reliance on the most successful producers created a bias favoring the large producers and threatened to make permanent the existing distribution of power within the agricultural economy. Moreover, as some top officials in the USDA, including Tugwell and Frank, tried to use agricultural policy to force economic reforms and address rural poverty, they threatened the close relationship between the major commodity producers and the AAA. The administration sought to nurture its relationship with major producers who had gained a fair deal of political influence, thus undercutting the reformist tendencies of some of Roosevelt's advisers.

The AAA was successful in organizing farmers and promoting high participation rates. Between 93 percent and 98 percent of the corn acreage in the top corn-producing states was covered by the production agreements, along with up to 89 percent of the wheat acreage in key wheat-growing states such as Kansas, Montana, and North and South Dakota. The AAA had under contract more than 75 percent of the cotton acreage, with similarly impressive sign-up rates in other commodities.[9] Despite the high levels of participation, however, the Agricultural Adjustment Act engendered a fair amount of political controversy. Farmers objected to the timing of the payments, the levels of support, and the amount that they could sell under the production controls. The protests grew in strength when commodity levels were not announced early enough to affect planting. Although problems of this type were to be expected during the early stages of the program, they still fostered concerns about whether the act would establish an effective system of regulation while promoting the growth of farm incomes. Moreover, the need to impose immediate production controls forced the wholesale destruction of crops and livestock—a highly publicized event. The attempts to bolster farm incomes through production controls seemed perverse, given the reduction in wages and the problems of underconsumption in the nonfarming population.

A host of internal problems plagued the AAA, owing in part to the diverse set of interests and contradictory strands within the administration. The conflict between production controls and the marketing of surpluses came to a head during the tenure of George Peek. His attempts to circumvent production controls and his conflicts with Henry Wallace led to his removal from the AAA. With this conflict out of the way, another quickly took its place. The commodity-specific focus of the AAA and the dominance of large agricultural producers disheartened those who envisioned a movement toward comprehensive agricultural planning. The dominance of large farmers was hindering the promotion of conservation, the reorganization of agriculture on a regional basis, and efforts to address rural poverty. However, the administration would not give up the goal of promoting increased prices for farm commodities, nor would it sacrifice its close relationship with large farmers. These conflicts led, ultimately, to the firing or resignation of a number of influential New Dealers, including Jerome Frank and Rexford Tugwell.[10]

In the end, the success of the AAA must be gauged not by the intensity of political conflicts or the agency's internal rifts but by the effects of policy on farm prices and incomes. Between 1932 and 1935, farm prices increased by 66 percent, and farmers' income as a percentage of the national income more than doubled. Net farm incomes increased from $1.9 billion in 1932 to $4.6 billion in 1935. Although the increase in farm income was in part due to the high level of transfer payments, which had reached $573 million by 1935, it was also due to the drought that ravaged the western states in 1934–35.[11] The drought eliminated surpluses of grains and even necessitated the importation of wheat. The overall effect was an increase in the cost of agricultural goods, which benefited farmers.

Despite the AAA's growing popularity among major agricultural groups, many of the processors and distributors who had to weather a decrease in the demand for their services strongly opposed the new regulatory system. They challenged the constitutionality of the core legislation before a sympathetic Supreme Court. In 1936, in *United States v. Butler*, the Supreme Court invalidated the tax on processors because it was a tax for a special interest rather than the general interest. Moreover, the Court questioned whether agricultural regulation fell within the jurisdiction of the national government.[12]

The Agricultural Adjustment Act Revisited

Congress responded almost immediately to the *Butler* decision by passing the Soil Conservation and Domestic Allotment Act, a thinly veiled attempt to preserve the main points of the Agricultural Adjustment Act. The act once again announced the goal of parity. It attempted to reinstate production controls by providing for payments—this time taken from general revenues—to those farmers who substituted soil-building crops for soil-depleting crops. (The latter category included crops that ran persistent surpluses—e.g., corn, wheat, cotton, and tobacco.) Further steps in the reconstruction of the AAA were made after the Supreme Court's strategic movement to the left: Congress passed the Agricultural Marketing Act of 1937, which authorized the creation of producer committees to formulate marketing agreements that would regulate production. The USDA enforced these agreements through its Agricultural Marketing Service.[13]

The legislation after *Butler* failed to restrain the level of production sufficiently. Indeed, the surpluses in many commodities were such that prices and farm incomes once again fell rapidly. Roosevelt responded by tying future price-support loans to the passage of legislation to fill the gaps left by the *Butler* decision and the subsequent collapse of the AAA. Congress responded in 1938 by passing a second Agricultural Adjustment Act, a revision of the original act which did not include the problematic processor tax. This legislation provides the basic framework within which agricultural regulation takes place today. The act authorized the Commodity Credit Corporation to provide nonrecourse loans at 52 to 75 percent of parity, and also created a number of mechanisms to control production levels. The Commodity Credit Corporation could deny payments and loans to farmers who exceeded their acreage allotments. Moreover, on a positive vote of two-thirds of the farmers producing a certain commodity, the secretary of agriculture could establish quotas backed by penalties. The act also created new mechanisms for disposing of surpluses. In addition to authorizing export subsidies for cotton and wheat, the act created a free school lunch program and the Food Stamp Plan, notable attempts to address farm surpluses by increasing domestic consumption.[14]

Like its predecessor, the second Agricultural Adjustment Act placed a premium on farmers' participation, using committees of farmers to administer policy at the local level. Regulators working in close consultation with agricultural groups set restrictions on how much could be produced. However, the expanded use of loans administered by the Commodity Credit Corporation promoted the production of surplus crops, which quickly became the property of the federal government. Moreover, the USDA's Extension Service promoted the further expansion of surpluses by disseminating new technology and information that allowed farmers to become more productive. Thus, in some years, such as 1938, agricultural production increased even though the total acreage under cultivation decreased.[15]

The organizing principles that characterized the associational regime are evident in the agricultural regulatory system established during the New Deal. First, Congress delegated authority to a highly professionalized agency, the Department of Agriculture. Indeed, the USDA has a deserved reputation as one of the most expert of all government agencies, with close connections to the agriculture schools and the agricultural economics departments at major land grant institutions, and a continual exchange of personnel between government service and the universities.[16] Second, the agricultural regulatory system placed a premium on producer organizations, for they were needed to make and implement policies under the supervision of USDA regulators. Where these organizations did not exist, the USDA created them and vested them with significant public authority.[17] Third, the goal was not to return to a market-based order or to replicate marketlike outcomes but rather to render the market unimportant and to assure farmers a stable income sufficient to guarantee purchasing power well above that which they would have had without regulation. Indeed, the benefits of regulation were so great that the USDA did not need to force farmers to submit to the regulations. The incentives provided by the government programs were sufficient to promote high levels of participation.

The agricultural regulatory system established during the New Deal evolved and became relatively insulated. Organized commodity producers, the USDA, and the relevant congressional committees monopolized policy. To facilitate the interaction of so many interests, the USDA organized its Agricultural Stabilization and Conservation Service, which administers price supports, and its Agricultural Marketing Service, which facilitates the formulation and implementation of marketing orders, on a commodity-specific basis. A similar level of disaggregation characterizes the organization of the agriculture subcommittees in Congress. The close relationship between members of Congress, the USDA, and the commodity groups, combined with norms of voluntarism and a devolution of public authority to producers, created a relatively stable system of self-regulation that allowed farmers to increase prices and income. Within this system of self-regulation, the majority of the benefits have accrued to the large farmers, at the expense of smaller farms and consumers. Indeed, by the 1970s the largest 19 percent of the nation's farms claimed more than 62 percent of the benefits from the farm commodity programs, and 42 percent of the total benefits went to the top 7 percent. In contrast, 50 percent of the farms—those that were the smallest units in terms of annual incomes—received approximately 9 percent of the subsidy benefits. Stated in another way, the richest farms in the nation gained 42 percent of their income from the commodity programs, whereas the farms in the bottom half of the income distribution received only 5 percent of their income from the program.[18]

REGULATING INDUSTRIAL RELATIONS

The New Deal gave rise to the first comprehensive regulatory system for labor. The centerpiece of this regulatory system was the Wagner Act of 1935, a direct product of the National Industrial Recovery Act and the conflicts it engendered. Prior to the New Deal, Congress had made a few significant advances toward greater recognition of, and protection for, organized labor. Some progress had been made during World War I, under the supervision of the National War Labor Board. After the war, the Railway Labor Act of 1926 prohibited employers from interfering with or using coercion to block the unionization of railway workers, and established a mechanism for the settlement of labor disputes. In 1932 Congress expanded the legal protections by passing the Norris–La Guardia Act, which affirmed workers' right to organize free from employer interference, prohibited "yellow dog" contracts, and limited the use of injunctions in labor disputes. Norris–La Guardia was a hollow victory for labor, owing to the lack of an effective enforcement mechanism and, more important, the dramatic decline in employment during the Great Depression. Because unemployment rates were high, employers felt little compulsion to recognize unions and negotiate over wages.[19]

Industrial Relations in the Early New Deal

The New Deal brought unprecedented gains for organized labor. The new regulatory system would play a decisive role in stimulating the organization of workers and compelling employers to meet with workers' representatives within the context of collective bargaining. Although unions would ultimately become a central component of the New Deal coalition, labor had been of little importance in the Democratic victory of 1932. Roosevelt promoted organized labor at the urging of influential presidential advisers such as Rexford Tugwell and Senator Robert Wagner, who believed that the purchasing power of labor was a central component of recovery. Moreover, many of Roosevelt's advisers believed that recovery and economic stability could be facilitated by the creation of a system of industrial self-governance in which the representatives of economic groups would act according to negotiated agreements. As long as such a system was absent, they thought, the economy would be prone to industrial conflict.

The Roosevelt administration had fulfilled some of the traditional demands of organized labor with the section 7(a) labor provisions of the National Industrial Recovery Act. It was William Green, president of the American Federation of Labor, who initially recommended the inclusion of section 7(a); Senator Wagner, one of the prime architects of the legislation, made his support for the recovery program contingent on the incorporation of these very provisions.[20] Though the act required businesses to meet the labor provisions in each code, it did not provide a useful mechanism for overseeing compliance or determining maximum hours and minimum wages. The business-dominated code authorities, usually with little input from labor, initially determined whether codes satisfied section 7(a). The National Recovery Administration's Labor Advisory Board recognized the conflict of interests inherent in such an arrangement and demanded that labor and consumer representatives be included in the code authorities—a demand that had little actual effect.[21]

During the summer of 1933 there was an explosion of strikes. Workers' militancy increased as labor activists interpreted section 7(a) as an invitation to organize and recoup some of the membership losses incurred during the first years of the Great Depression. Others simply reacted to employers' unwillingness to negotiate the terms of the codes. The NRA's advisory boards representing industry and labor responded to the strikes by calling for the creation of an intermediary in the labor-management conflicts, a body that would implement section 7(a). Roosevelt, in turn, established a tripartite National Labor Board chaired by Senator Wagner. Although the board had limited authority, it proceeded to state a few important principles. It determined that the right to collective bargaining granted by section 7 obligated businesses to meet with workers' chosen representatives and negotiate regarding the terms of the codes. Also, it established the principle of secret-ballot elections with majority rule when it adopted the Reading formula, which stated that the bargaining unit receiving a majority of the votes would become the sole authoritative representative of the workers.[22]

Hugh Johnson, head of the NRA, generally supported the National Labor Board and backed its decisions by threatening to remove the NRA Blue Eagle insignia from the products of employers that failed to comply with the board's election decisions. However, there was soon a parting of the ways. Johnson promoted proportional representation, believing it necessary to allow one bloc of workers within a corporation to claim membership in a labor union while allowing another bloc to belong to a company union. Roosevelt's support for Johnson in a major auto industry settlement led corporations to discount the board's power. One can interpret Roosevelt's support for proportional representation as an expression of his conviction that economic organization was imperative, regardless of its form. The NRA and much of Roosevelt's overall recovery plan depended on the organization of economic interests and the forging of agreements that would promote stability.[23]

The New Deal could not afford to retreat from its initial position on unionization because of the high levels of labor militancy in 1934. In that year alone, there were 1,856 strikes involving almost 1.5 million workers, or 7 percent of the labor force. Many workers engaged in sit-down strikes, occupying strategic industrial installations to halt production. Indeed, the largest strike thus far in American history took place in August 1934, involving some half a million workers in the textile industry.[24] Wagner's lobbying, together with the high levels of labor militancy, promoted further legislative action that, with Roosevelt's participation, resulted in the creation of the first National Labor Relations Board. The public resolution that created the board restated the right of employees to organize and to select their representatives for collective bargaining. It granted the NLRB greater investigative powers than its predecessor, as well as independent enforcement powers, which the National Labor Board had not had. Rather than having to rely on the NRA or the Justice Department for the enforcement of its decisions, the NLRB could appeal to the courts to issue mandatory injunctions.[25] However, the new board was soon plagued by the same problems that had faced its predecessor. It lacked detailed statutory authority, and resources; and thus employers continued to challenge and ignore its decisions. These problems were short-lived. In 1935 the Supreme Court's *Schechter* decision eliminated the NLRB along with the NRA.[26]

The Wagner Act

Following *Schechter*, Congress moved quickly to pass Wagner's labor relations bill; Roosevelt's support was forthcoming only after it was clear that the new legislation was going to pass in both chambers. The Wagner Act (also known as the National Labor Relations Act of 1935) continues to provide the basic institutional framework for the regulation of industrial relations. The act created a new National Labor Relations Board, which was to be composed of three individuals appointed by the president and confirmed by the Senate. Expanding on the provisions of the National Industrial Recovery Act, the new legislation established workers' right to elect via majority rule their own exclusive representatives. Several other points also deserve mention. The act explicitly prohibited a number of unfair labor practices, including attempts to restrain or coerce employees seeking representation; interference with labor organizations; discrimination against union members or those seeking to protect their rights under the provisions of the act; and refusal to bargain with the chosen representatives of labor. It also empowered the NLRB to issue cease and desist orders, and to appeal for court injunctions in response to violations of these orders. Finally, it authorized the NLRB to determine the appropriate unit for elections and representation.[27]

The new NLRB quickly became a highly professional agency, dominated by a large and growing legal staff. It inherited the 14-member legal staff of the National Labor Board and quickly expanded upon this core of lawyers. By 1939 its legal staff had grown to 252, representing the nation's best law schools.[28] Under the direction of general counsel Charles Fahy, the NLRB was organized along functional lines and included a litigation section, a review section, a trial examiners section, and an economics division. The central office immediately assigned its Washington-based lawyers to regional offices for three reasons: (1) at the time there was but one attorney stationed in the field, and it was critical to create a greater legal presence at the local level; (2) assigning attorneys to the regional boards would let them become familiar with the policy process at the grassroots level and gain experience with corporate lawyers; and (3) this strategy provided a means of imposing centralized control over the policy process. The NLRB lawyers were in direct contact with the board, and thus they could circumvent the regional directors. Because there were concerns over potential court challenges, the regional boards had to receive Washington approval before issuing any complaints.[29]

These attempts to create the bureaucratic culture of the new NLRB encountered a number of barriers. Regional directors resented the intrusion of the Washington office and found their old role as mediators difficult to reconcile with the NLRB's quasi-judicial functions. Moreover, there were problems within the Washington office. The economics division challenged the legal ethos of the agency. Rather than assuming a limited role in supervising industrial relations, division personnel promoted much more ambitious goals, hoping that the NLRB would develop and implement long-term plans for the evolution of industrial relations. As part of this vision, the division director recommended that economists be paired with attorneys on each important case and that the lawyers receive training in economics. The board's lawyers, especially General Counsel Fahey, rejected this expansive vision of the NLRB's mission and opposed a central role for economists within the agency. The opposition of the legal staff and the low levels of staffing within the economics division were sufficient to ensure that attorneys had the central role in the policy process.[30]

As Christopher Tomlins explains, the NLRB's early innovations "ensured that from the outset its model in both organizational and procedural matters would be one rooted firmly in professional legal practice. This reflected trends which had already been apparent during the tenure of the first NLRB. It also reflected the preferences and professional socialization of the senior staff of the new Board."[31] The new legal ethos of the NLRB was also part of a deliberate strategy to construct precise and consistent procedures that would help insulate the board from judicial challenges while making it seem neutral. The question of neutrality was critical. When Congress debated the Wagner Act, it explicitly addressed the objectivity and independence of the new board. The debates focused in large part on whether to place the NLRB in the Department of Labor—an option supported by those who wished to promote that department's interests—or to make it formally independent. As the

House Commerce Committee's minority report suggested, the NLRB's "prestige and efficacy must be grounded fundamentally in public approval and in equal confidence in its impartiality by Labor and Industry. If the Board is placed in the Department it will suffer ab initio from the suspicion that it is not a court, but an organ devoted solely to the interests of laboring groups."[32] It was critical that the NLRB be seen as objective, for otherwise corporations would discount or disregard the board's decisions. Corporate intransigence could force the agency to devote ever-greater time and resources to individual cases, thus placing severe limits on the board's regulatory capacity. Moreover, contested decisions could end up before the Supreme Court, which had recently invalidated the NRA.

Congress decided to maximize the NLRB's neutrality by making the board independent of the Department of Labor, and also placed a premium on the board's legal ethos. The legal profession values procedural propriety and due process within the adversary system. Attorneys seek to resolve conflicts within a neutral system through the application of relatively stable legal rules. These norms of the legal profession, once incorporated into the agency through a process of legal professionalization, gave the NLRB an appearance of objectivity and expertise. Because the law could only address a relatively limited set of issues—precisely those issues that did not threaten the existing distribution of economic power—it added a certain stability to the system and set distinct parameters for industrial conflict.[33]

The Wagner Act and the new NLRB were vulnerable to challenges until ruled constitutional in 1937.[34] Although there were many legal challenges to the NLRB, the agency took great care to select an appropriate test case. In spite of uncertainty regarding the ultimate constitutionality of the Wagner Act, the board's performance was truly impressive. By the end of 1939, more than twenty-five thousand cases involving nearly 6 million workers had been filed with the NLRB. The NLRB had conducted twenty-five hundred elections for union representation, and settled some two thousand strikes.[35] In the four years following the passage of the Wagner Act, union membership almost doubled, increasing from some 3.75 million to more than 6.55 million. The organization of labor and the selection of labor representatives—both processes promoted and facilitated by the New Deal's labor policies—allowed for a relatively stable regulatory structure that would promote collective bargaining without the violence and turmoil of the past.[36] Although there were ongoing conflicts between the American Federation of Labor and the Congress of Industrial Organizations, and the NLRB had a role in promoting the expansion of the latter, labor had clearly won a victory with the passage of the Wagner Act. Of course, labor rewarded Roosevelt and the Democratic party for their efforts. By 1940, union funds were the largest single source of contributions for the Democrats, and union members constituted a large and consistently loyal body of Democratic voters.[37] Labor became a core member of the New Deal coalition.

However, the stability that the Wagner Act introduced into industrial relations came at a high price—namely, the autonomy and ambitions of the labor movement. Before the New Deal, unions had largely been the product of self-organization. Any gains came through the actions of the unions and the workers, with the federal government not only providing little assistance but also often overtly resisting labor's efforts. After the Wagner Act, the NLRB essentially accepted responsibility for organizing labor by means of NLRB-supervised elections and a certification process. Labor-management relations were recast in highly legalistic terms; disputes were subjected to quasi-judicial hearings. Although these changes brought stability to industrial relations, they had three effects that would be of concern. Because the NLRB certified labor unions, the advances of organized labor became dependent on the support of regulators. In addition, the highly complex legal discourse that the NLRB introduced into industrial relations effectively excluded rank-and-file union members from the debates over management-labor contracts. Moreover, the centralization of power in the leadership of the unions, and the narrow set of issues addressed by the NLRB, fostered greater conservatism in the labor movement. Questions of workplace control were replaced by limited debates over wages, hours, and benefits. Of course, this was precisely the point: the New Deal's legacy in the regulation of labor was similar to its legacy in agriculture. The goal was to promote and supervise the organization of the regulated interests in hopes of promoting stability.

REGULATING CORPORATE CAPITAL

The New Deal initiatives in financial regulation were every bit as thoroughgoing as those in agriculture and industrial relations. Given the complexity of financial regulation and the events of the New Deal, it is necessary to explore the policy initiatives in some detail. Prior to the New Deal, financial regulation at the national level was less than comprehensive. Until the passage of the Banking Act of 1863, state governments had chartered banks, which subsequently operated under state regulations. Congress passed the Banking Act not only to facilitate the funding of the Civil War but also to superimpose a federal regulatory structure on this decentralized banking system. The act authorized the issuance of national charters for banks that met specific capital and reserve requirements, subject to the supervision of the comptroller of the currency. This dual regulatory structure allowed banks to function at either the state or the national level. The regulatory fragmentation was exacerbated by the decentralization of the banking industry—a product of state laws' restrictions on interstate banking and on the opening of branches. With the McFadden Act of 1927, Congress essentially extended the restrictions on branching to national banks.

The lack of a comprehensive regulatory structure, and the high levels of decentralization, made finance vulnerable to shocks, and this vulnerability was exacerbated by the close linkages between commercial and investment banking. During the 1920s, larger banks commonly used time deposits as a source of funds for their investment banking activities. Through securities affiliates, they used the funds to underwrite new issues and buy securities for their own portfolios. Moreover, the dramatic rise in the stock market between 1926 and September 1929 attracted new investors, many of whom purchased stocks on margin. Investors leveraged their purchases by borrowing funds from brokers, who in turn borrowed from the commercial banks. Between the end of 1927 and October 1929, broker loans almost doubled, increasing from $4.4 billion to $8.5 billion. Commercial banks and the time deposits they used as a source of funds were tied up in the stock market, and thus, were highly susceptible to market fluctuations.[38]

Although the stock market crash of October 1929 was not the cause of the Great Depression, the financial crisis it created made the depression all the more difficult to address. The panic sales of those who had purchased stocks on margin accelerated the decline. During the next three years, the value of all the stocks on the New York Stock Exchange plummeted by 83 percent, from approximately $90 billion to $16 billion. Likewise, the bonds listed on the exchange declined in value from $49 billion to $31 billion. The global depression also undermined the value of an already questionable $6.3 billion worth of foreign bonds purchased in the United States during the 1920s.[39]

The plunging values of stocks and bonds had a monumental effect on banks, reducing the value of their investments and making it far more difficult to collect on the loans made to investment brokers. This, when combined with depositors' panic and a drop in corporate receipts, resulted in the collapse of some nine thousand banks and caused additional losses of some $2.5 billion for depositors and stockholders.[40] Beginning in the fall of 1932, several states responded to the financial crisis by declaring bank holidays. In cities such as Philadelphia and Pittsburgh, the banks declared their own holidays to stave off the outflow of deposits. In early March, a bank holiday was declared in New York. This protected the largest banks in the nation, headquartered in the nation's money center, New York City. On March 5, 1933, the day after his inauguration, Roosevelt declared a national bank holiday. Congress passed the Emergency Banking Act four days later, ratifying the president's proclamation and authorizing the comptroller of the currency to reorganize the closed banks. On March 10, an executive order authorized the Department of the Treasury to reopen solvent banks. Roosevelt's reaction to the banking crisis restored confidence in the system and brought a rapid return of money to the nation's banks.[41]

The financial collapse in itself might have been sufficient to force new regulatory initiatives. However, the hearings held by the Senate Committee on Banking and Currency, under the direction of committee counsel Ferdinand Pecora, gave this collapse even greater significance. The Senate authorized the Pecora hearings in 1932 to investigate the causes of the stock market crash, and over the course of the next two years the hearings expanded to examine the practices and personalities that made up the investment banking industry. The investigations of the National City Bank and J. P. Morgan and Company drew national attention, with their stories of high salaries, falsified prospectuses, market manipulations, tax evasion, outright bribery, and the subtle use of preferred lists to allow influential political officials to use insider information to gain risk-free profits on new securities issues. These hearings politicized financial mismanagement.[42] The combination of financial collapse, highly publicized accounts of corruption, and vigorous presidential support was sufficient to force financial reform legislation through Congress. The legislation of 1933 and 1934 completely transformed the regulation and structure of American finance.

One cannot address the regulation of investment banking by the Securities and Exchange Commission without first examining the changes in the financial industry following the 1933 passage of the Glass-Steagall Act, which instituted a number of important reforms in the banking industry and created the Federal Deposit Insurance Corporation to insure deposits. For the purposes of this discussion, however, the act was important primarily because it mandated the separation of commercial banking (deposit-taking and loan-making) from investment banking (underwriting and dealing in securities). The separation of banking functions was not a new idea; it had been advocated by President Hoover and a number of representatives and senators concerned with potential conflicts of interest. The revelations of the Pecora hearings were sufficient to create the level of support necessary for legislative action. The Glass-Steagall Act prohibited national banks and state banks that were members of the Federal Reserve System from dealing in anything other than U.S. Treasury securities and general obligation state and municipal bonds. It also banned banks from underwriting and dealing in corporate securities. Congress enacted general prohibitions of interlocking directorates between commercial banks and securities firms, thus forcing the complete separation of these institutions.[43]

The Securities and Exchange Commission

After the passage of the Glass-Steagall Act, commercial and investment banking became two separate endeavors regulated by separate agencies. The Securities Act of 1933, drafted by James Landis and Benjamin Cohen under the direction of Felix Frankfurter, created a regulatory mechanism that Louis Brandeis had championed a decade earlier. Despite its Progressive roots, it was quickly shaped by the basic principles of associationalism. The legislation was designed to regulate through information. All public offerings of corporate stock in excess of $100,000 had to be registered with the Federal Trade Commission and accompanied by a prospectus disclosing relevant information regarding the corporation's business, its officers, and the terms and purposes of the financing. After the necessary information was filed, the FTC had twenty days to examine the contents and, if necessary, bar public sales through the issuance of a stop order. The issuing corporation, its directors, and the investment bankers underwriting the issue could be held liable only if they had failed to exercise "due diligence" in investigating and verifying the sales document. It was believed that the registration process and civil liability would compel issuers and underwriters to provide the information necessary for rational investment decisions.[44]

New legislation designed to regulate the stock exchanges themselves quickly strengthened the Securities Act of 1933. This was part of Roosevelt's overall goal of regulating both the issuance and exchange of securities. As with other New Deal initiatives, Roosevelt's advisers prepared several competing legislative plans. Sensing that some form of regulation was imminent, Richard Whitney, president of the New York Stock Exchange, implemented a number of reforms. New rules required that margin accounts be backed with a specified minimum balance and that stock pools, syndicates, and joint trading accounts file weekly reports with the exchange. Moreover, the exchange encouraged brokers to place their employees on salary to reduce the temptation to engage in high-pressure sales.[45] When these reform efforts failed to have the intended effect, Whitney recommended creating a new supervisory stock exchange authority composed of seven members, including two representatives of the exchanges. However, support for Whitney's plan was limited by a growing body of evidence of corrupt exchange practices collected through the Pecora hearings.[46]

Whitney orchestrated a massive lobbying effort that mobilized numerous corporate and financial interests that would be subject to the proposed regulations. They argued that regulating the stock exchanges would increase unemployment in the financial districts and impede recovery by increasing the costs of capital. In the end, Congress passed a modified version of a bill prepared by James Landis, Benjamin Cohen, and Tommy Corcoran. The Securities Exchange Act of 1934 required that the New York Stock Exchange and twenty-two other national exchanges register with a newly created independent regulatory commission, the Securities and Exchange Commission. The sec was directed to register all securities listed on the national exchanges, thus extending the coverage of the Securities Act to new and existing securities issues. The act forced corporations with stocks listed on the exchanges to register, and to submit quarterly financial reports. In addition, they had to abide by sec-established procedures in the solicitation of proxies and report the securities transactions of corporate officers and directors when these involved the stock of the individual's own company. To regulate the conduct of the traders, the act established antifraud provisions, mandated the registration of dealers, and prohibited a number of activities, including insider trading and wash sales (large-scale sales designed to manipulate the price of a security). Finally, in hopes of limiting speculation, the act set margin loan limits of 55 percent of the current market price of a security, allowing the Federal Reserve Board to change these limits at its discretion. The sec would become the most prestigious regulatory agency created during the New Deal.[47]

It would be easy to interpret the financial regulatory legislation of the New Deal as an extension of the older Progressive tradition that called for the fragmentation of economic power. The legislation was written by students of Brandeis who opposed any scheme that entailed planning. The regulatory system reflected the influence of Brandeis's classic book *Other People's Money*, which called, in essence, for regulation by means of disclosure and publicity.[48] Many were critical of the initiatives, suggesting that the decentralization of finance was difficult to justify in view of the evolution of the corporate economy during the previous few decades. William O. Douglas, in an article written before his appointment to the sec, suggested that the Securities Act was "a nineteenth-century piece of legislation" that was "wholly antithetical to the programme of control envisaged in the New Deal and to the whole economy under which we are living." He went on to note that the legislation was regressive in that it would force Americans to "unscramble our large forms of organization" and "bring back into business organization a simplicity and directness consistent more with our beginnings than with our present status."[49]

Although the regulatory legislation bore the imprint of Progressivism, the implementation of the new regulatory policies revealed great consistency with other initiatives of the associational regime. The sec enforced disclosure provisions and prohibitions of certain forms of activity. However, there was a large measure of industry self-regulation through the activities of industry trade associations. Moreover, the SEC played a critical role in giving these associations the necessary authority and, in one important case, actually facilitated the creation of a private association that had the authority to regulate its members. Let us explore briefly the SEC's regulation of the stock exchanges and the over-the-counter markets.[50]

Regulating the Stock Exchanges

One of the first acts of Joseph Kennedy, the first SEC chairman, was to direct the staff to complete a report on the stock exchanges. The final report was highly critical of the centralized control of of the New York Stock Exchange exercised by Richard Whitney and the Old Guard that he represented. The report called for a number of reforms in the governance of the exchange but suggested that they be carried out by the exchange itself. In a largely symbolic move, Charles Gay replaced Whitney in the 1935 elections, although the latter remained firmly in charge of both the exchange and the body in charge of exchange policies. In another symbolic act, the exchange adopted sixteen rules proposed by Kennedy, although they remained largely unenforced.[51]

James Landis, appointed chairman after Kennedy's resignation in 1935, was one of the architects of the securities legislation and a strong proponent of self-regulation. Addressing the New York Stock Exchange in 1935, he explained: "Self-government is, of course, the desirable thing. Everyone will admit that the less regulation there is, the better it will be, provided the objectives are always kept clear; and the better the self-government, the less need there is for regulation."[52] What Landis had in mind was a system of mixed regulation, one that "welded together existing self-regulation and direct control by government" and backed "existing powers by the force of government, rather than absorbing all authority and power to itself."[53] Despite the obvious attractions of such a system, Whitney and the exchange rejected any serious reforms and refused to enforce the rules they had only recently adopted at the SEC's request. Because Landis hoped to establish effective self-regulation, he responded to the exchange's intransigence by cultivating the SEC's relationship with exchange dissidents and with the public brokerage houses.[54]

In 1937 Landis left the SEC to assume the deanship of the Harvard Law School and was replaced by William O. Douglas. In the past, Douglas had been highly critical of Wall Street; given the uncompromising position taken by the New York Stock Exchange, Douglas was reluctant to forestall regulation. The only question was the form that the regulation would take. The exchange could either accept supervised self-regulation or submit to a more direct form of regulation imposed by the SEC. New evidence regarding further abuses at the exchange and Charles Gay's attempts to discredit the SEC by ascribing the 1937 drop in the stock market to excessive regulation led Douglas to move quickly. After a series of meetings initiated by the more progressive members of the exchange and representatives of the public brokerage houses, he issued an ultimatum: the exchange could begin formulating a reorganization and reform program or accept "an immediate and more persuasive administration by the Commission."[55]

In response to Douglas's threats and in spite of Whitney's opposition, Charles Gay named a committee to design a reorganization plan. The committee included a number of nonmembers of the exchange, as well as Adolf Berle, representing the Roosevelt administration. Ironically, tough new disclosure rules forced by the dissident commissioned brokers revealed that Whitney had engaged in numerous illegal and unethical activities during his years at the exchange. By March 1938 he had been indicted for grand larceny—a charge that ended in his conviction. With the Old Guard discredited, the exchange quickly adopted the reorganization plan.[56] The plan was essentially that formulated and suggested by Douglas during earlier negotiations. The exchange streamlined its organization and placed itself under the control of a salaried president who was a nonmember and was supported by an expert staff. The new president was William McChesney Martin, a reformer and Wall Street outsider who had served as the secretary of the reorganization committee. The governing board, formerly dominated by the Old Guard specialists and bond traders, was reduced in size and completely reconstituted so that twenty of the thirty-two seats were to be occupied by the commissioned brokers, and another three by nonmembers of the exchange. Moreover, the exchange's committees were to be supported by a large professional staff in hopes of preventing floor members from returning to the manipulative practices of the past. As an aftermath of these reforms, commissioned brokers who were largely supportive of the self-regulatory emphasis of the SEC took control. Under Martin's leadership and the direct supervision of the SEC, the exchange adopted many new rules and regulations governing the behavior of its members. Self-regulation of the exchange had been established.[57]

Regulating the Over-the-Counter Markets

The self-regulation of the over-the-counter market can be traced to the National Industrial Recovery Act rather than to the securities legislation of 1933 and 1934. Under the National Recovery Administration, the Investment Bankers Association formed a code committee to compile a code of fair competition. The code essentially adopted the disclosure provisions and the prohibitions included in the Securities Act and made them binding upon the members of the IBA. After the Supreme Court declared the National Industrial Recovery Act unconstitutional, the IBA, at the request of the SEC, tried to promote voluntary compliance with the code. The code committee was subsequently incorporated as the Investment Bankers Conference, and the conference quickly set about establishing rules to govern the OTC markets. However, the conference was ineffective owing to low participation rates: by 1937, it represented less than one-third of the registered dealers. This lack of participation and the need for more comprehensive regulations in the OTC markets led the conference, the IBA, and the SEC to draft new legislation and to plan the creation of a national association that would be responsible for regulating investment banking under the direct supervision of the SEC.[58]

The Securities and Exchange Commission promoted OTC organization to address the practical difficulties of regulating so decentralized an industry. As SEC commissioner George Matthews explained: "The problem of direct Government regulation of the over-the-counter market is a little like trying to build a structure out of dry sand. There is no cohesive force to hold it together, no organization with which we can build, as authoritatively representing a substantial element in the over-the-counter business."[59] A trade association would facilitate regulation by providing the cohesive force that was lacking. Moreover, self-regulation by means of a trade association held three additional promises: (1) if regulatory authority were vested in a private institution representing the OTC brokers and dealers, the administrative costs of regulation could be borne by the regulated themselves; (2) because the rules would be drafted and enforced by a voluntary organization, any members that rejected a particular regulation could simply leave the association, thus limiting the SEC's exposure to legal challenges; and (3) the use of an association as an organ of self-regulation could prove more effective than government regulation, allowing an extension of regulation to activities normally beyond the detection of the SEC. As William Douglas noted: "By and large, government can operate satisfactorily only by proscription. That leaves untouched large areas of conduct and activity; some of it susceptible of government regulation but in fact too minute for satisfactory control, some of it lying beyond the periphery of the law in the realm of ethics and morality. Into these large areas self-government, and self-government alone, can effectively reach."[60]

The Maloney Act of 1938 amended the Securities Exchange Act by authorizing the SEC to register national OTC associations that were charged with developing and enforcing rules "designed to prevent fraudulent and manipulative acts and practices, to promote just and equitable principles of trade, to provide safeguards against unreasonable profits . . . and, in general, to protect investors and the public interest" without simultaneously fixing rates or engaging in unfair discriminatory practices. The National Association of Securities Dealers was registered as the sole regulatory organization for the OTC market. To promote membership, broker-dealers who joined were offered wholesale prices on their purchases of securities from other members; nonmembers were required to pay the same prices and commission fees as the public. With this important incentive, the association expanded to include 90 percent of the eligible broker-dealers.[61] In close consultation with the SEC, the association quickly developed a set of rules for its members. As Thomas McCraw notes, the National Association of Securities Dealers "assumed the functions and structure of a regulatory agency. At the SEC's insistence, it began to develop its own professional staff which eventually included several hundred examiners and investigators."[62] It conducted investigations both on its own initiative and at the request of the SEC. Failure to adhere to the rules could be met with fines, suspension, or expulsion—sanctions that carried significant economic costs given the benefits of membership.

The New Deal initiatives to regulate land, labor, and capital had many elements in common. Like the initiatives of the Progressive Era's market regime, the New Deal initiatives showed a great reliance on administrative expertise. The USDA, the NLRB, and the SEC were highly professionalized agencies that quickly gained a reputation for expertise. Moreover, in all three regulatory arenas policies were designed with the explicit goal of promoting economic stability. In the case of agriculture, the focus was on reaching parity by controlling the supply of commodities; in the case of labor, the NLRB sought to introduce greater stability into labor relations by creating a system for collective bargaining which delimited the scope of industrial conflicts; and in the case of securities, the SEC introduced stability by imposing rigid disclosure rules and regulations on the conduct of those involved in the issuance and exchange of various debt instruments. Finally, the New Deal initiatives relied heavily on economic associations to assist in the definition and implementation of policy. In all three cases, the agencies were primarily responsible for organizing the economic interests in question and vesting them with public authority. Particularly in agriculture and investment banking, this entailed creating a system of government-supervised self-regulation.

THE ASSOCIATIONAL REGIME AND
THE LEGACY OF PROGRESSIVISM

The New Deal regulatory initiatives presented above clearly exemplified the fundamental principles of the associational regime. Some other initiatives of that era, however, did not. Two regulatory systems in particular—the regulation of air transportation and the regulation of public utility holding companies—showed great continuity with the Progressive past. The former was an example of regulation that closely paralleled the regulatory system established for railroads half a century earlier: a regulatory board controlled exit, entry, and rates so as to guarantee an acceptable rate of return. The latter, in contrast, was an example of populism taken to an extreme. Public utility holding companies were broken up and the industry was completely restructured, in spite of the utilities' strong and vociferous objections.

Populism Revisited: The Public Utility Holding Company Act

The discussion of the financial system presented above focused on two important issues: the separation of commercial and investment banking, and the creation of a regulatory system that devolved a significant amount of authority to the dealers and brokers. The question of public utility holding companies was closely tied to investment banking because of the key role of financiers in the creation and management of the holding companies. In view of the New Deal's other policies regarding the financial industry, and the emphasis these policies placed on self-regulation, the approach to public utilities was in many ways an astounding testament to the older strands of Progressivism which were latent in the New Deal.

The Federal Trade Commission conducted an investigation of the public utility industry over the period 1928–35, compiling more than eighty volumes documenting significant problems that ranged from the centralization of control in a few mammoth holding companies (the top three holding companies controlled 45 percent of the electrical energy generated in the United States) to the falsification of corporate records to manipulate rates. Moreover, the holding companies commonly floated much larger stock issues than they could justify given the earnings of the company and the underlying assets. The revelations of the FTC investigation and a subsequent House investigation created an environment conducive to new regulatory initiatives. Moreover, Roosevelt denounced the "Power Trust," arguing that the concentration of economic power in the holding companies was simply too great for effective state-level regulation. He sought some means of addressing the existing industrial structure and returning control to local managers and state-level regulators.[63]

Roosevelt's commitment to restructuring the industry stimulated the introduction of a number of competing bills. However, the administration backed a bill that prohibited many common abuses and required that public utility holding companies register with the SEC, which would thereafter exercise considerable control over their financial affairs. Thus far, the proposed legislation was not a significant departure from the securities regulations. However, at Roosevelt's insistence the bill included a "death sentence" provision that required the elimination of all public utility holding companies within five years unless it was determined that their continued existence was necessary. The administration supported nothing short of the wholesale eradication of the holding companies.[64]

After a dramatic lobbying effort on the part of the holding companies, Congress and the administration modified the "death sentence" provision. However, the final legislation, the Public Utility Holding Company Act of 1935, retained much of its force and stood as the most severe of the New Deal regulatory policies. The act authorized the SEC to regulate the holding companies' acquisitions and their issuance of securities, and to regulate the financial relationships between the holding companies and their operating subsidiaries. Most important, however, was the section 11 "death sentence." The act required the "simplification" of the public utilities systems "to provide as soon as practicable for the elimination of public utility holding companies," and directed the SEC to prepare plans for reorganization. The holding companies were to divest themselves of any subsidiaries not necessary to the maintenance of a physically interconnected and coordinated system within a geographical region. The act allowed the holding companies to submit their own plans for voluntary reorganization. However, it empowered the SEC to seek court orders to force the divestiture of subsidiaries that the agency had determined to be economically unnecessary.[65]

The act also required that all public utility holding companies register with the SEC by a specified date. If they chose not to comply, the federal government could bar them from interstate commerce and deny them the use of the mails. When the December 1935 deadline arrived, however, none of the major holding companies had registered. Rather, they filed more than fifty suits against the SEC in hopes of obtaining an injunction. The SEC carefully filed charges against the largest of the holding companies, the Electric Bond and Share Company, to shape the ultimate determination of the act's constitutionality. Because the legislation had been skillfully written to allow the registration requirements to stand separately from the death sentence, the district court and finally the Supreme Court decided only on the registration requirements, which they found to be sound.[66] After this victory, the holding companies quickly complied with the registration requirements.[67]

The SEC was initially cautious in the enforcement of the death sentence owing to concerns about the measure's constitutionality. However, by 1940 changes in the Court's composition led the SEC to implement the death sentence with great vigor. The SEC's authority to impose compulsory reorganization and divestiture led a vast majority of public utility holding companies to submit divestiture plans of their own for SEC approval. Voluntary divestiture was critical: it minimized both the courts' role in implementation and the costs and delays of lengthy litigation. Because the SEC adopted a narrow interpretation of the conditions under which a holding company could continue to control multiple utility systems, the holding companies usually submitted drastic divestiture plans. The success of divestiture was apparent. The public utility holding companies that had originally registered with the SEC had controlled 1,983 subsidiaries. By 1953, more than 1,600 had been divested. This record of success led Joel Seligman, an expert on the history of the Securities and Exchange Commission, to call the geographic integration and simplification of the holding companies "the agency's single most significant achievement."[68]

Progressivism Revisited: The Civil Aeronautics Authority

Technological change poses interesting challenges for public officials because of the obvious temptation to regulate a new technology by drawing analogies with earlier technologies. Policy-makers tend to subsume new technologies under existing regulatory frameworks. For example, in the Motor Carrier Act of 1935 Congress made the Interstate Commerce Commission responsible for regulating the trucking industry because the legislators considered this to be a natural and reasonable expansion of the commission's existing regulatory functions. And when designing policies to address civil aeronautics, Congress looked to the regulation of surface transportation. The final product was the Civil Aeronautics Act of 1938, which created the Civil Aeronautics Authority (renamed the Civil Aeronautics Board in 1940).[69]

Despite a number of attempts to regulate the aeronautics industry, it was not until more than two decades after the first successful flight that Congress passed national regulatory legislation. The federal government had favored promotion over regulation. In 1915 President Wilson created an advisory committee to coordinate and direct aeronautical research. Ten years later, the Air Mail Act authorized the postmaster general to transport U.S. mails on private aircraft in hopes of further stimulating economic development in the aeronautics industry. While the federal government was promoting the expansion of the industry, state governments busily expanded their regulations. By 1925, nineteen states were regulating various aspects of the aeronautics industry. Finally, in 1926, Congress passed the Air Commerce Act, giving the secretary of commerce the authority to regulate the safety of the industry. The act required that aircraft acting in interstate commerce be registered with the Department of Commerce and meet specified safety requirements. Likewise, Congress directed pilots to pass an exam and receive a license from the Department of Commerce. The department also began promulgating safety rules and, in 1934, gained the authority to investigate aviation accidents.[70]

The federal government continued to pursue a promotional mission after the Air Commerce Act was passed. The Watres Act of 1930, for example, gave the postmaster general the authority to subsidize the industry by paying airlines more than necessary in exchange for carrying the mails. However, a Senate investigation conducted three years after the passage of the act revealed a history of questionable practices, including bid-rigging in awarding government contracts. In response to the investigation, the postmaster general canceled all contracts for domestic mail transportation in February 1934, and President Roosevelt assigned the duties of mail transportation to the army—a task it was unprepared to undertake. In response to an immediate and substantial increase in aviation accidents, Congress passed the Air Mail Act of 1934, creating a piecemeal solution to the problem at hand. The act returned mail delivery to the private carriers but placed them under the direction of the Post Office, which awarded contracts and approved routes; the Interstate Commerce Commission, which set rates; and the Department of Commerce, which licensed pilots and planes. In addition, the Air Mail Act established the Federal Aviation Commission to investigate the aeronautics industry and recommend a comprehensive policy.[71]

During the next three years a number of legislative proposals were made concerning the further regulation of the industry. Although there was remarkable agreement on the goals of the new legislation, there were deep conflicts over the selection of the appropriate regulatory agency. The Federal Aviation Commission, authorized to study the industry and propose a comprehensive policy, presented a list of 102 policy recommendations. The commission called for the creation of an air commerce commission as the agency responsible for administering the new policy. Roosevelt's support for the vesting of regulatory responsibilities in the ICC created a deadlock, as the Department of Commerce

and the Post Office sought to preserve or expand their existing jurisdictions. An interdepartmental committee tried to eliminate the stale-
mate and recommended, once again, the creation of a new agency.[72] The
Senate and House debates increasingly echoed the committee's recommendation. The House report on the proposed legislation, for example,
called for "the coordination of all governmental functions relating to
civil aeronautics in a newly created independent agency."[73]

The Civil Aeronautics Act of 1938 established a five-person independent agency, the Civil Aeronautics Authority. In terms of its responsibilities and authority, the CAA was in many ways the equivalent of the
Interstate Commerce Commission. As the ICC licensed railroads and
trucking companies, the new agency licensed air carriers, giving them
certificates of necessity which acknowledged that the carrier was capable of performing the service under the provisions of the Civil Aeronautics Act and that the transportation and service was necessary and
in the public convenience. The Civil Aeronautics Act also echoed the
earlier railroad legislation in that it gave the CAA the power to approve
both the creation of new routes and the abandonment of existing routes,
and the responsibility to determine whether such creation or abandonment was in the public interest before granting approval. In addition,
the act empowered the CAA to approve consolidations within the aeronautics industry. Closely following the model of the ICC's railroad and
trucking regulations, the legislation required that all air carriers file
their rate schedules with the CAA. Rates had to be "just and reasonable,"
and the CAA had the authority to reject or adjust rates and rate changes
if it found them unreasonable. The act also prohibited rebates and price
discrimination. The CAA exercised rate-making authority in determining the compensation air carriers would receive for carrying the U.S.
mail. Finally, the act gave the CAA's Air Safety Board the responsibility
for regulating the safety of air carriers by licensing pilots and aircraft
and promulgating air traffic rules.[74]

Although the system for civil aeronautics regulation was similar to
that created a half-century earlier for the railroads, one must examine
the priorities that were established through implementation. The CAA's
goals—restraining competition and promoting industrial development
—were in keeping both with the regulatory focus of the other New Deal
initiatives and with the practices the ICC had by this point in its history adopted. Stability was emphasized, rather than competitive market
structure or low prices. In the case of the ICC, the large capital investments and the existing structure of the railroad industry suggested that
a natural monopoly existed. Thus, using railroad regulation as a model
for public utility regulation seemed quite appropriate. In the case of air
transportation, however, competition was not strictly precluded by the

nature of the industry. Yet the core principles of the associational regime found a clear expression in aeronautics regulation.

As the ICC had done in its regulation of the railroads, the CAA interpreted its mandate as requiring the regulation of competition. As it explained in its first annual report: "For the first time air carriers and the public are safeguarded against uneconomic, destructive competition and wasteful duplication of services by the statutory requirement that no person or company may engage in air transportation without first receiving a certificate of public convenience and necessity."[75] The congressional debates repeatedly expressed the fear that excessive competition would undermine stable growth and force carriers to deemphasize safety. The agency thus sought to manage competition while guaranteeing a rate of return sufficient to fund orderly expansion. This entailed the erection and maintenance of significant barriers to entry, primarily implemented by the agency's control over carrier certification. Indeed, during the first four decades of its existence, despite tremendous increases in the amount of air traffic, the agency refused to allow even one new trunk carrier to begin service on a major route. Owing to mergers within the industry, the number of carriers actually declined from sixteen (the number that were grandfathered in under the provisions of the 1938 legislation) to eleven. Ultimately, concern over the lack of competition and the inflated fares led to the passage of the Airline Deregulation Act in 1978, which removed major regulations and eliminated the Civil Aeronautics Board.[76]

The New Deal initiatives that comprised the associational regime shared common elements. In particular, they relied on expert agencies, the organization of economic interest groups, and government-supervised self-regulation as means of promoting economic stability and creating a distribution of income different from that which would have been possible under market conditions. Given these goals, the initiatives were in many ways successful. However, during the postwar period critics would accuse the agencies of enforcing anticompetitive regulations that fostered monopoly power, raised prices, and limited the entry of new competitors, all to the detriment of the consuming public. Self-regulation would be interpreted as government-sponsored cartelization that provided the structural basis for monopolistic abuses. The same conclusions were ultimately reached with respect to the other regulatory initiatives of the associational regime. These persistent critiques of the New Deal regulations would have significant consequences for institutional reforms during the postwar period. I turn now to an examination of the critique of traditional economic regulation as developed in the late 1960s and the 1970s.

6

Compensating for Capitalism:
The New Social Regulation

THE LATE 1960S AND THE 1970S SAW THE EMERGENCE OF A
new regulatory regime. This period, like the Progressive Era and the era
of the New Deal, was characterized by the formation and mobilization
of new interests demanding a new role for the state in the economy. The
demands were shaped and translated into policies and institutional
change by new visions of the political economy and a new administrative philosophy. There were, however, significant differences between
the period in question, on the one hand, and the Progressive Era and the
New Deal, on the other. Most importantly, the postwar period was a
period of sustained growth in real incomes. Owing to active macroeconomic management, the fluctuations in the business cycle during
the first two decades after World War II were mild by comparison with
those during the previous half-century; and thus, during this later period, unlike the earlier ones, structural transformations in the economy
did not drive group mobilization. In addition, the new regime differed
with respect to the kinds of policies initiated. Whereas earlier regimes
had focused on questions of economic regulation, the new regime concentrated on new social regulations. These two differences are linked:
the change in regulatory focus was possible because the record of prolonged growth concentrated attention on other aspects of the capitalist
production process.

Before addressing the sources and central characteristics of this new
regulatory regime, it is useful to explore the distinction between social
and economic regulations. The economic regulations of the Progressive

Era and the New Deal extended governmental controls over the price and supply of goods, the number of participants in certain regulated industries, and the conditions of entry into these industries. Depending on the period in question, policy-makers justified the initiatives on the grounds either that markets were failing to function efficiently owing to inherent features of the sector in question, or that market competition was simply too destabilizing. A less-than-comprehensive listing of the major economic regulatory agencies created as part of earlier regimes would include the Interstate Commerce Commission (1887), the Justice Department's Antitrust Division (1890), the Commerce Department's Bureau of Corporations (1906), the Federal Reserve Board (1913), the Federal Trade Commission (1914), the Federal Power Commission (1920), the Commodity Exchange Authority (1922), the Food and Drug Administration (1931), the Federal Home Loan Bank Board (1932), the Federal Deposit Insurance Corporation (1933), the National Recovery Administration (1933), the Agricultural Adjustment Administration (1933), the Federal Communications Commission (1934), the Securities and Exchange Commission (1934), the National Labor Relations Board (1935), the Federal Maritime Commission (1936), and the Civil Aeronautics Board (1938).[1]

Unlike economic regulations, social regulations focus on fundamental aspects of the production process and on its negative externalities. Thus, social regulatory policies address the quality of the goods and services that are produced, and the by-products of the industrial economy which threaten human health and life, and the environment. Rather than protecting corporations, social regulations seek to place constraints on their activities in hopes of protecting the general public; and rather than seeking to secure competitive conditions or protect competitors, social regulations may involve compliance costs that limit the viability of smaller firms. During the 1970s, Congress initiated policies to reduce air and water pollution, to control toxic wastes and chemicals, to prevent occupational accidents and disease, and to promote consumer safety. The passage of the new regulatory legislation was commonly obtained through a combination of political entrepreneurship, the mobilization of advocacy groups, and the effective exploitation of highly publicized events or reports that focused public attention on a related set of policy problems. Agencies such as the National Highway Traffic Safety Administration (1970), the Environmental Protection Agency (1970), the Occupational Safety and Health Administration (1970), and the Consumer Product Safety Commission (1972) are the best known of the social regulatory agencies.

In this context, we must note that some of the policies initiated in earlier decades were social regulatory in nature. For example, the Food and Drug Administration and the Federal Trade Commission—both created well before the contemporary period—performed some social regulatory functions. However, during the 1960s and 70s there was a dramatic expansion of social regulation. The change in focus becomes strikingly clear when the social regulatory initiatives are examined in historical perspective. Congress successfully passed five consumer protection and health laws during the Progressive Era and an additional eleven such laws during the New Deal. In contrast, during the period considered in this chapter Congress passed sixty-two laws in this area. Similar differences are evident in the area of occupational safety and working conditions: the Progressive and New Deal periods produced five laws; the period 1960–78, twenty-one. Progressive and New Deal efforts also produced seven pieces of legislation addressing energy and the environment, whereas the contemporary period produced thirty-two.[2] The sheer level of legislative activity suggests that a new regime was created which was as distinctive as those created during the Progressive Era and the New Deal.[3]

Regulation gained broad acceptance following the New Deal. The shift in regulatory focus limited the opposition of the regulated interests, and with it the acrimony and antagonism that characterized earlier decades. In many industries, stability and ongoing profitability depended on the maintenance of existing regulations. State-economy relations became more antagonistic, however, during the late 1960s and the 1970s. The creation of many new advocacy groups transformed regulatory politics. These groups demanded that the state play a qualitatively different role in the economy, one that would entail a significant diminution of corporate autonomy. Drawing on the New Left's critiques of capitalism, policy advocates rejected policies that merely promoted industrial stability and prohibited the more egregious forms of corporate abuse. Instead, the groups demanded that the government create and vigorously enforce standards addressing various dimensions of the production process itself. The social regulatory legislation of the 1960s and 70s forced regulators to extend controls over numerous corporate decisions that had previously been the domain of corporate managers. The new, ambitious policy initiatives were accompanied by the creation of new institutions, as well as innovative mechanisms for structuring administrative discretion and promoting the integration of group interests, and—most significantly—an expansive role for scientific and social-scientific expertise in the definition and implementation of policy. The components of the societal regime are shown schematically in Figure 6.1.

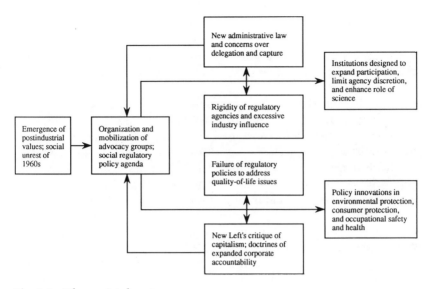

Fig. 6.1   The societal regime.

THE ORIGINS OF THE SOCIETAL REGIME

The regulatory initiatives of the 1960s and 70s differed dramatically from their historical predecessors. Economic regulatory agencies such as the Interstate Commerce Commission, the Federal Communications Commission, and the Civil Aeronautics Board distributed benefits (e.g., routes, frequencies, and rate changes) among a limited number of corporations within a single sector of the economy. The policies, although they may have hurt consumers and excluded potential competitors, promoted stability and profitability and thus received the support of the regulated interests. Indeed, the close relationship between the regulatory agencies and the regulated firms raised persistent complaints that the former were using their powers systematically to increase the revenues of the latter.[4] The new social regulations, in contrast, addressed problems that cut across industries and sectors of the economy. One could not effectively address air and water pollution, faulty and dangerous consumer products, and occupational accidents and disease with an industry-specific focus. To reduce the severity of these problems, it was necessary to establish standards on an economy-wide basis. Thus, rather than promoting stability and profitability, and thus furthering the interests of the regulated industries, the new social regulations imposed significant costs that were often of uncertain magnitude, timing, and competitive effects. The new regulatory focus and the high costs of compliance fostered an adversarial relationship between the regulated and the regulators, a sharp shift from the mutually supportive relationships that had previously existed between regulators, corporations, and congressional committees.

Legislative initiatives that impose concentrated costs and yield diffuse benefits are notoriously difficult to pass. Those forced to bear the costs have strong incentives to mobilize in opposition. Potential beneficiaries, in contrast, lack similar incentives. If such measures are successful at the legislative stage, the regulated interests can continue their opposition at the implementation stage.[5] Many of the social regulatory policies (e.g., environmental protection, consumer safety, and occupational health policies) fall into this category. Skilled political entrepreneurs in the Senate, such as Paul Douglas, Philip Hart, Robert Kennedy, Warren Magnuson, and Abraham Ribicoff, played a critical role in securing the passage of early social regulatory legislation such as the National Traffic and Motor Vehicle Safety Act (1966), the Flammable Fabrics Act (1967), and the Wholesale Meat Act (1967). Often, skilled legislators were able to use the public attention provoked by salient events or by exposés to put into place new policies addressing the problems in question.

As David Vogel has argued, consumer-oriented legislation was politically attractive for several reasons.[6] For one thing, it was an extension of the Great Society reform agenda that provided benefits to a middle-class constituency. For another, public opinion in the United States—as in other industrialized nations—supported the government's playing a greater role in improving the quality of life. The "postindustrial" quality-of-life values emerged as the economic growth of the postwar period alleviated widespread poverty and the most striking economic problems.[7] Moreover, the initiatives were attractive because they made minimal demands on the national budget—an important factor in light of the expenditures associated with the Great Society programs and the Vietnam War. The costs of the initiatives were borne by corporations. Given the corporate profitability and extended economic growth of the postwar period, the capacity of the regulated to absorb these costs was not in question.

The early consumer protection legislation of the 1960s depended on the efforts of a few entrepreneurs who found the populist focus of the new social regulations attractive and politically promising. Although we must acknowledge the role played by political entrepreneurs, they were soon eclipsed by newly organized consumer and environmental advocacy groups. There was a virtual explosion in the number of citizen or public-interest groups during the late 1960s and the 1970s. Fully

76 percent of the public-interest groups in existence in the mid-1980s had been founded in the 1960s and 70s; 57 percent had been established in the 1970s alone.[8] Some of the more influential public-interest groups formed during in this period were the Environmental Defense Fund (1967), the Consumer Federation of America (1968), Friends of the Earth (1969), the Natural Resource Defense Council (1970), Common Cause (1970), the Center for Auto Safety (1970), Environmental Action (1970), Public Citizen (1971), and the Children's Defense Fund (1973).[9] The new public-interest groups played a critical role in promoting new regulatory legislation and regulatory initiatives at the agency level.

What explains the proliferation of public-interest groups during this period? Many citizens became active in response to the modern muckraking activities of consumer advocates such as Ralph Nader. Nader's report *Unsafe at Any Speed* was instrumental in focusing public attention on the question of auto safety; subsequent "Nader's Raiders" reports on regulatory agencies or potentially serious policy problems had similar effects in other policy areas. Moreover, Nader provided the seed money necessary to create many of the consumer-oriented interest groups. The experiences of the 1960s had also inspired many people and encouraged them to organize, thus reinforcing Nader's efforts. The successes of the civil rights and antiwar movements had revealed the role that citizen action could play in forcing significant shifts in public policy at the state and national levels.[10] However, as Richard Harris and Sidney Milkis have revealed in their book *The Politics of Regulatory Change*, one cannot understand the regulatory initiatives of the period without exploring the New Left critique of capitalist democracy. It gave the events greater meaning and theoretical significance and provided a useful reference point for many participants.[11]

The New Left, made up of radical scholars writing during the 1960s and the early 1970s, formulated a critique of power in contemporary society and developed a distinctive vision of democracy and political action. Although the works commonly considered representative of the New Left are in many ways diverse, they present a common vision of society, asserting that it is dominated by large corporate, military, and governmental bureaucracies and the elites that control them. G. William Domhoff, for example, echoed the earlier writings of C. Wright Mills when he argued that a "business aristocracy" or "governing class" dominates the United States. It "owns a disproportionate amount of the country's wealth, receives a disproportionate amount of the country's yearly income, and contributes a disproportionate number of its members to the controlling institutions and key decision-making groups in the country."[12] This power elite controls the major social and governmental institutions, and by promoting the priorities of corporate profitability and social stability it influences these institutions to serve its own interests. In this political-economic order, policies are determined via elite consultation, then justified by means of the symbols of democracy. Despite the populist rhetoric surrounding early regulatory initiatives, Domhoff and a number of radical historians subjected regulation to the same critique. As Domhoff notes, "The power elite did not merely pervert or take over regulatory agencies—they planned and developed them as an alternative to public ownership, destructive competition, and uneven state regulation."[13]

Society accepted corporate hegemony as the best and brightest were coopted and infused with corporate values by the educational system controlled by the power elite. The culture of consumerism seduced the general population into embracing the new social order. Citizens uncritically adopted the proposition that the technologies and power structure of the industrial system provided the only means of meeting their material needs.[14] As Charles Reich argued in his influential book *The Greening of America:* "What happened to the American people? In a word, powerlessness. We lost the ability to control our lives or our society because we had placed ourselves excessively under the domination of the market and technology. Finally, we totally abandoned ourselves to the Corporate State, cutting ourselves off from our sources and our consciousness to such an extent that we were threatened with destruction as a species . . . We must recapture the ultimate sovereign right to choose values for ourselves."[15]

Although some members of the New Left freely appropriated the rhetoric of class warfare, more common was a rejection of hierarchy and an affirmation of individualism and participatory democracy. As Herbert Marcuse explained: "The new radicalism militates against the centralized bureaucratic communist as well as against the semi-democratic liberal organization . . . The initiative shifts to small groups, widely diffused, with a high degree of autonomy, mobility, flexibility."[16] This was, of course, in keeping with established traditions of populism and the American suspicion of large-scale economic and political organizations. The New Left critique was compatible with traditional American demands for the creation of grass-roots organizations to serve as countervailing forces to balance and contest the power of the corporate state. Whereas many of these "parallel institutions" emerged as part of the antiwar movement on the college campuses, a growing number focused on what could be considered quality-of-life concerns, such as pollution, the organization of work, and product safety. However, these issues could be integrated into a broader critique of capitalism, according to which a capitalist system organized around the mass production and marketing of consumer goods, and dependent on the maintenance of high profit margins, must necessarily produce the destruction of the environment, the alienation of workers, and the exploitation of consumers.[17] Concerns about the power of the corporate state; the vision of a participatory democracy consisting of multiple grass-roots organizations; and the salience of so-called quality-of-life issues motivated individuals to create, join, and support advocacy groups.

THE INSTITUTIONAL CRITIQUE

The New Left's vision of participatory democracy, and the successes of the civil rights and antiwar movements, promoted a dramatic expansion of the interest-group universe. New interest groups mobilized, each articulating a distinctive vision of regulatory authority. The newly founded public-interest groups, animated by the New Left critique of capitalist democracy and the experiences of the 1960s, demanded policies protecting consumers, workers, and the environment. They combined their demands with a new administrative philosophy and a critique of existing regulatory institutions and administrative practices.

Their new administrative philosophy was in many ways an expression of, and a response to, a growing body of work detailing the failure of past regulatory efforts. The goal was to surmount the problems that had effectively undermined earlier initiatives and to keep legislative victories from being subverted at the administrative stage. As noted in earlier chapters, Progressive and New Deal legislation commonly vested authority in independent regulatory commissions. Following the main thrusts of Progressive thought, policy-makers presented the commission as an organizational form providing a unique synthesis of policy expertise, administrative flexibility, and independence. Postwar critiques of regulatory commissions—critiques that were widely read and cited by participants in advocacy groups—suggested that these assumptions about the relative merits of this organizational form were patently false.

Perhaps the classic work on regulatory capture is Marver Bernstein's *Regulating Business by Independent Commission*. Bernstein discussed the intellectual foundations of the independent regulatory commission and the promise that it held as an organizational form. However, through an examination of agency performance he concluded that commissions pass through a life cycle of sorts. When the early stages—gestation and youth—are finished, independent regulatory commissions enter a period of maturity. During this period, "the commission becomes more concerned with the general health of the industry and tries to prevent changes which adversely affect it. Cut off from the mainstream of political life, the commission's standards of regulation are determined in light of the desires of the industry affected."[18] The commission eventually enters old age, a stage in which "the regulated interests become so fixed that the agency has no creative force left to mobilize against the regulated groups. Its primary mission is the maintenance of the *status quo* in the regulated industry and its own position as recognized protector of the industry."[19] In short, independent commissions tend quite naturally toward capture. Because formal independence insulates them from the electoral system, their incompetence goes unnoticed. The only support on which they can rely is that provided by the very interests that Congress has directed them to regulate.[20]

The institutional critique expressed doubts concerning the merits of the independent regulatory commission. However, the critique went beyond the question of organizational form to address the very nature of the policy process. Most influential in this respect was Theodore Lowi's *The End of Liberalism*, originally published in 1969. Lowi describes the system based on the delegation of authority as "interest group liberalism." He explains: "It is liberalism because it is optimistic about government, expects to use government in a positive and expansive role . . . It is interest group liberalism because it sees as both necessary and good a policy agenda that is accessible to all organized interests and makes no independent judgment of their claims . . . It defines the public interest as a result of the amalgamation of various claims."[21] When Congress delegates authority without clear statutory standards, administrators commonly define policy through reference to the demands of interest groups that have gained access to the implementation process.

According to Lowi, the interplay between the delegation of authority, the lack of precise statutory standards, and a public philosophy supportive of interest groups' access to the administrative process generates several problems. Because Congress initiates policy without providing a clear statutory plan, there is little legislative guidance for directing implementation actions or evaluating policy. Moreover, this decentralization of decision-making power promotes inefficiency and frustrates coordination across agencies. According to Lowi, however, delegation is of paramount concern precisely because it devalues that which is central to any democratic system. Lowi writes: "Interest group liberalism possesses the mentality of a world universalized ticket-fixing. Destroy privilege by universalizing it. Reduce conflict by yielding to it. Redistribute power by the maxim of each according to his claim. Purchase support for the regime by reserving an official place for every major source of power. In the process, liberalism has promoted concentration of democratic authority but deconcentration of democratic power. Liberalism has opposed privilege in policy formulation only to foster it quite systematically in the implementation of policy."[22] Because the political system combines delegation with unlimited group access and a public philosophy legitimizing this access, private interests can succeed in subverting majoritarian politics by manipulating policy at the implementation stage. Delegation, for Lowi, was a serious matter precisely because it vitiates democratic norms and provides the structural basis for interest groups' capture of agencies, and the subsequent subversion of policies.

This administrative critique found a clear expression in the changing role of the courts. In a highly influential 1975 article, Richard B. Stewart reviewed some changes in court doctrines which had emerged over the course of the previous few decades. He suggested that concerns about delegation, agency capture, and the expansion of regulatory authority "changed the focus of judicial review (in the process expanding and transforming traditional procedural devices) so that its dominant purpose is no longer the prevention of unauthorized intrusions on private autonomy, but the assurance of fair representation for all affected interests in the exercise of the legislative power delegated to agencies."[23] Stewart noted that the new "judicial system of interest representation" is "indispensible if unorganized interests are to enjoy an acceptable measure of recognition." It is "an indispensible response to new conditions in the face of apparent legislative and executive inertia or incapacity."[24]

The "judicial system of interest representation" took several forms during the late 1960s and the 1970s. The courts (particularly the Circuit Court for the District of Columbia) eased standing requirements, thus allowing a broader range of interests access to the courts. Public advocacy groups and citizens anxious to promote more vigorous implementation of policy could appeal regulatory decisions—an opportunity formerly reserved for the regulated. Moreover, the courts expanded on the basic requirements of the Administrative Procedure Act by requiring agencies to offer interest groups far greater opportunities for participation in rule-making. In addition, the courts forced the agencies to take greater care in justifying their decisions through analysis and the examination of competing regulatory alternatives. By openly questioning the rationale for rules and forcing agencies to construct detailed explanations for their decisions, the courts have attempted to limit agencies' discretion. The courts' new activism, their advocacy of enhanced interest representation, and the new analytic demands placed on regulatory agencies influenced the activities of the latter and the regulatory initiatives of the period.[25]

The regulatory initiatives of the period reflected the critiques of existing institutional design and the new role of the courts. When Congress (and the president, in the case of the Environmental Protection Agency) created new regulatory agencies, they favored forms other than the independent commission. Thus, Congress placed the Occupational Safety and Health Administration within the Department of Labor, and President Nixon established the Environmental Protection Agency as an independent agency. The one significant exception to this generalization is the Consumer Product Safety Commission, created in 1972. However, the decision to promote an independent commission was due less to the perceived virtues of this organizational form than to the political context. For managerial reasons, Richard Nixon was strongly opposed to independent regulatory commissions. Because he advocated reorganizing the government to create a greater centralization of presidential control, he was critical of further decentralization at the national level. The Nixon administration thus suggested placing a consumer agency in the Department of Health, Education, and Welfare, and transfering to this agency the staff and the regulatory responsibilities of the Food and Drug Administration. Consumer advocates feared that a consumer protection agency thus constituted would be inordinately susceptible to business interests, particularly in view of the reputation of the FDA in its interaction with industry. In a largely defensive move, consumer advocates supported the independent commission and rejected the recommendations of the Nixon administration.[26]

Many stressed the importance of factors other than organization. As noted above, Lowi's influential critique dealt primarily with the problem of vague legislation and the delegation of authority such legislation entailed. In response to the critiques of delegation, the regulatory initiatives of the 1970s differed from their predecessors with respect to the extent and form of delegation. The new regulatory legislation had several features that distinguished it from earlier legislation. The first was that the new legislation was far more specific. The environmental legislation addressing air and water pollution described the substances the EPA was to regulate and provided relatively precise, if overly ambitious, implementation timetables. For example, under the provisions of the Clean Air Act of 1970 Congress directed the EPA to develop national ambient air quality standards within thirty days. The same legislation required that automakers reduce emissions of carbon monoxide and hydrocarbons by 90 percent by 1975, and make parallel reductions in nitrogen oxide emissions by 1976. These goals—backed by fines of ten thousand dollars per car—raised significant concerns on the part of the automobile industry because of the tremendous lead time required to affect changes in the production of cars and the more disturbing fact that no one had developed the technology needed to meet the new standards. Although the goals and timetables might have been unrealistic, they limited the EPA's discretion while fostering an adversarial relationship between the regulators and the regulated.[27]

Another distinguishing feature of the new legislation was the role of interest groups in the policy process. As noted earlier, the initiatives of the associational regime gave the regulated interests an unprecedented role in the definition and implementation of policy. The regulatory initiatives of the societal regime, however, were designed not only to minimize agencies' discretion—a point to which I shall return in a moment—but also to give advocacy groups a far greater role in regulation than would have been possible in earlier regulatory regimes. Congress promoted an expanded role for these groups in the regulatory process in three ways. First, the rule-making processes in agencies such as the EPA and OSHA were far more complex than required under the Administrative Procedure Act.[28] They included multiple layers of review and ample opportunities for group input. Second, legislation such as the Clean Air Act granted citizens standing to sue the agency for failing to fulfill its mandate. As a result, advocacy groups could use the courts to force an agency to comply with the regulatory initiatives—an opportunity they now use often. Third, some of the regulatory legislation of the period included authorization of intervener funding programs designed to give interest groups that lacked sufficient financial resources the means to participate in agencies' decision-making. The goal of all of these provisions is clear: to democratize the regulatory system and guarantee advocacy groups a continuous presence in policy implementation.

Even though the specificity of the new legislative mandates created an appearance of nondelegation, the new legislation could not completely eschew delegation. The problems addressed by the social regulatory agencies were far more complex than those addressed by the economic regulatory agencies. Determining the reasonableness of a given rate of return is relatively simple by comparison with determining chemical toxicity, exposure rates, and acceptable levels of risk. The new regulatory mandates required agencies to place a premium on scientific research. Legislation could require that the EPA develop national ambient air quality standards within a specific time frame and force predetermined reductions in pollution levels by a specific date, but there was no way to dictate which scientific assumptions and data would be used in this endeavor. Thus Congress delegated to the EPA the power to determine what would constitute an acceptable national ambient air quality standard. The action-forcing provisions, although politically attractive, came into direct conflict with the need to develop scientifically justified standards, because those provisions forced regulators to initiate actions that were not firmly supported by research programs, which were in relatively early stages of development.

Despite the critique of delegation, the ethos of participatory administration, and the New Left's rejection of hierarchy, the new legislation delegated authority to and vested responsibility in social-scientific and scientific experts in the agencies. In earlier regulatory regimes, experts had played an important part in the definition and implementation of policy. However, because of the goals of the new initiatives, the role the new regime assigned to experts was historically unprecedented. This delegation of authority was, in many ways, more problematic than earlier acts of delegation. Social-scientific and scientific professionals claim their authority on the basis of the highly specialized knowledge and skills they have mastered through intensive postgraduate education. The specialized language and methodologies used by such professionals allows for efficient communication and participation in a common set of research programs. It also serves to exclude from the pertinent debates those who lack the necessary training. This creates a tremendous barrier for those who would attempt to oversee the activities of scientific and social-scientific professionals. Whereas legislation could provide ample opportunities for group participation in rule-making, it could not give the interested parties the expertise necessary to make significant contributions or to expose the regulators to anything resembling efficacious oversight.

The unprecedented dependence on expert analysis made policy highly dependent on the quality of the scientific assumptions and research used in the policy process. It should be no surprise that the adequacy of the underlying analyses and data increasingly became the focus of regulatory politics in the 1970s and 80s. As one might expect, this promoted an ever-closer correspondence between a group's resources and its influence, thus favoring corporations and trade associations over the less well-financed advocacy groups. Those groups capable of employing their own professional staffs or consultants possessed a great advantage in the rule-making process and in subsequent attempts to shape implementation. Indeed, this is the most ironic aspect of the societal regime. The very groups that proved to be so influential in shaping the regulatory agenda discovered that the resource demands associated with participation limited their ability to engage in regulatory politics. One response to the expense of long-term interaction with the agencies was the adoption of a litigation-based strategy in order to influence regulatory decision-making. However, this created problems of its own. Resources devoted to litigation could not be devoted to regulation. Moreover, the reliance on the courts opened the door to a new set of actors (e.g., public-interest groups) lacking, in many instances, the expertise necessary to make sound decisions about highly technical issues.

FROM REGULATORY EXPANSION TO REGULATORY REVERSAL

The social regulatory initiatives of the late 1960s and the 1970s came to fruition as a result, in part, of the mobilization of advocacy groups. As noted above, many of these groups were formed during the late 1960s and the early 1970s, a critical period with respect to the passage of new regulatory legislation. Businesses and trade associations failed to mount effective political resistance. As a number of analysts have noted, a supportive liberal political culture and attentive elected officials have always given business a privileged position. Corporations in the United States, unlike their European counterparts, are largely free from the challenges of labor or radical parties. As Andrew Shonfield correctly noted in his classic work *Modern Capitalism* (1965), "The United States is indeed one of the few places left in the world where 'capitalism' is generally thought to be an OK word . . . Among the Americans there is a general commitment to the view, shared by both political parties, of the natural predominance of private enterprise in the economic sphere and of the subordinate role of the public initiative in any situation other than a manifest national emergency."[29] Under such circumstances, in which business exercised what amounted to ideological hegemony, one should not be surprised that corporations were not prepared to mobilize effectively in response to challenges like those posed by the newly formed public-interest groups.[30]

The regulatory victories of the period would not go unchallenged for long. Because the new regulations addressed complex externalities (e.g., air pollution or occupational disease) on an economy-wide scale, compliance was often quite costly. The policies in the area of environmental protection and occupational safety and health were the most expensive regulations in U.S. history. The EPA and OSHA commonly required businesses to implement elaborate engineering measures to control the release of pollutants or exposure to workplace toxins. The costs of complying with standards that required changes in workplace design, for example, were so great that corporations found lobbying and litigation to be cheaper than compliance.

Presidents Nixon, Ford, Carter, and Reagan were highly sensitive to corporate concerns about the costs of the new regulations because of the growing problems of macroeconomic performance. An OPEC oil embargo and increases in food prices placed great pressure on the inflation rate, which reached 12 percent in 1974 and continued at a high level for the remainder of the decade. The high levels of inflation were combined with low levels of growth and persistent unemployment, the second component of economic stagflation. As the dual problems of slow growth and high levels of inflation placed macroeconomic performance at the top of the domestic policy agenda, the costs of regulation and cases of regulatory excess became a chief concern. Increasingly, presidents, some members of Congress, and analysts within the regulatory agencies became committed to the belief that established and proposed regulations, in order to be considered justified, must yield net social benefits—as determined through economic analysis.

Beginning in the early 1970s, attempts were made to blame excessive regulation for inflation and low growth rates. Regulatory review processes centralized in the Executive Office of the President were initiated and then expanded. The executive review processes began in earnest in 1974 with President Ford's Executive Order No. 11821, which required that agencies accompany major regulations and rules with an inflationary impact statement. The Council on Wage and Price Stability and the Office of Management and Budget reviewed these statements. The Carter administration continued these activities, expanding the inflationary impact statement (renamed the economic impact statement) and creating the Regulatory Analysis Review Group and the Regulatory Council in 1978. Finally, during the Reagan administration, a new executive order required executive agencies to provide a cost-benefit justification for major rules and regulations. These justifications were analyzed by the OMB's Office of Information and Regulatory Affairs, which had to approve all regulations prior to promulgation. This review process remained in place during the Bush administration, enforced in large part by the President's Competitiveness Council, chaired by Vice-President Dan Quayle.

The review process aroused some concern, particularly during the Reagan administration. The economic analysis required for executive review forced agencies to integrate new decision-making rules into the policy process. The value of each specific environmental protection regulation, for example, had to be justified by a comparison of the costs and benefits associated with alternative policies. Regulators and public-interest groups charged that the economic analyses conflicted with the objectives set forth in the original legislation. When Congress wrote social regulatory legislation, it commonly discounted cost considerations and emphasized the importance of public health or environmental preservation. Thus, the imposition of economic analysis seemed to many to entail a subversion of politically defined goals. Moreover, the executive review processes commonly gave various business associations an additional point of access to the policy-making process, an opportunity to contest administrative decisions that they found unduly intrusive or costly. Opponents of the review process charged that the communications between the OMB and the regulated fell outside of the procedural safeguards of the Administrative Procedure Act.[31]

The nation's poor economic performance in the 1970s also stimulated ever-greater waves of deregulation, particularly in the economic regulatory subsystems established during the Progressive Era and the New Deal. Congress passed legislation deregulating surface transportation, air transportation, financial institutions, and energy. Although it was Congress that passed major deregulatory statutes, the initiatives commonly originated in the agencies themselves.[32] Throughout the 1960s and 70s, economic regulatory agencies underwent professionalization. Many agencies that had been essentially large litigation shops created economics staffs and offices for the planning and evaluation of policy. These economics staffs increasingly brought their disciplinary paradigms to bear when evaluating the justifications for policy. The concern over the potential inflationary impact of regulation led economists and policy-planning staffs to initiate deregulatory activities at the agency level, and Congress passed a number of acts that authorized and extended the bureaucratic initiatives. Because the economic regulatory policies and the historically close relationship between the regulated and the regulators had earned the scorn of the public-interest groups that emerged during the early 1970s, deregulation went largely unopposed.

The events of the late 1970s and the 1980s are of interest for two reasons. First, the introduction of new interests, ideas, and institutions suggests that a new regulatory regime was established, one based on a return to the market, and the supremacy of economics in regulatory decision-making. Second, unlike the three regulatory regimes that have been addressed thus far, the new efficiency regime was not the product of popular politics. Although the last five presidents have attacked excess regulation, opinion polls reveal little public support for a reduction in the federal government's regulatory activities. Change has been a product of agency professionalization, revisions in the administrative process, and executive politics. These events will be examined in chapter 8. Before exploring deregulation and regulatory reform, however, it is necessary to address the regulatory initiatives of the societal regime in greater detail. These policies are the subject of chapter 7.

7

Regulating Risk: The Political Economy of the Societal Regime

THE SOCIETAL REGIME EMBODIED A DISTINCTIVE VISION OF the role of the state in the economy. The new regulatory initiatives were based on the conviction that government had to accept responsibility for preventing or minimizing hazards to human health and the environment, and had to extend its regulatory authority to encompass a broad array of decisions traditionally reserved for corporate managers. The complexity of the regulatory problems also required a synthesis of scientific research and administration within highly professionalized agencies. However, the agencies' expert administrators had to operate under severe constraints. The public-interest groups and legislators who had played a central role in shaping policies tried to ensure maximum group access to the administrative process and place strict statutory limits on agencies' discretion. They did this by combining an extended rule-making process with a host of safeguards, including precise implementation guidelines, action-forcing provisions, and expanded access to the courts.

The regulatory focus of the societal regime is significant for three reasons. First, some of the risks that the new policies sought to control are invisible for all practical purposes. Regulators address the long-term effects of exposure to substances measured in parts per million or parts per billion.[1] Second, the new regulations require a close interplay of science and administration.[2] Regulators must assess the risk entailed by exposure to a variety of substances, often on the basis of incomplete data and highly tenuous assumptions regarding critical exposure levels and the proper means of extrapolating from limited evidence. They must then determine means of managing the risks—a task that may require developing entirely new control technologies. Third, the costs of addressing risks are commonly great: managing exposure to a variety of chemical substances, for example, often requires costly engineering solutions.

This chapter explores the history of two of the most significant and controversial components of the societal regime, the Environmental Protection Agency and the Occupational Safety and Health Administration, from their creation to the 1990s. On the one hand, the complexity of the regulations issued by these agencies and the high costs of compliance with these regulations generated great corporate resistance. On the other hand, the time required to promulgate standards, a direct reflection of the complexity of the questions involved and the multiple layers of review, provoked constant criticism from the proponents of regulation.

THE ENVIRONMENTAL PROTECTION AGENCY

Until the 1970s, environmental policies focused primarily on conserving limited natural resources to preserve their recreational value and commercial life. In contrast, the new regulatory legislation of the 1970s was protective, seeking to defend Americans from the hazards associated with pollution and to preserve the nation's air, water, and wildlife regardless of commercial value. Earlier policies had failed to establish rigorous standards and federal control over state and local efforts. The contrast with the 1970s could not be more pronounced. The new policy initiatives set up stringent guidelines and established the supremacy of national policy. Congress backed highly specific and costly standards enforced by heavy fines. Let us examine a number of major pieces of legislation—the National Environmental Policy Act, the Clean Air Act, and the Clean Water Act—before addressing the organization and activities of the EPA.

The Legislative Foundations of Environmental Protection

The contemporary regulatory system has its origins in several pieces of legislation passed during the late 1960s and the 1970s. The first of these was the National Environmental Policy Act of 1969. Section 101(a) of the act declared it to be "the continuing policy of the Federal Government . . . to create and maintain conditions under which man and nature can exist in productive harmony." The act created the Council on Environmental Quality to advise the president on environmental policy. Most important, it mandated that federal agencies complete environmental impact statements assessing the environmental consequences of "proposals for legislation or other major Federal actions significantly affecting the quality of the human environment" (Sec. 102[c]).

The EIS was important because it forced agencies to consider certain potential repercussions of their actions. The National Environmental Policy Act stated that, in writing the impact statements, agencies were to adopt an interdisciplinary approach, integrating scientific and social-scientific data and considering both "unquantified environmental amenities and values" and "economic and technical considerations" (sec. 102[b]). In 1971 alone, agencies filed approximately two thousand EISs. By guaranteeing other agencies and citizens access to the statements, the act forced agencies to assume a greater degree of accountability. Environmental groups regularly challenged agencies' decisions by filing court cases to force the filing of EISs. Approximately 10 percent of the filings ended in litigation, often causing significant delays on government construction projects.[3]

Although Congress passed many laws regulating pesticides, toxic wastes, and pollution control, this discussion focuses on the legislation addressing air and water pollution. Federal efforts to address air pollution date back to the mid-1950s, when Congress passed the Air Pollution Control Act. Early efforts were hindered by insufficient funding, excessive decentralization, and a lack of adequate sanctions. In 1969, as Congress began to consider amendments to the Clean Air Act, advocates of environmental policy demanded that Congress establish more rigorous regulations. Senator Edmund S. Muskie, chairman of the Senate Subcommittee on Air and Water Pollution, initially advocated a relatively conservative air pollution policy based on regional standards and a consideration of economic costs and technical feasibility. Fearing that Muskie would be the Democratic candidate in the 1972 presidential election, the Nixon administration introduced a more rigorous policy proposal based on national standards. The turning point came in May 1970, with the release of a Ralph Nader report entitled *Vanishing Air*, a highly caustic critique of the federal air pollution control efforts which was particularly critical of Senator Muskie. Muskie then modified his position on national standards and the relevance of economic and technological feasibility, producing the most sweeping regulatory legislation in U.S. history.[4]

The Clean Air Act Amendments of 1970 (generally referred to as the Clean Air Act) directed the EPA to establish within 30 days national ambient air quality standards for pollutants that have "an adverse effect on the public health or welfare," and to issue within 120 days final standards (secs. 108, 109). The EPA had to determine primary and secondary standards for each substance. Primary standards establish exposure thresholds to protect the public health and allow for an adequate margin of safety. Secondary standards go beyond health concerns to protect the public from any known or anticipated adverse effects. Under the provisions of the Clean Air Act, all air quality regions had to achieve the primary standards by 1975 (with possible extensions to 1977) and the secondary standards within a reasonable period. To achieve this ambitious timetable, the Clean Air Act provided new regulations for automobile emissions and for pollution discharged from stationary sources such as factories. Automakers were required to reduce the carbon monoxide and hydrocarbons in auto emissions by 90 percent by 1975, with parallel decreases in nitrogen oxide emissions by 1976. Under the provisions of the legislation, the EPA could grant a one-year delay in the enforcement of these standards. Congress backed the policy by establishing fines of ten thousand dollars for each car produced in violation of the standards. New stationary sources of pollution (e.g., factories) had to abide by pollution control specifications established in the EPA's new-source performance standards. The standards would incorporate "the best system of emission reduction . . . taking into account the cost of achieving such reduction" (sec. 111). As for existing stationary sources, the Clean Air Act required each state to write and submit for approval an implementation plan, complete with control strategies, for each of the regulated substances, emission limits, and compliance schedules. The EPA had to approve the state implementation plans by 1972. If states did not write acceptable implementation plans, the act directed the EPA to impose plans of its own.[5]

Two points are worth noting. First, the Clean Air Act of 1970 was the first in a series of technology-forcing statutes, for some of the goals it mandated were not achievable by existing technology. This introduced a good deal of uncertainty into implementation and gave the EPA the responsibility for developing new control technologies. Second, the legislation was action forcing. It established specific implementation timetables and authorized citizen suits in district courts to force the execution of nondiscretionary duties. As explained in Chapter Six, such provisions were an innovation of the period attributable to the critiques of delegation and agency capture.

In 1977 Congress passed amendments to replace the initial attainment guidelines with more realistic implementation targets. States had to meet primary standards by 1979, with a 1982 deadline (1987 with an extension) for pollutants from mobile sources. Congress redefined automobile emissions targets as well, and extended the deadlines for compliance with the hydrocarbon and carbon monoxide standards. The amendments directed the EPA to assess, by 1979, the state implementation plans for nonattainment areas (i.e., areas that failed to realize at least one of the NAAQS). New sources in attainment areas had to apply the "best available control technology," whereas new sources in non-attainment areas had to employ technologies producing the "lowest achievable emission rate" (sec. 171). This latter standard required that new sources achieve "the most stringent emission limitation" contained in any state implementation plan or "achieved in practice" (sec. 171). The 1977 amendments also formalized the policy that required the prevention of significant deterioration in regions that met or exceeded NAAQS, a policy that had resulted from an early court decision.[6]

The third strand of environmental protection legislation was the Federal Water Pollution Control Act amendments (also known as the Clean Water Act) of 1972. Federal legislation addressing water pollution dates back to the turn of the century (e.g., the Refuse Act of 1899). Federal efforts changed in focus as a result of the Water Pollution Control Act of 1948, which authorized the provision of sewage treatment grants to local governments. The program degenerated into a large "pork barrel" program that provided federal funding for local projects. The Water Quality Act of 1965 was an improvement on earlier legislation in that it tied the distribution of sewage treatment grants to states' development of clean water standards. The act gave the federal government the authority to establish standards for states that refused to establish their own.[7]

The revolution in water pollution policy closely parallels the revolution in air pollution policy described above. President Nixon called for new water pollution legislation in February 1970, but although Muskie's subcommittee held hearings, a bill was not reported out of committee until 1971. Muskie advocated a strict policy with potentially great economic consequences, forcing Congress to devote a year to reconciling the provisions of the Senate bill with those of the more moderate House bill. The final legislation, passed over a presidential veto, established an ambitious goal: "to restore and maintain the chemical, physical, and biological integrity of the Nation's waters," with zero discharges by 1985 (sec. 101). The legislation directed the EPA to promulgate technology-based effluent standards on an industry-by-industry basis by 1973. By 1974 the EPA had to issue effluent permits to corporations that were discharging wastes in the waterways. The permits were critical because they would control effluent levels on a plant-by-plant basis, requiring the adoption of the "best practicable control technology" by 1977, and the "best available technology" by 1983 (sec. 301). In addition, the legislation addressed municipal sewage treatment plants, requiring that they meet "any applicable water quality standards established pursuant to this act" and adopt the "best practicable waste treatment technology" by 1983 (secs. 301, 201). The EPA could punish violators with civil injunctions, as well as criminal penalties of up to twenty-five thousand dollars per day and one year's imprisonment. The agency was also authorized to close facilities that failed to meet the 1983 guidelines.[8]

In the Clean Water Act as in the Clean Air Act, Congress produced technology-forcing legislation. Because the effluent permits would establish the proper technological standards, the success of the legislation depended on the EPA's capacity to determine by 1973 what constituted the best practicable technology and the best available technology. This was an incredibly complex task given the diversity of the more than two hundred thousand polluters under the EPA's jurisdiction. The deadlines forced the EPA to adopt effluent guidelines without subjecting them to serious internal review or an assessment of economic consequences. Indeed, in many cases the interim standards on which the issuance of permits was based became the de facto standards. The inevitable delays in the release of guidelines were combined with conflicts between the standards established in the interim and final guidelines, and those applied in the effluent permits. Predictably, further delays and legal challenges were the consequences. Congress'responded to the failed implementation efforts and amended the Clean Water Act in 1977, once again extending the deadlines and introducing greater flexibility. Congress provided an extension (to July 1, 1979) for industries that did not meet the 1977 deadline for the adoption of the best practicable technology. Under the 1972 act, industries had been required to adopt the best available technology by 1983. Congress now retained this deadline for sources releasing toxic pollutants and required conventional polluters to adopt the "best conventional pollution control technology" (a category intermediate between the best practicable technology and the best available technology) by 1984.[9]

The Creation and Organization of the Environmental Protection Agency

To appreciate the difficulties of implementing the new environmental policies, it is useful to examine the EPA's origins and its internal organization. The EPA was the product of a larger effort to reorganize the executive branch initiated during the early days of the Nixon administration. In January 1969, Nixon created the President's Advisory Council on Executive Organization (the Ash Council), which unveiled plans for the consolidation of the existing executive departments into four new departments to facilitate coordination and presidential control. Although this grand reorganization proved politically unfeasible, it did result in the creation of the Environmental Protection Agency. Nixon submitted Reorganization Plan No. 3 to Congress on July 9, 1970. He summed up the rationale for the new agency by saying, "Our government today is not structured to make a coordinated attack on the pollutants which debase the land that grows our food." He spoke of the need to "identify pollutants, trace them through the ecological chain

. . . [and] identify where . . . interdiction would be most appropriate."[10] On December 2, 1970, the EPA began operation.

The EPA consolidated offices and programs from fifteen agencies and placed some 5,743 people under the official control of a new executive, creating a holding company for the nation's environmental regulators.[11] The EPA inherited a bureaucratic nightmare. Many of the programs and offices were of questionable quality, reflecting the low priority attached to environmental protection prior to the 1970s. As one official involved in EPA planning noted, "These programs have been buried so low that there's a real gap in management capability."[12] Rather than integrating these units, EPA officials made efforts to preserve the offices' autonomy and preexisting routines. A programmatic organizational structure facilitated these efforts by insulating many of the subunits and allowing them to execute overlapping functions. Although EPA administrators hoped to introduce parallel functional divisions and phase out the programmatic structure, the efforts were largely unsuccessful.[13]

Despite a series of reorganizations, the EPA's basic organizational structure has remained relatively stable. The agency is under the control of an administrator, a deputy administrator, and a number of assistant administrators, all appointed by the president. The attorney-dominated general counsel's office represents the EPA before reviewing courts; and because the basic environmental legislation provides extensive opportunities for private parties to file suit, the general counsel's office is involved in the agency's decisions at an early stage. The enforcement office files suits and monitors compliance. The legal staff is highly decentralized, working in the regional offices, where it can more effectively monitor compliance. An office of policy planning and evaluation, staffed largely with economists, reviews the economic effects and the cost-benefit justifications of proposed and existing regulations. In addition, there are programmatic offices responsible for air pollution, water pollution, solid waste, pesticides, and toxic substances. Each of these offices combines a diverse set of professional disciplines. For example, the air pollution office is staffed by attorneys and by a number of research specialists, including mechanical and chemical engineers, meteorologists, and environmental scientists.[14]

One cannot understand the internal workings of the EPA without examining the role of scientists in the agency and in the policy process. The air and water pollution statutes forced the agency to rely heavily on scientific expertise and the conclusions of numerous research programs. The EPA inherited established research staffs and thirty-one laboratories in nineteen states, but there was little interaction among the science staffs because they had previously been in different agencies. The staffs' established missions were often difficult to reconcile with the new responsibilities. For example, the Department of Agriculture's pesticides regulation division had traditionally directed its research toward promoting agricultural productivity, and had established close relationships with various commodity groups and pesticide producers. When the division was transferred to the EPA, it was difficult for the agency to reorient it to promoting public health and identifying violations of environmental regulations.[15]

Moreover, there were conflicts between professional groupings in the agency. The EPA's research scientists worked in tandem with other bureaucrats who fulfilled the more traditional roles of program managers. The different professional orientations created significant tensions within the agency and in the policy process. The program managers looked to the scientists for the technical support and information needed to fulfill administrative and litigation-related duties. The scientists, however, found these demands difficult to reconcile with the ethos of the research staff. As Alfred Marcus explains: "Research scientists were discipline oriented. They saw their purpose as expanding the state of the art and making contributions to the environmental sciences that would have a long-term impact . . . [They] were in touch with the work done by their professional counterparts in academia and industry. They maintained that since the environmental disciplines were underdeveloped, pure research was more important than practical research. The needs of the programs and regions were too immediate and particular. They argued that these programs focused too much on technical support and service, on the knowledge and equipment that applied to unique problems."[16] The conflicts between the program managers and the research scientists were only part of the problem. By 1972, the EPA had more than fifty laboratories employing more than two thousand employees, who represented, in turn, more than sixty different disciplines and subdisciplines. Integrating the activities of so diverse a group of professionals, who had different disciplinary norms and were engaged in a broad variety of research programs, proved impossible. Because the researchers (particularly those in the field offices) claimed professional autonomy and were wedded to long-term research projects, they resisted attempts to redirect their activities toward the legislatively mandated activities.[17]

The Policy Process

The EPA's difficulties in managing a diverse staff and fulfilling a complicated and demanding mandate are exacerbated by a complex and lengthy policy process. The procedural requirements imposed on the agency's decision-making are more rigorous than those specified in the Administrative Procedure Act, reflecting a recognition of the value that legislators and the courts placed on analysis and participation.[18] The agency's rules originate from the requirements of enabling legislation, from court orders, and from the findings of scientific studies conducted by researchers both in the agency and in universities. Once it has been decided to make a new standard, the EPA administrator creates a working group chaired by a representative from the office specializing in the appropriate policy area. The working groups commonly also include members from offices dealing with enforcement, and research and development. The working group is the primary locus of decision-making with respect to new rules, although its activities are under the constant oversight of the EPA administrator and his or her staff.

During the first phases of the rule-making process, the working group compiles a rule-making package, presenting the proposed rule, a discussion of the goals of the rule, and a discussion of alternative approaches. The development plan integrates these components, specifies the demands that the rule will place on the agency's resources, and presents an overall schedule for the development of the rule. The staff supports the proposed rule with scientific and technical analyses that specify the nature and magnitude of the problem; the costs and benefits of the proposed rule and its alternatives; the rule's economic effects; methods of lessening the regulatory burden on small business; and the rule's ecological effects. Additional analyses address the costs of implementing each of the alternatives, and the means by which the agency will evaluate the performance of the rule after promulgation.

In preparing the preliminary rule package and the supporting documentation, the working group relies heavily on the suggestions of numerous offices and private contractors. The support documents require the synthesis of scientific, technical, and economic analyses. Ad hoc advisory groups composed of representatives of federal, state, and local agencies, and interest groups, also provide support. The EPA administrator, a steering committee (representing the assistant administrators and other officers), and the ten regional administrators review the preliminary rule package and the supporting documentation. Upon review and approval by the Office of Management and Budget under Executive Order No. 12291 (see chapter 8), the EPA publishes a notice of proposed rule-making in the *Federal Register*. With the commencement of the public-comment period, the EPA gathers information, analyses, and comments at public hearings and conferences, and through correspondence. Transcripts of the meetings and the submitted comments become part of the public record. The agency then compiles a final rule-making package, revising earlier analyses and including new information and studies assembled during the comment period. The final rule undergoes additional review within the agency and receives final OMB approval, and is then published in the *Federal Register.*

Three points regarding the EPA rule-making process are worthy of emphasis. First, the development of new rules takes a considerable amount of time, commonly several years. Second, the interplay of interests, science, and institutions is highly complex. The development of new rules requires the integration of multiple offices and professional staffs, and environmental legislation has established a process designed to provide interested parties with maximal opportunities for participation while subjecting the proposed rule to intensive review. Concerned parties can force modification at multiple points in the process—or stall the process altogether. Third, standards are routinely challenged in the courts, forcing the rejection or modification of standards. Parties commonly argue that rules are unsupported by the analyses or fail to reflect the letter or the spirit of the laws.

Limitations on the Agency's Autonomy

One might argue, with some justification, that active oversight of highly professionalized agencies is not essential because professionals act within the normative parameters established by their academic disciplines. Professionalized agencies are less likely than unprofessionalized ones to engage in opportunistic behavior, especially when the professional norms are supportive of the agency's mission. As noted in chapter 2, this view was one of the central factors supporting Progressive efforts to professionalize the civil service. Moreover, when an agency addresses scientifically complex issues, other agencies and elected officials may lack the competence to interpret the regulatory decisions. However, the White House, Congress, and the courts do subject the EPA to intensive oversight and review.

Presidents play a role in shaping the EPA's activities through their selection of the administrator, and deputy and assistant administrators. As will be shown below in the discussion of the agency's implementation efforts, the choice of administrators plays an important role in determining the agency's orientation. However, because legislation imposed strict implementation timetables and the courts have actively forced the agency to execute its functions, the EPA administrator is perhaps less important than his or her counterpart in other regulatory agencies. Arguably, the president's greatest opportunity to influence policy is through the executive review processes. The EPA is part of the executive branch and thus is subject to a series of executive orders requiring that new initiatives be justified by cost-effectiveness or cost-benefit analysis. The review processes have become more stringent over time, making ever-greater claims on the agency's resources. Although the extent to which executive review has shaped EPA standards is unclear, the review processes have forced the agency to rely more heavily on its economists.[19]

Congress also plays a critical role in limiting the EPA's autonomy. Although President Nixon created the agency through an executive reorganization, the major pieces of environmental legislation were written by Congress, and Congress is responsible for the environmental protection policies and the action-forcing provisions that have limited the EPA's discretion. Of course, these policies and provisions were influenced by the ongoing tensions between a series of presidents who were gravely concerned about macroeconomic performance, and committee chairs who sought to protect their legislation from future challenges at the hands of unsympathetic presidents and their appointees.[20]

The EPA has the largest budget of any regulatory agency. During the 1970s, however, when new legislation and court orders expanded the EPA's responsibilities, and executive review processes increased the need to conduct analyses of regulatory impacts, the new demands were not accompanied by sufficient increases in the agency's budget. This reflected, in part, the decentralization of Congress. Although Muskie's Senate subcommittee strongly supported bold regulatory objectives and vigorous enforcement, the House Appropriations Subcommittee on Agriculture, Environment, and Consumer Protection was chaired by Jamie Whitten, an opponent of environmental protection policy. Thus, there was a disjunction between what was mandated and what was appropriated.[21] During the early 1980s, when control of Congress was divided and the President was strongly opposed to regulation, the EPA's lack of resources translated into rapid staffing reductions and a decline in enforcement.

Finally, with respect to oversight, Congress encounters the kinds of problems common in complex policy areas. Because members of Congress are generalists, they lack the specialized competence necessary to appreciate the more complicated facets of policy and the limitations of the data and studies. Although the staffs of the Senate and House committees are known for their skill and expertise, they are no match for the analytic and financial resources of the EPA, trade associations, and major environmental advocacy groups. Moreover, during most of the 1970s oversight was directed toward assuring that the EPA was actively enforcing environmental regulations free from the intrusions of the White House. This support for the EPA prevented those engaged in oversight from questioning the scientific assumptions underlying policy.

Over the course of the past two decades, the courts have expanded the EPA's responsibilities.[22] The role of the courts is partially the product of institutional design: key legislation allowed citizens to sue the agency in if it failed to fulfill its nondiscretionary regulatory responsibilities. It is also a product of compliance costs. Because the EPA's rules commonly force businesses to make large capital investments, corporations and trade associations have been anxious to use the courts to gain delays or weaken standards. With environmental groups and industrial groups willing to use the court to shape environmental regulations, few EPA rules have gone unchallenged. Although the sheer bulk of the litigation involving the EPA precludes an adequate survey of the court decisions, it is important to stress two major points.

First, the courts have played a very active role in forcing the EPA to broaden its regulatory focus. Unfortunately, although the courts can force the EPA to expand its regulatory activities, they cannot determine budgetary allocations. Thus, the courts have forced the agency to redirect scarce resources to fund court-mandated programs that are often of less importance than other enforcement activities.[23] For example, in 1972, in *Sierra Club v. Ruckelshaus*, the District Court for the District of Columbia decided that the provisions of the Clean Air Act required the EPA to prevent the erosion of air quality in regions that met or exceeded the national ambient air quality standards. The court reasoned that when Congress directed the EPA to "protect and enhance" air quality, it established the dual goals of reducing pollution and preventing the degradation of existing resources. Assuming that this had been Congress's intent, one would conclude that the use of new-source performance standards in areas meeting NAAQS would provide sufficient means of realizing this goal. However, the decision forced the EPA to adopt policies that worked at cross purposes, because one strategy for reducing pollution in urban areas is to relocate existing sources and require adherence to rigorous performance standards. A polluting facility is thus replaced by one that achieves higher levels of pollution control, and pollutants are dispersed. To prohibit "significant deterioration" in more pristine regions is to eliminate this strategy.[24]

Second, the courts have affected the policy process by ruling on the adequacy of EPA analysis and the kinds of information considered necessary in arriving at regulatory decisions. Here it is critical to differentiate between the courts' position in cases addressing standards and its position in cases addressing enforcement. Early on, the courts forced the EPA to defend its standards on the basis of the underlying analysis. In *Kennecott Copper Corporation v. Environmental Protection Agency*, the D.C. Circuit Court refused to approve the secondary standard for sulfur dioxide until the EPA provided the supporting analysis. The EPA was forced to drop the standard when it was discovered that the standard was based on a misreading of the evidence.[25] Judicial demands that agency analyses provide the basis for standards have greatly increased the time that the EPA must spend compiling the case for new standards. Indeed, the D.C. District Court required the EPA to expand its rule-making process and its record to include an explanation of the standard; a discussion of the methodology and data used; and a record of the comments offered during the rule-making process and the agency's responses to these comments. This expanded record gives the courts a more substantial body of evidence on which to base subsequent reviews.[26]

Although the courts have forced the EPA to devote greater resources to the development of standards, they have not vigorously questioned the underlying assumptions of the standard-setting process. One cannot adopt a standard without accepting the assumptions that (1) there is a threshold level at which exposure to a substance constitutes a health risk; and (2) one can manipulate exposure to reduce the size of the population subject to disease. However, for most substances the threshold concept is irrelevant: there are simply different levels of risk associated with different levels of exposure. Between the extremes of unlimited exposure, which would be detrimental in terms of public health, and no exposure, which would be prohibitively costly or impossible, there are innumerable possibilities. Acknowledging that the applicability of the threshold assumption was limited would force the EPA to justify standards on the basis of socially desirable levels of risk and cost-effectiveness. Because the threshold assumption is retained, the courts essentially determine whether existing standards are supported by research findings.[27]

With respect to the factors weighed in the standard-setting process, the courts have based their position on a reading of congressional intent. The Clean Air Act directed the EPA to develop air quality standards to protect health and provide an adequate margin of safety, not to balance those goals against economic growth. In a 1980 decision, the D.C. District Court went so far as to state that the EPA "may not consider economic and technological feasibility" when determining standards, and that these issues, while germane in designing state implementation plans, are of no relevance when setting standards.[28] Indeed, the courts have allowed the EPA to set standards that are stricter than of the evidence would support. This tendency to promote overregulation is derived from a reading of congressional intent. The courts interpret the goal of protecting health and establishing an "adequate margin of safety" as justifying standards based on worst-case assumptions. This position is supportive of the professional biases of the health professionals working in the EPA, many of whom adopt a highly protective stance in their work.[29]

When corporations have challenged enforcement decisions and implementation plans in court, judges have been willing to address a wide variety of issues. The Clean Air Act did not make compliance with state implementation plans contingent on the feasibility of these plans; and it did not provide exemptions based on the capacity of a given corporation or industry to absorb the economic costs of adopting a new control technology. The legislation was strict and technology-forcing. Yet courts have proven willing to address questions of feasibility. In a series of challenges to the enforcement of state implementation plans, the courts in question prohibited the EPA from forcing compliance without showing that the required control technologies are both technically and economically feasible. The decisions required that the EPA either examine the state and industry feasibility studies or conduct feasibility studies of its own. The Supreme Court addressed the issue in 1976, deciding that the EPA could enforce regulations without proving the feasibility of the required control technologies. However, the Court noted that in enforcement proceedings state and federal courts could consider economic and technological factors relating to feasibility. The EPA thus remained vulnerable to these challenges. The contradiction is striking. The EPA is urged to set overly cautious standards to maintain the margin of safety; at the same time, it must remain prepared to defend the practical feasibility of the implementation plans.[30]

The role of the courts in environmental policy is, in many ways, conducive to policy failure. The courts have expanded the EPA's duties without simultaneously expanding its resource base, and they have promoted the creation of stringent standards without careful consideration of the underlying scientific assumptions or the technological and economic data. Yet in hearing and responding to challenges to state implementation plans, they have acknowledged the relevance of these very factors. As a consequence, ambitious goals are established without sufficient resources, and the EPA promulgates stringent standards, only to be challenged during implementation.

The Implementation of Environmental Policies

The EPA has faced many problems during its short history. When he created the agency, President Nixon appointed William Ruckelshaus, a former head of the Justice Department's Civil Division with little experience in environmental policy, to serve as the first administrator. Environmentalists questioned whether such an appointee would be committed to rigorous environmental protection. Nixon's public statements did nothing to reduce this suspicion. In one speech he asserted that the administration was "committed to cleaning up the air and cleaning up the water" but that it was also committed to economic growth. He warned, "We are not going to allow the environmental issue to be used sometimes falsely and sometimes in a demagogic way basically to destroy the system—the industrial system that made this the great country that it is."[31] Ruckelshaus developed support by distancing himself from the administration. He questioned the concept of "production at any cost" and argued that what really matters "is not the rate of growth but the quality of life."[32] He continually appealed to environmental groups and sought to use the press to nurture their support and that of Congress. Most significantly, he pursued a strategy of vigorous enforcement and targeted actions against significant polluters: within the first few months of his tenure, the EPA filed 185 suits against a number of prominent manufacturers. This cultivated an image of a highly active and committed agency and created a prosecutorial ethos that unified an otherwise fragmented bureaucracy.[33]

Of course, Ruckelshaus faced additional responsibilities that challenged his legal expertise. As noted above, the Clean Air Act required the EPA to propose NAAQS within thirty days and to adopt final standards within four months. The EPA established 247 air quality control regions and set NAAQS for particulate matter, sulfur dioxide, nitrogen oxides, carbon monoxide, hydrocarbons, and photochemical oxidants. Ruckelshaus relied on a newly constituted pollution control staff to determine appropriate standards. Because of the timetable presented in the Clean Air Act, there was no opportunity for careful consideration of the new standards. Indeed, Ruckelshaus received the proposed NAAQS just three days before the deadline. There was a broad recognition within the EPA that the standards were difficult to justify on the basis of scientific evidence and, in many cases, were simply unachievable. Ruckelshaus delayed the transportation controls because of the "uncertain status of existing knowledge."[34] Surprisingly, only the secondary standard for sulfur dioxide was invalidated when a court determined that it lacked scientific foundations.[35]

Ruckelshaus was in an unenviable position: Congress had directed the EPA to establish and enforce standards without allowing the agency sufficient time and resources. The courts only added to the EPA's responsibilities, thus placing greater pressure on the agency. On top of this, the EPA had to struggle with an administration that was highly sensitive to compliance costs. Ruckelshaus responded to the administration's hostility by creating a steering committee led by an economist, Robert Sansom. The steering committee coordinated the various offices within the EPA, including the Office of Enforcement and the Office of Research and Development. Attorneys determined whether the agency was in compliance with the legal requirements imposed by Congress; scientists reviewed the analyses supporting regulatory standards and recommendations; economists assessed the costs and benefits of the regulations. Ruckelshaus gave these activities a more permanent status when he created the Office of Planning and Evaluation.[36]

Russell Train, former chairman of the Council on Environmental Quality, became the second administrator of the EPA in the summer of 1973 and served until the end of the Ford presidency. Train successfully expanded the agency's programs and its staff, particularly in the regional offices responsible for the initiation of most enforcement actions. He emphasized enforcement to build the EPA's reputation as an aggressive agency, but he also promoted an expansion of the agency's research efforts. The emphasis on research was reflected in the EPA's budget: from fiscal year 1974 to fiscal year 1975, the research budget increased from $168.9 million to $357.7 million. Equally important, however, were Train's efforts to redefine the EPA's relationship to the president. Following Ruckelshaus's example, Train demanded and received written confirmation that the EPA administrator rather than the White House would determine the content of the agency's regulations. To further insulate the agency from White House interference, Train cultivated the EPA's relationship with Congress and with Muskie's subcommittee.[37]

Early in Train's tenure, it became clear that the deadlines established in the Clean Air Act and the Clean Water Act were simply unachievable. In response, the EPA asked Congress to extend the deadlines, something that was done with the 1977 amendments to both acts. One response to the failure to meet the air quality deadlines was a policy innovation, the "offset." Under the offset policy, new sources (of pollution) could be constructed only if they met regulatory emission standards and obtained from existing plants emissions reductions that would offset the emissions introduced by the new plant. This policy allowed industrial development while reducing aggregate emissions from new and existing sources. Although corporations initially used offsets on an intrafirm basis, emissions trading gradually emerged. By putting a price on emissions, the policy created financial incentives for the development of new control technologies. Congress officially authorized the offset program in 1977, with the passage of the new Clean Air Act amendments.[38]

President Carter appointed Douglas Costle, a former staff member of the Ash Council and head of the Connecticut Department of Environmental Protection, as EPA administrator, and also appointed to the agency a number of individuals from environmental groups.[39] Costle's tenure saw some substantial successes. Using the enforcement powers provided in the 1977 amendments, the EPA forced many corporations that were actively polluting to comply with the regulations. By 1980, there had been significant advances toward realizing the NAAQS for sul-

fur dioxide and particulate matter.[40] Most significantly, Costle shifted
the agency's priorities away from ecology and toward protecting public
health. In a series of speeches he emphasized the risks associated with
exposure to toxic substances and carcinogens, and the EPA's expanded
efforts of the to address these problems through research and enforcement. He noted that the "EPA is now a preventive public health as well
as an environmental agency." The new emphasis paid off. Whereas stagnant economic growth forced most agencies to accept modest budgetary
increases, Congress expanded the EPA's operating budget by 25 percent
in 1979 alone.[41]

Costle's tenure was also a period of experimentation, with further
examination of incentive-based programs, a continuation of the efforts
initiated under Train. Incentive-based programs promoted policy goals
while lowering compliance costs by allowing firms to determine where
reductions could be realized most cost-effectively. These efforts were
most pronounced in the implementation of the Clean Air Act, in which
the EPA used bubbles, offsets, and banking. The incentive-based approach gained gradual acceptance after lengthy debates within the EPA
policy office and between the staff and their counterparts in various environmental groups. This consensus-building was necessary because an
incentive-based approach was a departure from established patterns of
enforcement.[42]

Compliance costs can be overwhelming when regulators require that
corporations bring all sources of pollution into compliance with a single
standard. Under the bubble concept, regulators focused on the emissions of a plant or a regional grouping of plants rather than a single
smokestack. In essence, they created an imaginary bubble over a related
cluster of emission sources. The EPA first used the bubble in December
1975, when it allowed the owners of a plant to violate new-source performance standards in the expansion of existing facilities as long as
there was an equivalent reduction in the same pollutants from another
emissions source. In a subsequent challenge, the D.C. Circuit Court
found that in adopting the bubble the EPA had exceeded its authority.[43]
The EPA promulgated a revised bubble policy in 1979, giving existing
sources greater flexibility in controlling emissions. It allowed corporations to reduce their emissions where this could be done most cost-
effectively, essentially bringing the average emission in line with the
regulatory standards. However, before there could be widespread use of
the bubble states had to revise their implementation plans—a process
fraught with delays. Another innovation was the offset policy, discussed
above, which allowed corporations to offset new emission sources by
acquiring reductions from other sources. The EPA experimented with
offsets, as well as with the bubble, under Train. Expanded use of the

offset policy was facilitated in 1979, when the EPA allowed for a third innovation: the banking of emissions credits for subsequent sale. Banking enhanced the offset program in that it created financial incentives for making greater reductions in emissions than were needed to offset new sources. Banking has been of limited consequence because only a few emissions banks were established, and corporations commonly retained their credits to offset future expansions.

The Carter appointees to the EPA and other regulatory agencies reflected the president's goals of promoting deregulation and regulatory reform, a point that is explored in greater detail in chapter 8. These goals entailed eliminating regulations that interfered with competition and introducing incentive-based mechanisms to replace "command and control" regulations wherever possible.[44] Ronald Reagan also promoted deregulation and regulatory reform, seeking to eliminate or transfer regulatory authority to the states, and subjecting those regulations deemed necessary to economic analysis. However, some of the Reagan appointees failed to show the care their predecessors had shown. Rather than reforming regulation, they occasionally chose to disable the agencies. No better example exists than Reagan's first EPA administrator, Ann Gorsuch.

Gorsuch's brief tenure at the EPA was characterized by modest regulatory reforms, dramatic budget reductions, comparable reductions in enforcement activities, and scandals that ultimately led to her resignation. The reforms included an acceleration of the agency's delegation of policy authority to the states, as well as efforts to promulgate generic standards that would give state agencies the greatest possible discretion in implementation. The EPA also streamlined its approval of state plans. Whereas an expanded state role could eventually reduce the demands on the EPA, the budget cuts were immediate. During 1981 and 1982, the EPA's budget (excluding the Superfund established to clean up chemical dump sites) was reduced by more than one-quarter; the number of staff positions declined by 22.6 percent. Indeed, in 1981 alone, approximately 1 percent of the EPA staff resigned per month. Sluggish attempts to fill positions at the assistant administrator level, and frequent reorganizations (the enforcement staff was reorganized every eleven weeks in the first year), only exacerbated the effects of the staffing reductions. By the end of 1982, the number of cases the agency referred to the Justice Department had fallen by 50 percent, resulting in a one-third reduction in enforcement orders. In addition, regulatory relief measures implemented by the EPA stalled or weakened several regulations.[45]

Disheartened by the changes at the agency, EPA staffers began to leak documents to Congress. One document given to Congress was a request to the OMB for $17.6 million in severance pay and related expenses associated with firing thirty-two hundred employees over the next two years. Gorsuch's public statements and initial actions provoked a great reaction on the part of environmental advocacy groups, which met to coordinate their litigation strategies so that each group would focus on the implementation of different environmental policies. Even businesses and trade associations reacted negatively to the changes, fearing that they would be forced to comply with as many as fifty different sets of state regulations rather than a single set of rules administered by the EPA. As the midterm elections approached, there was growing recognition that the events of the past few years had made Gorsuch's EPA a political liability to the president. In an attempt to minimize the agency's antienvironmentalist image, Gorsuch and her team unveiled a number of initiatives, including a regulation requiring the inspection of schools with loose asbestos; a new position on lead additives in gasoline; and the reinstitution of a ban on the disposal of liquid hazardous wastes in landfills.[46]

The efforts to limit the political damage failed. In response to suggestions that the EPA had distributed Superfund monies for political ends, John Dingell, chairman of the House Energy and Commerce Committee, opened an investigation and subpoenaed Gorsuch to testify and provide documents on three toxic waste dumps. On the advice of the Justice Department, Gorsuch refused to comply under executive privilege. Congress responded by citing Gorsuch for contempt. Ultimately, Superfund administrator Rita Lavelle and a number of her assistants were fired by Gorsuch for mismanagement of the Superfund. This scandal undermined whatever support remained for Gorsuch within the administration. She was forced to resign in March 1983, and was soon followed by more than twenty other EPA officials.[47]

The Reagan administration responded to the events at the EPA by appointing as administrator William Ruckelshaus, who had headed the agency under Nixon. Ruckelshaus brought an experienced team to the EPA and tried to reemphasize enforcement and to further the mission that had been challenged for the past several years. Congress was anxious to support the agency's revitalization. However, the agency's 1984 budget (excluding the Superfund and construction monies) was one-third less than its last budget during the Carter administration, and the research funds had been reduced by almost one-half. Ruckelshaus immediately requested, and was given, an additional appropriation of $165.5 million. After Reagan's reelection Ruckelshaus resigned and was replaced by Lee Thomas, formerly an EPA assistant administrator. Under Thomas, the EPA continued its departure from the public health issues addressed by Costle, focusing once again on ecology—albeit global ecology—because of the growing international concerns about global warming and ozone depletion. Continuing an effort initiated by Ruckelshaus, Thomas began to evaluate EPA priorities on the basis of risk assessment, hoping to allocate resources to the areas in which expenditures could produce the greatest gains.[48]

Although many environmentalists welcomed the efforts of Ruckelshaus and Thomas to compensate for the excesses of the Gorsuch years, those efforts were, at least initially, insufficient. The firings and resignations during the early 1980s had brought about a stunning loss of administrative and scientific expertise, and the vacant positions were not easy to fill given the low morale and recent events at the EPA. Moreover, the budget cuts prior to Ruckelshaus's return were not offset by subsequent increases. Thus, the agency remained underfunded and understaffed. Although it is impossible to anticipate the long-term effects of the 1980s on environmental policy, there can be little question that by the end of the decade the EPA was less capable of managing its complex tasks than it had been at the beginning.

THE OCCUPATIONAL SAFETY AND HEALTH ADMINISTRATION

Regulatory complexity, heavily scientific foundations of policy, and political-institutional constraints are not unique to environmental protection. Indeed, these same factors characterize many of the occupational safety and health regulations initiated in the 1970s. Occupational safety and health became part of the federal policy agenda in the latter half of the 1960s, when President Lyndon Johnson and his aides adopted it as a quality-of-life issue that could broaden the social reform program and appeal to organized labor. However, Johnson's decision not to run for reelection dramatically undermined congressional support for his proposal. With the election of Richard Nixon, the effort to promote workplace safety found a new proponent. However, the administration's proposals fragmented enforcement powers and located standard-setting outside the Department of Labor, reflecting the administration's concerns about the influence of organized labor in that department. In the end, Congress passed Democratic legislation written with the assistance of labor representatives. This legislation unified standard-setting and enforcement authority in a new agency located within the Department of Labor. Moreover, the act established a much broader mandate than that envisioned by the administration.[49]

The Legislative Foundations of Occupational Health Regulation

Section 2 of the Occupational Safety and Health Act gave the agency it created a broad mandate: "to assure so far as possible every working man and woman in the nation safe and healthful working conditions and to preserve our human resources."[50] Significantly, the duty fell primarily on the employer, who had an obligation to "furnish to each of his employees employment and a place of employment which are free from recognized hazards that are causing or are likely to cause death or serious physical harm to his employees" (sec. 5(a)1). To realize the broad goal of assessing occupational health and safety, the act authorized the secretary of labor and OSHA to promulgate and enforce standards for all private-sector employees. The Bureau of Occupational Safety in the Department of Health, Education, and Welfare was renamed the National Institute for Occupational Safety and Health. Its research and reports were to provide a basis for many of OSHA's standards. More specifically, it was charged with developing and recommending health standards, especially those addressing toxic substances. The act also created the Occupational Safety and Health Review Commission, an appellate body to review contested decisions.

It is critical to note that the Occupational Safety and Health Act did not require the agency to weigh the benefits of new health regulations on the basis of costs. Section 6(b)5 instructed the secretary of labor to promulgate the standard "which most adequately assures, to the extent feasible, on the basis of the best available evidence, that no employee will suffer material impairment of health or functional capacity even if such employee has regular exposure to the hazard dealth with by such a standard for the period of his working life." Of course, the use of the phrase "to the extent feasible" would raise a number of objections from corporations seeking to interpret this phrase as requiring an examination of cost-effectiveness. The chief objectives of the Occupational Safety and Health Act are problematic, for one simply cannot achieve a risk-free economy. Anything approaching this ideal would involve tremendous costs and place distinct limits on growth. At what point would the costs limit the efficacy of additional gains in safety and health? Obviously, some threshold must exist beyond which one cannot justify additional advances. However, the Occupational Safety and Health Act did not establish this threshold, nor did it direct the agency to consider costs to arrive at this determination.[51]

The Occupational Safety and Health Policy Subsystem

Although OSHA, NIOSH, and OSHRC are formally separate, they are integral parts of a single policy-making unit in which OSHA executes the primary functions, being responsible for the development, promulgation, and enforcement of safety and health standards. The research arm of the policy-making unit is NIOSH, which provides the research that is essential for the development of health rules; and OSHRC adjudicates disputes, a function that most regulatory commissions internalize. Although it is useful to examine OSHA, NIOSH, and OSHRC separately, one must not lose sight of the fact that they are integrated parts of a single policy subsystem.

The head of OSHA is the assistant secretary of labor for occupational safety and health. The assistant secretary is a presidential appointee confirmed by the Senate. Although OSHA has undergone minor changes in its organization during its brief history, its offices can be divided into three distinct groupings. A number of offices (e.g., the Policy Office) provide technical support, engage in planning and evaluation, and also assist the secretary in maintaining external relations with Congress and the OMB. Other offices—the Health Standards Office and the Safety Standards Office—deal with the formulation of standards. Each of the standards offices is divided into specialized units. For example, the Health Standards Office has a unit that specializes in the regulation of workplace carcinogens and a unit that specializes in toxins. A third set of offices deals with the administration of programs at the state level, and the performance of on-site inspections. To facilitate implementation, OSHA maintains regional and field offices.

All three of the agencies that deal with occupational safety and health—OSHA, NIOSH, and OSHRC—are highly professionalized, albeit each with a different mix of professionals. A number of professions are represented, including industrial hygiene, toxicology, epidemiology, industrial engineering, economics, and law. With its research-related duties, NIOSH is dominated by scientists; OSHRC is involved in addressing legal challenges and thus is staffed with lawyers; and OSHA has a large contingent of attorneys and a large number of health professionals. As noted above, professionalization commonly creates organizational problems. The professional norms and aspirations of the scientific and social-scientific experts are often difficult to integrate. Moreover, it is often difficult to reconcile these norms with an agency's broader goals. A carefully conducted scientific research program may take several years to complete. The time required to do the underlying research may conflict with the political pressures to develop and enforce rules. Likewise, the standards derived from the research findings may require regulatory remedies that are impossible to implement.

Although OSHA, NIOSH, and OSHRC have a wide variety of professionals, these agencies' organizational culture is dominated by the industrial hygienists and health professionals who have been central to the development of health and safety rules. As Steven Kelman details in his work on OSHA, professionalization created distinctive biases that shaped the design of regulatory remedies. Kelman explains: "Officials have worked in the occupational safety and health professions (safety engineering or industrial hygiene) or take courses in these fields after joining the agencies. Members of these professions share a body of knowledge. They also tend to share, like members in many professions, values that comprise a professional ideology. For occupational safety and health professionals, these are pro-protection values. They believe strongly that workers ought to be protected from hazards and that larger reductions of risk are preferable to smaller ones (without much thought of cost)."[52] By their training, industrial hygienists and engineers are socialized to promote technical design standards rather than piecemeal approaches to occupational hazards. The goal is to solve a problem—not simply to limit exposure. As will be explained in greater detail below, this has had a distinct impact on the costliness of compliance with OSHA regulations.[53]

Coordination problems are common in agencies that seek to synthesize scientific or social-scientific research and administration, but OSHA has had some rather unusual problems. The separation of OSHA and NIOSH has impeded communication. Some OSHA administrators have claimed that there is little or no effective communication between OSHA and its research arm. As a consequence, the activities of OSHA and NIOSH have often revealed a phenomenal lack of coordination and the existence of different priorities. The latter agency has often devoted time and resources to developing data on the risks associated with exposure to certain workplace substances only to discover that the substances in question were of little concern to the standards offices at OSHA. This is a problem because NIOSH in large part drives OSHA's agenda through its submission of criteria documents containing research findings and recommendations.[54]

The Policy Process

The mandate of OSHA encompasses the development, promulgation, and enforcement of standards addressing safety and health. Safety problems (such as poorly designed machinery) are relatively easy to address by establishing design standards. The vast majority of OSHA standards have addressed safety problems, commonly relying on existing industry codes and the recommendations of standard-setting organizations. The agency's health regulations, in contrast, aim at reducing or eliminating workers' exposure to substances that promote disease. The health regulations have been a source of controversy. Some of the controversy has been tied to the complexity and uncertainty of the risk-assessment process. For the most part, OSHA relies on academic and federally funded research studies when conducting risk assessment and determining whether to regulate exposure to a substance. Thus, a crucial question is how to combine and weigh existing research. The high dosages used in bioassays (i.e., animal experiments) often produce positive findings. Relying more heavily on bioassays than on to epidemiological studies will commonly produce more risk-averse regulations. Likewise, the mathematical models used to extrapolate from animal to human populations are fraught with uncertainty. However, OSHA has freely relied on conservative, risk-averse assumptions in deciding to promulgate rules.[55]

Health regulations have also been a source of conflict because of the high costs of compliance. Administrators at OSHA must determine how to manage risks and must decide how to distribute the burdens of the regulatory remedy among employers and employees. In risk management, OSHA, reflecting the professional norms of its staff, has generally supported technical design standards (which require the application of specific technologies) in preference to less-costly performance standards. As noted above, the Occupational Safety and Health Act does not force the agency to consider the cost-effectiveness of its health regulations. The high compliance costs are particularly troublesome because of the lack of clear evidence regarding policy success. Owing in large part to long latency periods, most of OSHA's health regulations will yield their benefits years if not decades after their introduction. The multicausal nature of many diseases and the possible effects that exposure to certain chemicals may have on future generations only exacerbates this problem. In any event, the lack of clear results may make the compliance costs seem more oppressive.[56]

The Occupational Safety and Health Act empowered OSHA to adopt temporary standards to address emergency situations. However, most standards emerge as a product of the rule-making process established in the Administrative Procedure Act and the Occupational Safety and Health Act, and refined by the agency over the course of the of the 1970s and 80s.[57] Even when the agency establishes emergency standards, it must initiate the formal rule-making procedure to promulgate a permanent rule. Except in emergencies, the agency develops most standards in response to reports compiled by NIOSH or OSHA researchers, and petitions filed by state and local officials or private parties and associations. Once an opportunity for rule-making has been identified, OSHA routinely establishes an advisory committee consisting of members representing the Department of Health and Human Services, state and local agencies, business, and labor. These committees also include relevant professionals, and representatives from one or more standard-setting organizations. Although OSHA is not required to create advisory committees, they provide early access to analysis and competing perspectives.

Within the agency, project teams consisting of attorneys, scientists, and economists bear the responsibility for the development of new rules. These teams, headed by members of the Health Standards Office or the Safety Standards Office, formulate each rule and guide it through the administrative process. After developing a proposed standard on the basis of the scientific evidence and literature, and receiving OMB approval, the agency publishes a notice of rule-making in the *Federal Register*. During the next thirty days the proposed rule is subject to public comment. Interested parties may submit supplementary evidence and analysis and written comments on the rule. Hearings routinely follow the public-comment period. Agency officials, management and labor representatives, members of pertinent professional groups, and advocacy groups commonly testify, subject to cross-examination. Testifying parties commonly submit additional reports and data to support their positions, often providing tens of thousands of pages of additional documentation. At the conclusion of the hearings, the project team reviews and revises the proposed rule in light of the new evidence. After OMB review, the agency publishes the final rule in the *Federal Register*.

Limitations on the Agency's Autonomy

The Occupational Safety and Health Administration promulgates rules addressing workplace health and safety. In so doing, it seeks to regulate the relationship between management and labor, albeit in a less explicit fashion than other regulatory agencies, such as the National Labor Relations Board. The broad mandate of OSHA, the basic assumption of the Occupational Safety and Health Act (i.e., that business is responsible for preventing workplace injuries and work-related diseases), and the high compliance costs of OSHA's rules make the agency very susceptible to challenges from affected parties. It should be no surprise that the rule-making process is checked by a host of internal review processes and that the agency's actions are closely scrutinized by the White House, Congress, and the courts.[58]

The president appoints the assistant secretary for occupational safety and health. As will be shown below, the choice of administrators can have an important effect on the agency's posture and agenda. The assistant secretary and a regulation review committee continually supervise the policy process and appraise the preliminary research supporting new standards and all the analyses leading up to the promulgation of a final rule. Additional reviews are conducted within the Department of Labor. In addition, all proposed and final regulations are subject to reviews conducted by other executive-branch agencies. Like other executive-branch agencies, OSHA is required to submit its proposed rules for OMB review, but because OSHA's organic mandate establishes feasibility as the proper criterion, executive orders cannot force the agency to adhere to cost-benefit analysis. However, Thorne Auchter, assistant secretary during the Reagan administration, imposed cost-effectiveness analysis on the agency's decision-making. Because cost-effectiveness is but one of many factors considered in OSHA's regulatory design, the administration did not consider this a contradiction of congressional intent.

The role of Congress in monitoring the agency's performance and supporting its efforts has been limited. Congress's oversight of OSHA, like its oversight of the EPA, is conditioned by the complexity of the policy area. The technical complexity of risk assessment and management places natural limits on legislators' capacity to intervene on a routine basis in the development of health standards. Congress has generally supported OSHA through appropriations. However, because the agency's regulations affect millions of businesses (each of which falls within a distinct congressional district) there have been many attempts to ease the regulatory burdens on certain sectors of the economy and on small businesses. During the 1970s, legislators introduced numerous bills and riders to exempt small businesses, farms, and recreational facilities from OSHA regulations. Moreover, riders on appropriation bills further restricted OSHA's jurisdiction and limited the agency's discretion in the use of its resources. More significant, at least from a symbolic standpoint, have been the numerous bills introduced to amend or repeal the Occupational Safety and Health Act. Quite naturally, the tenuous support for OSHA has limited the agency's authority. Corporations may be hesitant to make large capital investments to comply with OSHA standards if the agency's future is unclear.[59]

The courts' relationship with OSHA resembles their relationship with the EPA: they play the most important role in checking the exercise of the agencies' discretionary authority. Almost every health regulation promulgated by OSHA has been met with a court challenge. Indeed, one could consider legal challenges to be a part of the regulatory process, because they are routine. This vulnerability to the courts has affected the agency's policy-making. As Graham Wilson explains: "OSHA must always anticipate Court battles when it frames standards. Indeed, the framing of standards within the agency usually involves a constant quarrel between the expert advocates of a proposed standard, anxious to tackle a health problem quickly, and the lawyers of the agency, anxious to prepare the strongest possible case for the Court battles which almost certainly lie ahead."[60]

It is useful to examine the courts' position with respect to the scientific and economic factors that need to be addressed in OSHA standard-setting. The need to provide a relatively precise scientific foundation for standards became clear when a court challenged OSHA's benzene standard. Benzene has been cited as a cause of leukemia when exposure levels are above 100 parts per million. Although there is little proof of significant risks at much lower levels of exposure, OSHA set conservative standards to provide for a margin of error. In 1978, the agency revised its benzene standard, lowering it from 10 part per million to 1 part per million. When industry challenged the new exposure levels, the Fifth Circuit Court of Appeals rejected the benzene standard because OSHA had failed to determine whether the benefits of a more stringent standard could justify the additional costs. The Supreme Court reviewed the case and accepted the lower court's decision without affirming the basis of its decision. The majority interpreted OSHA's mandate as requiring that standards be "reasonably necessary." The necessity of the new standard could be proved only by demonstrating that a 1-part-per-million standard was more beneficial than a 10-part-per-million standard. In short, the agency had to "make a threshold finding that a place of employment is unsafe."[61]

The courts have been less certain when addressing the relevance of economic factors, particularly the economic effects of OSHA standards and the potential role for cost-benefit analysis. In 1971, OSHA adopted an emergency standard to limit exposure to asbestos to 5 fibers per cubic centimeter and initiated efforts to promulgate a permanent standard. A NIOSH criteria document recommended tightening the asbestos standard to 2 fibers per cubic centimeter in two years. Although an OSHA-commissioned study concluded that a 5-fiber standard would achieve 99 percent of the benefits, OSHA decided to accept NIOSH's recommendation, albeit allowing four years before the 2-fiber standard would be put into effect. The hope was to retain a margin of safety and allow more time for compliance. The AFL-CIO challenged the standards, arguing that this lengthy transition period reflected an inappropriate concern with compliance costs.[62]

The court of appeals that decided the case accepted the standard, but the decision was significant in that it provided some insights into the meaning of "feasibility." As will be recalled from the above discussion, the Occupational Safety and Health Act empowered OSHA to promote making the workplace as safe as was feasible. Because feasibility was the only factor limiting the agency's authority, the interpretation of this clause was no trivial matter. In *Industrial Union Department v. Hodgson*, the court acknowledged that feasibility had an economic basis: "It would comport with common usage to say that a standard that is prohibitively expensive is not 'feasible' . . . Congress does not appear to have intended to protect employees by putting their employers out of business—either by requiring protective devices unavailable under existing technology or by making financial viability generally impossible." The court stressed that a regulation might be considered feasible even if its compliance costs could affect profitability and even put some employers out of business. However, the regulation's feasibility would come into question as "the effect becomes more widespread within an industry."[63]

In 1976, OSHA proposed a new standard revising the acceptable exposure levels to cotton dust, a substance widely acknowledged to be a cause of byssinosis in workers in the cotton textile industry. Since 1965, federal regulations had set acceptable exposure levels at 500 micrograms per cubic meter. On the basis of subsequent studies and after rather contentious debate involving the president, the Council of Economic Advisers, and the Department of Labor, OSHA decided to change exposure levels to 200 micrograms per cubic meter for yarn production and 750 micrograms per cubic meter for fabric production. The Textile Manufacturers Association, the trade association representing the financially troubled textile industry, challenged this costly regulatory response. The association based its objections on two arguments. The first, which echoed the appellate court's decision in the benzene case, was that OSHA had not shown a reasonable relationship between the costs and the benefits of the cotton dust standard. The second, which echoed the reasoning in the asbestos decision, was that the rule was not economically feasible in light of the troubles of the industry.[64]

The court of appeals stayed the implementation of the standard, and the decision was appealed to the Supreme Court. The newly inaugurated Reagan administration asked that the Court remand the case to OSHA for a new determination of the justification for the rule. The Court, however, rejected the administration's request and heard the case. The Court determined that OSHA did not have to subject regulations to cost-benefit analysis, arguing that "Congress itself defined the basic relationship between costs and benefits, by placing the 'benefit' of worker health above all other considerations."[65]

These three decisions suggest the pressures placed on OSHA's decision-making. Indeed, they understate the situation, for several appellate courts have ruled on these issues, but few attempts have been made to present compatible interpretations of feasibility.[66] To determine whether a regulation is feasible, OSHA must consider the regulation's economic consequences, particularly its effects on the industry in question. However, the economic analysis need not take the form of cost-benefit analysis, because the Occupational Safety and Health Act clearly emphasized the benefits of occupational health. Moreover, although the Court has allowed the agency to use safety margins in its regulations, it has ruled that the agency must justify its standards scientifically. There must, in short, be some reasonable expectation that a given standard will produce greater benefits than a less rigorous standard will. This comes very close to suggesting that some form of cost-effectiveness analysis is appropriate in rule-making in the area of occupational health.

The Implementation of Occupational Safety and Health Policies

The Occupational Safety and Health Administration and the Environmental Protection Agency have much in common. Both are responsible for addressing complex problems that require a heavy reliance on scientific expertise. Both force the regulated interests to absorb significant compliance costs. And in both, as in all regulatory agencies, the priorities of the agency and the administration of policy are sensitive to the influence of political executives and the presidents they represent. During the Nixon administration, osha focused on the promulgation of safety standards, placing very little emphasis on occupational disease. The Occupational Safety and Health Act empowered the agency to bypass normal rule-making procedures to adopt consensus national safety and health standards during its first twenty-eight months. The vast majority of the more than forty-four hundred consensus standards adopted were safety standards formulated by standard-setting organizations or imposed by the federal government on corporations that had federal contracts in excess of ten thousand dollars. Although the Occupational Safety and Health Act had given the agency twenty-eight months to accept consensus standards, Assistant Secretary of Labor George Guenther moved to adopt the standards after one month. This wholesale adoption entailed the acceptance of many standards that were grossly outdated, irrelevant, or extraordinarily detailed. Some of the more memorable rules included the requirement that toilets have hinged, open-front seats, that all rest room stalls have hooks for coats, and that "ice in contact with drinking water shall be made of potable water."[67]

During Guenther's tenure, osha slowly developed enforcement priorities as inspectors were directed to focus on industries with high injury and fatality rates (e.g., longshoring, roofing and sheetmetal work, meat processing, and the manufacture of transportation equipment and of lumber and wood products). Moreover, there were some minor achievements in health regulations. In May 1971, osha issued a list of more than four hundred substances thought to be harmful and urged employers to guard against exposure levels above the thresholds established by the American Conference of Governmental Industrial Hygienists. Moreover, in 1972 osha promulgated a standard on asbestos. However, resource constraints and Nixon's policy agenda limited the agency's efforts to develop health regulations. The administration imposed employment ceilings and average-grade controls as cost-cutting measures, limiting the ability of OSHA and NIOSH to hire upper-grade health professionals. This was particularly a problem for NIOSH, which was unable to fill one-sixth of its authorized positions. Dr. Marcus Key, director of NIOSH, cited the shortage of research scientists as the primary cause of the delays in developing criteria for toxic substances. Effective regulation was also frustrated by Nixon's "New Federalism." The administration tried to shift power and responsibility to the states, setting aside a large percentage of OSHA's overall budget for state grants. Labor advocates feared that a successful transfer of power to the states would promote local variations in coverage, as well as more conservative policies.[68]

During its first three years of existence, OSHA had earned the scorn of the business community and organized labor. Business associations were concerned with the agency's enforcement of trivial standards; labor was critical of the small appropriations, the small number of inspectors, the protracted policy process, and the Nixon administration's alleged attempts to limit enforcement efforts in exchange for corporate contributions to the 1972 reelection campaign. One indicator of dissatisfaction was the legislative reaction: in the Ninety-third Congress more than eighty bills were introduced to amend the Occupational Safety and Health Act. The proposed amendments would have reduced OSHA penalties, lengthened the rule-making process, and required a broader dissemination of information, as well as on-site consultation services for small businesses.[69]

Despite this hostile environment, there were during the Ford administration signs of meaningful efforts to enhance OSHA's the administrative capacities and performance. Chief among these efforts was the appointment of Morton Corn as assistant secretary. Corn was a former professor of occupational health and chemical engineering. He hoped to create the agency "Congress mandated with no extraneous influences," noting that the agency's success "rests on its professionalism."[70] Corn stressed numerous goals, which included enlarging the professional staff and placing a greater reliance on scientific research. To this end, he expanded the professional staff of the Standards Development Office to thirty and began bringing scientists into the agency to work with OSHA staff. Moreover, Corn planned to focus the agency's efforts on serious health problems by bringing about closer interaction with NIOSH, and to focus inspections on industries with high death, injury, and illness rates and/or high levels of exposure to toxic chemicals. Finally, he sought to enhance OSHA's political standing by clarifying standards and expanding the congressional affairs staff. Although business and labor provided some support for Corn's vision, his influence was limited by Ford's brief term in office and by the antiregulatory environment promoted by the president. During 1976 Ford consistently degraded OSHA in his public statements about the inflationary effects of regulations. The agency had become a symbol of overregulation and was a convenient target. As part of the growing support for deregulation, Ford established a presidential task force, headed by Paul MacAvoy of the Council of Economic Advisers, to streamline regulations. The creation of the task force and Ford's antagonism toward OSHA's policies mobilized the opposition of organized labor. In the end, the task force was not given the authority necessary to redefine the agency's duties. Rather, it assisted the agency in the critical examination and screening of consensus standards. This environment limited Corn's efforts to enhance OSHA's capacities.[71]

The agency reached its peak during the Carter presidency. Carter appointed Eula Bingham, a noted toxicologist and environmental health expert, recommended for the position by the AFL-CIO, as assistant secretary. Her appointment was a sign of the administration's commitment to the promotion of occupational safety and health. Bingham declared three goals for the agency. The first was to focus the agency's efforts on health regulations. An emergency standard was immediately released regulating exposure to benzene. During Bingham's tenure, OSHA promulgated permanent standards for benzene, dibromochloropropane (DBCP), inorganic arsenic, cotton dust, acrylonitrile, and lead. All told, the number of health standards more than doubled during her tenure. The focus on health regulations required an expansion of the scientific staff and the devotion of a greater proportion of the agency's resources to health inspections. This attempt to focus the agency's use of its resources forced a decline in the number of investigations. However, the proportion of serious violations addressed, and the penalties imposed, increased dramatically, indicating the positive role of the new priorities.[72]

Bingham's second goal was to improve the agency's approach to regulating health hazards. During the previous few years, OSHA had adopted a rather inefficient case-by-case approach to making health regulations that addressed workplace toxins. In 1974, NIOSH had identified forty-two thousand chemical substances used in industry, including some two thousand possible carcinogens.[73] Because a case-by-case approach could not be sustained, OSHA adopted a generic approach to regulating exposure: it regulated on the basis of effect rather than on the basis of chemical composition. Thus, in 1980 it released its cancer policy and a list of 207 substances that would be affected immediately. The controversial subject matter and the potential implications of a legally binding cancer policy generated great publicity. The agency received more than a quarter of a million written comments during the public-comment period. Under the cancer policy, OSHA divided suspected carcinogens into two categories. Category I included substances that had been conclusively linked to cancer through epidemiological studies, or through a single mammalian bioassay (if the results were supported by other evidence). These substances OSHA would ban, or if no substitutes for them existed, the agency would require that exposure be reduced to the lowest feasible level. Category II included suspected carcinogens, which would be regulated on a case-by-case basis. Although the Reagan administration relaxed the cancer policy, the generic approach to health regulation remained an important innovation.[74]

Bingham's third and final goal was to eliminate or revise some eleven hundred of the safety standards that the agency had adopted wholesale in 1971. Two factors frustrated the standards deletion project. First, whereas the Occupational Safety and Health Act allowed OSHA to adopt consensus standards with relative ease, the process for deletion closely paralleled the formal rule-making process and required the agency to present the standards in question for public comment. Second, OSHA quickly discovered that many of the standards had constituencies: interested parties commented on 90 percent of the standards. Most distressingly, the AFL-CIO demanded that elimination of standards take place only after public hearings. In the end, OSHA avoided the expenses of formal hearings by consulting with union representatives, and it targeted some nine hundred standards for revocation.[75]

During the tenures of Corn and Bingham, OSHA was rapidly maturing into an effective regulatory agency. The pursuit of clear priorities, the increase in the number of health standards, and the professionalization of the agency held great promise. However, the Reagan appointees to OSHA reversed the gains of the late 1970s, seeking to further reduce the regulatory burden and forge a more cooperative relationship with business. This was particularly the case during the tenure of Thorne Auchter. Unlike Corn and Bingham, who were health professionals, Auchter was an executive in a family construction company that had been cited for OSHA violations on numerous occasions, and he had been a Reagan campaign organizer in Florida. This raised concerns that the appointment was a reward for past loyalty.

Like Gorsuch at the EPA, Auchter took control at OSHA with the goal of transforming the agency into a "cooperative regulator."[76] Corn and Bingham had hoped to improve the agency's troubled relationship with business by increasing the agency's professionalism and eliminating frivolous standards. Auchter had something different in mind. During the first years of his tenure, the agency underwent significant resource reductions. Its budget was reduced from $213.6 million in 1981 to $200.6 million in 1982—far below the Carter administration's proposed fiscal 1982 budget of $242 million. Additional reductions came in later years. These cuts had a significant effect on staffing. In 1980 the agency had employed more than three thousand people, including more than sixteen hundred inspectors. By the beginning of 1982, the staff had been reduced by one-sixth, and the number of inspectors by one-fourth. This reduction in staffing had an immediate effect on the number of inspections performed and violations discovered, and on the aggregate fines imposed.[77]

To transform OSHA into a "cooperative regulator," Auchter stressed voluntary compliance rather than enforcement and promoted a greater role for the states. The agency routinely used informal conferences with violators to resolve violations before it became necessary to resort to prosecution. Moreover, OSHA encouraged businesses to conduct self-inspections, and provided the necessary training. It also authorized a number of states to administer their own occupational safety and health programs, removing OSHA inspectors from twenty-one states.[78] Although the changes at OSHA drew denunciations from labor and from many advocacy groups, business offered nothing but praise. As a representative of the U.S. Chamber of Commerce explained, "I don't think there's a regulatory agency in Washington that has delivered more on candidate Reagan's promises on regulatory reform—OSHA's way out in front in that respect." A representative of the National Association of Manufacturers agreed, noting, "For most of our members, OSHA is not the dirty word it used to be."[79]

Auchter combined the promotion of voluntarism and of state-level regulation with a concerted effort to revise existing standards. The agency attempted, albeit with only partial success, to revise, dilute, or delay standards for asbestos, benzene, cotton dust, ethylene dibromide, lead, and noise. Indeed, in most years OSHA devoted a larger proportion of its standard-setting staff to revising regulations than to developing new standards. The efforts to weaken health standards alienated OSHA's scientific staff. Gerston, Fraleigh, and Schwab explain that because of "Auchter's policy to weaken existing standards . . . many professional staff members, demoralized and disgusted, simply quit, tired of having both their advice on health matters and their concern with the direction the agency's regulatory policies ignored. Others were not so lucky, and were fired, demoted, or reassigned."[80] In essence, deregulation at OSHA was accomplished through a progressive elimination of the agency's administrative capacities.

Auchter resigned in March 1984 and was replaced by Charles Rowlands, former chair of OSHRC. Rowlands resigned the position before confirmation and was replaced by John Pendergrass, a former executive from 3M. There were no serious attempts to reestablish OSHA as a competent regulatory agency, and the events of the early 1980s colored the agency's performance for the remainder of the Reagan presidency.[81]

The Reagan appointees promoted voluntary compliance and embraced budget reductions that cut deeply into the overall pool of regulators. These efforts were largely successful. However, one may question their long-term significance. In light of the role that George Bush played in the Reagan deregulatory efforts as chairman of the President's Task Force on Regulatory Relief, one might have expected a continuation of the Reagan policies. However, the Bush administration promoted a mild revitalization of the EPA and of OSHA. The EPA's new administrator, William K. Reilly, had been president of the Conservation Foundation and the World Wildlife Fund–U.S. prior to his appointment. Reilly's expertise in and support for environmental protection seemed to reopen the possibility of an expansion of the EPA. Moreover, the passage of new Clean Air Act amendments—stalled for the entirety of the Reagan presidency—was an indication of reduced hostility toward environmental protection. Likewise, something of a revitalization of OSHA occurred under the direction of Secretary of Labor Elizabeth Dole and Assistant Secretary Gerald F. Scannell, an occupational safety and health professional with prior corporate and OSHA experience. Under the leadership of Dole and Scannell, new efforts have been initiated to address cumulative trauma disorders associated with repetitive work, as well as health care workers' exposure to infectious disease (e.g., hepatitis B and AIDS). Indeed, under Scannell OSHA proposed the largest fine in its history, a penalty of $7.3 million against USX for a number of health and safety violations.[82]

The shift in emphasis from the Reagan presidency was apparent to many regulatory analysts. Indeed, when one examines a host of indicators of regulatory activity (e.g., personnel, agency budget, and the number of new rules promulgated), President Bush seems to have more in common with Carter than with Reagan.[83] Concerns about the growing emphasis on regulation and the recession of 1991–92 led Bush to place a moratorium on new regulations, and through his Council on Competitiveness to once again pressure agencies to consider whether the costs of regulation can be justified by the benefits. Whether the regulatory agencies such as the EPA and OSHA can free themselves of the legacy of the deregulatory 1980s remains to be seen.

THE LIMITS OF THE SOCIETAL REGIME

An examination of the EPA and of OSHA, the two flagship agencies of the societal regime, reveals three major problems. The first is the incredible complexity of making policies in areas that require a reliance on scientific research. The difficulties can be seen most clearly in the case of the EPA. The research programs upon which regulators had to draw were yet in their infancy and thus incapable of providing anything resembling a firm foundation for standards—a situation exacerbated by statutory timetables. As Douglas Costle explained: "There's a credibility problem for everybody because people tend to expect yes-or-no, bottom-line answers. But the science of these problems is a lot more ambiguous than that. We live in a twilight zone of scientific uncertainty . . . Whoever is in charge of the science is going to be vulnerable on the grounds of credibility simply because he has to make policy judgments based on ambiguous science. Now, if you separate the science from regulation, you have some problems. How would you know the scientists are going after the right issues? If you don't have some control over the research that's done, you can't be sure of getting scientific data in time to meet congressionally mandated deadlines."[84] Of course, this latter problem was of great concern in the case of OSHA. With research centralized in NIOSH, the difficulties associated with scientific uncertainty were compounded by additional problems of coordination.

A second major problem comes in the area of institutional design. As explained earlier, the new social regulations were accompanied by significant institutional innovations. The regulatory legislation directed the agencies to fulfill incredibly ambitious mandates in hopes of promoting the maximum regulatory effect. Action-forcing provisions, an expanded rule-making process, and the promotion of citizen suits to force the execution of nondiscretionary functions provided means of forcing agencies to be accountable and responsive. However, these features had troublesome consequences. The broad mandates established expectations that simply could not be met. Failure to meet legislative deadlines or regulate all substances that posed a threat to public health exposed the agencies to the charge that they were failing to enforce their mandates with sufficient vigor. This undoubtedly led many businesses to discount the agencies' authority and the risks of noncompliance. Although the action-forcing provisions, such as the timetables in the Clean Air Act of 1970, compelled the EPA to move swiftly and establish standards, these actions were taken on the basis of tenuous assumptions, incomplete analyses, and insufficient internal reviews. Likewise, whereas an expanded rule-making process and citizen suits could enhance an agency's accountability, resources tied up in hearings and litigation could not be devoted to performing the agency's statutory duties.

A third major problem exists in the area of external constraints on agencies' activities. This has been addressed, in part, in the discussion of citizen suits and expanded rule-making. However, I want to focus on the courts and the White House review processes. The provisions encouraging citizen suits and the controversial and costly nature of the regulations, created ever-greater incentives for litigation. This gave the courts an extraordinary role in defining agencies' authority and the kinds of factors that had to be addressed in regulatory decision-making. Because of the complexities of social regulation, judges commonly found themselves at a loss. As one judge stated in an early suit involving the EPA: "Socrates said that wisdom is the recognition of how much one does not know. I may be wise if that is wisdom, because I recognize that I do not know enough about dynamometer extrapolations, deterioration factor adjustments, and the like to decide whether or not the government's approach to these matters was statistically valid."[85] Despite this admission of limited judicial capacities, many judges have been unwilling to acknowledge their lack of expertise. They have routinely opined on the quality of the evidence and on the scientific and economic foundations of agencies' actions. Given the decentralization of the judiciary, this has produced decisions that are difficult to reconcile with the agencies' mandates.

The executive review processes, in contrast, express a greater degree of coherence. The growing demands that agencies justify their regulatory decisions on the basis of economic analysis have forced an integration of economics into the agencies' decision-making processes. Regulators have become more careful to address the cost-effectiveness of alternative policies and to ensure that decisions are justified on the basis of the underlying scientific analysis. Although such requirements can potentially facilitate better regulatory decision-making, they also make the agencies far more vulnerable to budget cuts. Reductions can eliminate critical research staffs, thus making it impossible to muster the data and analyses necessary to justify new regulations. Indeed, much of the reduction in the level of regulatory action during the Reagan administration can be attributed to the staffing cuts. Even if there was a desire to regain former levels of activism, the barriers to new regulatory policy-making within the executive branch would make this impossible without further resources. The review processes and their effects on regulatory action are the subject of chapter 8.

8

Regulatory Reform and the Emergence of a New Regime

DURING THE 1970S, AS NEW LEGISLATION WAS EXTENDING regulation to numerous activities previously unaddressed, there was also a contraction of regulatory authority. Attempts to reform regulatory policy-making and deregulate a number of sectors of the economy began in earnest in the mid-1970s and were carried over into the 1980s. Although there was a broad commitment to reevaluating well-established economic regulatory policies, the costliness of the new social regulations stimulated efforts to introduce new economic criteria into the regulatory decision-making process and reconsider policies deemed too intrusive or too burdensome. The decade, which had begun with a significant expansion of regulation, ended with retrenchment.

Regulatory reform and *deregulation* are commonly treated as synonyms. However, there are differences worth exploring. *Regulatory reform* refers to attempts to improve the internal management of the regulatory agencies by promoting the consideration of the economic costs and benefits of alternatives. One aspect of this reform was the centralization of regulatory review and clearance in the Executive Office of the President and the Office of Management and Budget. Such centralization, it was believed, could facilitate efforts to coordinate agencies' actions and to minimize the economic impact of these actions. Making executive review a routine part of the regulatory process compelled agencies to enhance their own policy-planning and policy-evaluation staffs and internalize the review process. *Deregulation*, in contrast, refers to the elimination of "unnecessary" or "burdensome" regulations. Although existing economic regulations guaranteed a degree of industrial stability, these gains were realized at a cost: competition was limited and innovation was slowed. Increasingly it was argued that the market could effectively regulate economic activities in most sectors of the economy. Critics of regulation suggested that deregulation could benefit consumers by reducing prices; it could revitalize a stagnant economy by allowing for new competition and reducing the costs of inputs critical to the production process. Important initiatives that were passed during the period eliminated key regulations in telecommunications, commercial banking, surface transportation, energy, and air transportation.

Although regulatory reform and deregulation can be addressed as analytically distinct, they commonly worked in tandem. When analysts within an agency determined that existing policies imposed excessive costs on the economy or were not cost-effective, these policies became ripe for deregulation. As economic criteria were introduced into regulatory decision-making at the agency level, policy-makers increasingly sought incentive-based solutions to regulatory problems. Agency executives seeking to introduce market mechanisms as part of deregulatory initiatives could rely on the support of economics staffs created as part of the reform process. Economic professionalization created a natural constituency for deregulation.

This chapter examines the origins of regulatory reform and deregulation. Although the lack of historical distance prevents a definitive conclusion, the evidence suggests that these activities, when taken together, constituted a new regulatory regime. The efficiency regime of the 1970s and 80s differed from previous regimes not only in its focus but also in its genesis. Unlike earlier regulatory regimes, which originated in the demands of mobilized social groups seeking to control one aspect or another of the economic system, the new regime had its origins in elite politics and the institutional changes of the previous decades.

A NEW REGULATORY REGIME

The significance of the Reagan revolution in regulation has received serious attention in recent years. Was the Reagan administration responsible for a new regulatory regime? Richard Harris and Sidney Milkis address this very question in their fine study *The Politics of Regulatory Change*. After sorting through a wealth of information, they arrive at a negative response. While noting that "the Reagan presidency has certainly brought important changes that are likely to have an enduring influence," they conclude that no "firm consensus has developed in support of a market-oriented regulatory regime."[1] My analysis differs from that of Harris and Milkis on two grounds. First, it is my view that when the Reagan years are seen in a broader historical context, there is ample evidence to suggest that a new regime has emerged. To arrive at this evidence I must address events that preceded the Reagan presidency. Second, I contend that the question of whether or not a consensus exists concerning the central features of the new regime may not be crucial if, as I will argue below, the regime has its origins in elite politics and the analytic biases established as a result of administrative change.

The new regime can be characterized by several defining features. The first is an unprecedented centralization of regulatory authority in the OMB and in White House review bodies. The second is the requirement that initiatives must be justified on the basis of economic analysis. The third, reflecting faith in market mechanisms and in the self-regulatory capacities of corporations, is the use of the market as a benchmark in assessing the need for policies and in designing new policies. The fourth is the fact that the regulatory reform and deregulation efforts are driven by an overwhelming concern with corporate compliance costs. Social benefits are weighed against the costs incurred by corporations, and regulators are urged to seek the least burdensome form of regulation. Given the central role of efficiency in the new politics of regulation, it is appropriate to refer to this regime as the "efficiency regime."

The characteristics of the efficiency regime clearly distinguish it from earlier regimes. Unlike the Progressive Era market regime, which sought to revitalize or replicate decentralized markets, the new regime recognizes few sources of market failure. The market is, for the most part, thought to be a system of economic governance free from regulatory constraints. The new regime shares with the New Deal's associational regime a faith in the self-regulatory capacities of economic actors but deemphasizes the need for active government supervision and attacks the regulatory structures created to coordinate and monitor corporations' activities. Corporate practices and modes of organization, it is believed, will be eliminated by market forces unless they are efficient. Finally, the new regime departs from the societal regime of the late 1960s and the 1970s in the core assumption that corporate compliance costs must be considered when determining the justification for many of the new regulatory policies. Environmental protection and workers' safety are considered less important than corporate profitability and economic competitiveness.

The origins of the efficiency regime also distinguish it from its predecessors. As argued throughout this book, the regulatory initiatives of earlier regimes were largely products of democratic politics. Policies were initiated in response to the demands of various groups mobilized by salient economic crises or transformations and demanding a policy response. Although the final policies were rarely an accurate reflection of groups' claims—the demands of coalition maintenance, prevailing theories of state-economy relations, and administrative reform agendas were at all times central in shaping the legislative mandates and institutional design—the democratic origins remain evident. In contrast, a search for the democratic roots of the efficiency regime is fruitless. To be certain, during the 1970s and 80s the nation elected a series of moderate and conservative presidents. Particularly in the wake of the 1980 election, when Republicans claimed the presidency and the Senate, there were popular discussions of the growing conservatism of the electorate. Indeed, President Reagan and many other notable conservatives repeatedly interpreted the 1980 election as a popular referendum on the contemporary welfare state and regulatory system. However, there is little evidence that the choices at the presidential level were accompanied by a new hostility toward regulation or a greater faith in markets and in the self-regulatory capacities of corporations.[2]

The public's feelings about regulation can be estimated by examining poll data, although polls are imprecise and public opinion itself is transitory. Polls taken during the 1970s reveal the strength and consistency of public support for regulation. A series of polls conducted by Opinion Research Corporation during the 1970s revealed growing public concern about business profits, and increasing support for an expansion of government regulation. The percentage of the sample believing that businesses in competitive sectors were making excessive profits increased in each successive poll: from 26 percent in 1971 to 45 percent in 1975, and to 51 percent in 1979 and 1981. The percentage of the sample believing that the government ought to place legal limits on corporate profits increased in the same fashion, rising by 1979 from a low of 33 percent to a high of 60 percent. The public's concern about large corporations was expressed in additional polls. During the 1970s, the percentage of the sample believing that too much power was concentrated in the hands of large corporations increased from 66 percent in 1971 to a high of 79 percent in 1979, with an average of 73.8 percent for the period. Similarly, the percentage of the sample agreeing that many of the largest companies should be broken up into smaller companies increased during the decade, from a low of 47 percent in 1971 to a high of 57 percent in 1975 and again in 1979.[3]

Concern about corporate power translated into high levels of support for regulation. In a Cambridge Reports poll conducted during the period 1978–80, the sample was asked whether there was "so much regulation it interferes with efficient business operation" or whether there was not enough regulation "to protect consumers." In no year did the percentage of the sample citing excessive regulation exceed the percentage believing that the nation had the proper amount of regulation or needed greater regulation. In fact, a Harris poll conducted in 1976 and 1977 indicated that between 70 and 75 percent of the population believed that a one-third reduction in government regulation would result in moderate or serious losses to consumers. If there was strong popular support for deregulation, this support was not expressed in the opinion polls. The level of support for regulation which the polls demonstrated was remarkable in light of the arguments in support of deregulation and reform being presented by presidents, members of the policy community, and key members of Congress.[4]

Of course, support for regulation is difficult to gauge because the term *regulation* is vague. It could be the case that the public supported the *idea* of regulation—a direct reflection of the negative assessment of the equally vague concept "big business"—but opposed specific regulations. Although the available poll data are limited, they are nonetheless suggestive. A Roper poll conducted each year between 1973 and 1981 asked whether environmental protection laws and regulations had gone too far, had not gone far enough, or had struck the correct balance. The results reveal tremendous support for environmental protection. The percentage of the sample believing that the environmental regulations had either struck the correct balance or had not gone far enough ranged from 65 percent (in 1979) to 69 percent (in 1974 and 1981), and averaged 67 percent. The poll provides no evidence whatsoever that public support for environmental regulations was in decline.[5]

Similar trends can be found in the area of consumer protection. A Roper poll conducted each year during the period 1974–80 reveals consistently high levels of support for consumer protection. Those polled were asked whether they believed that the government had to devote somewhat greater efforts, much greater efforts, or no additional efforts to establishing more regulations to protect consumers. The percentage of the sample believing that greater consumer product safety regulation was necessary ranged from a high of 89 percent in 1976 to a low of 81 percent in 1978, with an average of 85.4 percent. Polls conducted between 1976 and 1978 revealed that a majority of the sample favored the creation of a new consumer protection agency. In a Harris poll conducted between 1974 and 1977, between 80 and 85 percent of the sample believed that if there were no governmental protection of consumer safety, "people [would] continue to risk many serious health and accident dangers."[6]

If the public was not generally supportive of regulatory reform and deregulation, what stimulated these reforms? There would appear to be three contributing factors worth exploring. The first of these is a change in the interest-group system. Public opinion is less important as a source of policy change than the opinions of the interests that actually mobilize. As explained in chapter 6, many new advocacy groups mobilized in the late 1960s and early 1970s, providing crucial support for legislation addressing environmental protection, occupational health, and consumer protection. These victories, combined with poor economic performance, rising inflation, and the Watergate revelations of corrupt business practices, marked a low point for business. Public confidence in corporations declined at a precipitous rate. Whereas in 1966 and 1967 some 51 percent of the public had a great deal of confidence in corporate leaders, by the mid-1970s the figure had dropped to 20 percent. During the same period, there was an escalation of compliance costs. By 1974, manufacturing corporations were spending more than $10.4 billion—almost 11 percent of capital investment—on the installation of pollution control and occupational safety equipment.[7]

The costs of regulation, when combined with declining productivity rates and growing competition from foreign producers, were sufficient to stimulate a new burst of business organization and mobilization. A number of business associations, including the U.S. Chamber of Commerce, expanded their membership and their resource bases. Moreover, a large number of new corporate and business associations were formed, and existing associations established Washington offices. Twenty-three percent of the trade associations that had Washington representation in 1980, and 6 percent of the corporations with such representation, had established their Washington offices during the 1970s. Indeed, by 1980 fully 72 percent of the organizations that had Washington representation were corporations or trade associations. For the most part, these organizations were represented by legal offices engaged in highly intensive lobbying.[8] Large corporations and trade associations combined professional lobbying with active grass-roots lobbying efforts. Various corporations also tried to redefine the terms of the policy debate over state-economy relations by funding research and publications at numerous conservative think tanks, such as the Heritage Foundation and the American Enterprise Institute. This financing provided much-needed support for studies that decried the effects of overregulation and reaffirmed the supremacy of the market.[9]

The new corporate presence in campaign finance is even more striking. Under the provisions of the Federal Election Campaign Act of 1974, organized interests began creating political action committees to channel campaign contributions to candidates in House and Senate elections. In less than a decade, the number of PACs increased from 608 to 3,371. Much of this increase was the result of a 1975 Federal Election Commission decision that allowed corporations to use corporate funds to establish and administer PACs, and to use payroll deduction plans to collect funds for campaign contributions. By the end of the decade, corporate and trade association PACS accounted for some 62 percent of all PACs and were responsible for 59 percent of all PAC contributions, approximately $32.4 million in 1980 alone. In contrast, the citizen groups that had been influential earlier in the decade accounted for less than 5 percent of the PACs. The high levels of corporate spending reinforced the expanded lobbying efforts and the attempts to shape the discourse surrounding regulatory policy.[10]

Presidential initiatives were the second factor contributing to change in the regulatory system. The regulatory review initiatives of the 1970s and 80s were put in place by means of executive orders and were centralized in the White House. Moreover, Presidents Nixon, Ford, Carter, and Reagan included deregulation and reform among their most important agenda issues, largely out of concern about economic stagflation. As noted earlier, regulatory reform and deregulation were linked rhetorically to the need to promote economic growth and price stability. Although there is mixed evidence for a political business cycle, in which electoral politics directly drives economic policy and performance, there is no question that voters are averse to inflation. Since the early 1970s, as revealed in a series of polls, economic performance has been a far more salient issue than domestic, political, and social problems. It should not be surprising that high inflation and unemployment rates adversely affected voters' support for incumbent presidents, making economic performance a key issue in the presidential campaigns of 1972, 1976, 1980, and 1984.[11]

Although there is little to suggest that regulatory reform and deregulation had a significant impact on inflation, there is no question that presidents repeatedly presented their initiatives in this light. For example, the 1979 *Economic Report of the President* justified deregulation and regulatory reform by making the connection between regulation and inflation explicit: "Once incurred, the costs of regulatory actions enter into the wage- and price-setting mechanisms of the economy. Most of the costs of regulatory action show up not as governmental budget expenditures, but as increased costs to industry." The report presented the necessary response: "Both the large impact of government regulation, measured by its costs and benefits, and the way in which the costs add to inflation, highlight the responsibility of all branches of government to make sure that regulations are both necessary and efficiently designed." In conclusion, regulatory reform was presented as "a top priority" of the administration.[12]

It is doubtful that the Nixon, Ford, Carter, and Reagan administrations truly considered regulation to be a significant cause of economic stagflation. However, in view of the failure of fiscal and monetary policies and the inability of economic theory to offer more promising responses to the economic maladies of the period, deregulation seemed to be a plausible response. By linking regulatory reform and deregulation to a broader economic program, presidents could compensate for the declining popular confidence in macroeconomic policies and claim to be engaged in a comprehensive effort to restore growth and price stability. Given the political salience of economic performance, such claims were symbolically important, for they were attempts to translate popular concerns about macroeconomic performance into demands for a reduction in regulation.

The third factor contributing to regulatory reform and deregulation may have been new administrative practices and staffing decisions at the regulatory agencies. As noted in chapter 1, administrative capacities shape policy. Because policy is essentially a pattern of action, one must be concerned with the factors that shape implementation, including the extent of agency professionalization, the intellectual tools applied in the policy process, and the role of interest groups in the regulatory process. The 1970s and 80s saw significant alterations in the policy process and in agencies' staffing practices. Many agencies responded to the regulatory reform efforts of the 1970s by creating planning and evaluation offices or expanding their economics staffs. These agencies integrated economic criteria into their internal policy process in hopes of anticipating many of the concerns that would be addressed during executive review. Quite naturally, the systematic application of economic analysis favored deregulation. Indeed, because economic analysis was integrated into the policy process rather than imposed from above, one can argue that these intra-agency changes may prove to be the most significant.[13]

These three contributing factors discussed above can be integrated to construct an account of the regulatory changes that took place during the 1970s and 80s. Corporations responded to the combination of new social regulations and deteriorating economic conditions by demanding regulatory relief. The demands of corporations and trade associations were clearly focused on regulation, whereas popular concerns focused overwhelmingly on inflation and stagnant economic growth. However, these popular concerns were linked with prevailing economic critiques of regulation and with the argument that regulatory administration could be reformed through the application of economic analysis in regulatory decision-making. These doctrines found a clear expression in a series of executive orders. The executive review processes, in turn, forced institutional changes, thus creating a bureaucratic constituency for deregulation and regulatory reform. Although it is difficult to deter-

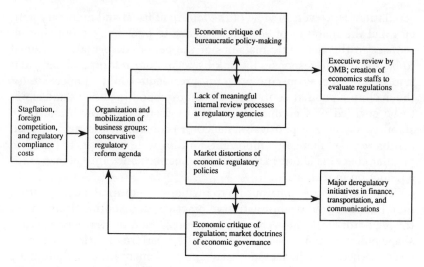

Fig. 8.1   The efficiency regime.

mine whether corporate PAC contributions were decisive, such funding reinforced the political expediency of deregulation and may have been instrumental in increasing congressional support for deregulation. The key elements of the efficiency regime are presented schematically in Figure 8.1.

THE REJECTION OF REGULATION

To understand the origins of the efficiency regime, it is critical to examine the events of the 1970s and 80s, focusing on both deregulation and regulatory reform. Proponents of these measures justified them, in large part, by the prevailing economic critiques of regulation. Deregulation was justified on the basis of significant concerns about how policies that empowered firms in some industries to function as members of government-managed cartels, deriving excessive profits free from market forces, were affecting competition. Regulatory reform, in contrast, was tied to concerns about the high compliance costs being absorbed by businesses. These expenses, it was argued, limited profitability and the incentive to reinvest. Deregulation and reform not only appealed to economists but also were supported by consumer advocates. Few chose to argue against the notion of eliminating unnecessary regulations, and deregulation was sufficiently vague and attractive to unite a diverse set of supporters. To understand the appeal of these ideas, it is useful to examine the critique of regulation.

In 1971 the economist George Stigler published an article entitled "The Theory of Economic Regulation."[14] Although it restated what had been long established in the political-science literature, it proved highly influential in the debates concerning regulation. Stigler argued that the public-interest interpretation of regulation was of little explanatory value because there was little evidence that many regulations actually advanced the public interest. Rather, he maintained, regulatory policies are designed and administered to provide benefits to the regulators and to the regulated corporations. According to Stigler, regulated industries demand and receive four kinds of policies: (1) those that create barriers to entry; (2) those that provide direct subsidies (although these are less beneficial than barriers to entry); (3) those that impose regulatory burdens on firms producing potential substitutes for the policy-seekers' products; and (4) those that impose price controls administered by a regulatory agency, thus allowing for higher rates of return and eliminating price competition. Policies that create barriers to entry can be seen in action when political officials awarding licenses, charters, broadcasting frequencies, new routes, or many other resources impose conditions that protect established firms from new competition. All four types of policy create a de facto cartel under the protective umbrella of regulatory policies; taxpayers and consumers absorb the costs of maintaining the cartel.

For Stigler, the causes of this situation were easy to understand. Members of Congress and regulators act self-interestedly, rationally exchanging policies for votes and resources (e.g., campaign funds). Although this convenient transaction forces the general public to bear the burdens of supporting industry (e.g., taxation, higher prices, and limited alternatives), this assignment of costs and benefits does not result in a negative electoral response because voter preferences are not registered on an issue-specific basis. Moreover, the high cost of informed activity and the lack of any mechanism that links the impact of an individual's vote to the depth of his or her knowledge means that most of the electorate are apathetic.

The economic interpretation of regulation evolved in the 1970s, as economists applying frameworks similar to Stigler's tried to bring greater sophistication to the model of regulatory capture and to assess the negative effects of regulation in specific industries.[15] The capture thesis caught the attention of many public-interest groups, and of consumer advocates as well. Regulatory capture, administrative mismanagement, bureaucratic rigidity, and political corruption became central themes in a series of Nader reports on regulatory agencies and government-business relations published during the early 1970s. For example, the Nader report on the Interstate Commerce Commission explained that "the crucial element impeding ICC performance . . . is the cumulative effect of many years of acculturation with the industry," and noted the commission's history of "influence peddling, incestuous job interchange with industry, [and] lack of appointment integrity."[16] Mark Green, then director of Nader's Corporate Accountability Research Group, claimed that government regulations "have undermined competition and entrenched monopoly." This was troublesome because "competition is to the economy what political freedom is to our polity: both oppose unchecked power and both value diversity in the contest for solutions." The remedy was clear: "Where there would be a viably competitive market but for economic regulation, that industry should be freed from regulatory restraint."[17]

Regulatory capture was seen as linked to inflation and economic stagnation, the dual concerns of the 1970s. The distortions and high prices that result from economic regulations were commonly cited as factors contributing to inflation. As the Nader study of the ICC explained: "Increasing inefficiency, increasing discrimination, misallocative transportation traffic between the modes, and an increasing misallocative effect directly upon the economy at large—all unquestionably have some impact on inflation. Since inflation may well turn out to be one of the most serious issues America will have to face in the twentieth century . . . transportation should be one of the first industries to be examined."[18] Similar connections were made regarding regulation in other sectors of the economy, the argument being that when prices for basic goods increased faster than the overall price level, they contributed to an inflationary trend. Reflecting these concerns, a number of agencies, including the Justice Department's Antitrust Division, the Office of Management and Budget, and the Council of Economic Advisers, began advocating deregulation. As the *Economic Report of the President* noted in 1975, deregulation "could save billions of dollars by releasing resources for other uses, helping combat inflation, and making the economy more efficient and more productive in future years."[19]

The costs of regulation—particularly the costs associated with the new social regulations in occupational health and environmental protection—were of great concern. Murray Weidenbaum attempted to estimate the costs of regulation, including both direct budgetary outlays and compliance costs. He noted that the administrative costs had increased dramatically during the 1970s, driven in part by the creation of new regulatory agencies. In 1974 the administrative costs were approximately $2.2 billion; by 1979 they had grown to $4.8 billion. In some years, their annual rate of growth was 22 percent, well above the infla-tion rate. Indeed, by 1979 there were approximately 215,000 federal employees working at the regulatory agencies. The increases in the regulatory budget were insignificant, however, when compared with the compliance costs and the overall costs borne by the economy. Wei-denbaum cited OSHA as an example. Whereas the agency had an an-nual budget of approximately $150 million, its regulations forced cor-porations to make capital outlays estimated at $3 billion per year. The aggregate effects of regulation were even more striking. Taking into ac-count a number of factors, including capital expenses, losses in effi-ciency, various economic distortions, and impediments to the rapid dif-fusion of technological innovations, Weidenbaum calculated that the direct and indirect costs of regulation had been $65 billion in 1976 and had increased above the $100-billion mark by the end of the de-cade. Because of the high cost of regulation, Weidenbaum urged policy-makers and analysts to assess the economic impact and justification of public policies.[20]

Weidenbaum's estimates were widely questioned, but Charles Noble is correct in saying that "the numbers were less important than the underlying ideas."[21] Because there was little doubt that regulations forced society to incur large costs, the key question was whether these costs were justified by the social benefits. Some critics of regulation—particularly economists, who claimed an ever-greater role in the policy debates—focused primarily on efficiency. When assessing regulation, they commonly asked whether it was compensating for some form of market failure. If the answer was negative, then they supported de-regulation. Even when markets could not be relied on, these critics still strongly supported a return to the market, given that the history of regu-lation was one of cartelization, barriers to entry, artificially high prices, and retarded innovation. These deleterious effects had to be weighed against any benefits resulting from regulation. Increasingly, economic critics of regulation demanded that a regulatory policy's net benefits be used to determine whether the policy was truly warranted. Even if the goals of the policy were praiseworthy, the costs might make an ongoing commitment to that policy prohibitively expensive, particularly in a period of declining growth rates, high inflation, and growing interna-tional economic competition.

Consumer advocates and representatives of public-interest groups tended to differentiate sharply between economic regulations and social ones. Many economic regulatory policies, they argued, could be elimi-nated as long as active enforcement of antitrust regulations was used to keep private restraints of trade from replacing the regulatory restraints. They thought, however, that although it was feasible and desirable to balance the costs and benefits of economic regulations, the same could not be said for social regulations, owing to the importance of the values being promoted and the difficulties of accurately monetizing the benefits (e.g., the value of a species, or of the prevention of a premature death). Despite these strong objections, however, cost-benefit analysis was in fact applied to social regulatory policies. As a result of a series of executive orders issued in the 1970s and 80s, all rules and regulations promulgated by executive-branch agencies were required to meet cost-benefit criteria before receiving the approval of the OMB. The lack of this clearance could stall the regulatory process indefinitely. These changes in procedures, well in place by the 1980s, were every bit as significant as those that defined the parameters of the regulatory regimes addressed earlier in this book.[22]

REGULATORY REFORM

Deregulation and regulatory reform occurred simultaneously and were linked to widespread concerns regarding the impact of regulation on economic performance. As noted above, the domestic policy agendas of the Nixon, Ford, Carter, and Reagan administrations were driven by those administrations' attempts to promote price stability and economic growth. Although there was little evidence to suggest that regulations were major contributors to the economic maladies of the period,[23] a series of presidents worked diligently to limit the "regulatory burden" by improving the management of the regulatory agencies and requiring that at an early stage in the policy process the agencies consider the economic impact of regulatory actions.

Regulatory Review in the Nixon and Ford Administrations

The regulatory reform movement had its origins in the Nixon presidency. In response to concerns over inflation, the administration made some modest efforts to impose executive review processes, thus providing a foundation on which subsequent administrations would build. Following the creation of the Environmental Protection Agency, the Nixon administration became increasingly concerned about the potential economic impact of environmental policy. The Department of Commerce had received from businesses numerous complaints about the large and uncertain costs of complying with the new environmental regulations. Moreover, the staff of the OMB was troubled by the potential budgetary implications of pivotal EPA programs. Through the activities of Secretary of Commerce Maurice Stans, OMB director George Schultz, and domestic policy aide John Erlichman, an interagency "quality of life" committee was established in June 1971 to study the need for regulatory review. In October 1971, Richard Nixon issued an executive order establishing the Quality of Life review process, centralized in the OMB.[24]

The Quality of Life review process required that an agency formulating a significant rule submit the proposed rule and analyses of it for OMB review thirty days prior to publishing a notice of rule-making proceedings in the *Federal Register*. These materials would then be open for examination by other agencies, whose written comments would be forwarded to the OMB and to the agency responsible for the proposed rule. Twenty days before the final rule was to be published, the issuing agency was required to submit to the OMB a copy of the final draft, and a summary of the public comments and the new issues raised during the rule-making process.[25] The review process was highly significant insofar as it gave the OMB a critical role in the review of regulations. However, the process relied on the agencies themselves to determine whether their regulations were "significant" and thus subject to OMB review. As a result, many agencies simply ignored the process. Moreover, the OMB's authority was limited by the fact that the agency retained final authority over the issuance of rules. The OMB could seek to shape the agency's decisions or to introduce additional facts, but it could not formally prohibit the promulgation of new rules. Finally, because of its origins, the review process focused almost exclusively on the EPA. Indeed, the conflicts between Secretary of Commerce Stans and EPA administrator Ruckelshaus, commonly over the relevance of economic factors in EPA standards, dominated the review process. Ultimately, Ruckelshaus made his continued service contingent on the president's willingness to give final authority over the EPA's rules to the administrator, rather than to the OMB or the Department of Commerce.[26]

Nixon's initiatives were expanded upon by Gerald Ford. In August 1974, as part of an attempt to promote price stability, Congress authorized the creation of a Council on Wage and Price Stability, in the Office of the President. The council had a dual mission: to monitor private-sector events affecting price stability, and to review government programs and determine their inflationary impact. Ford's Executive Order No. 11821 created the inflationary impact statement as a means of standardizing this review. In essence, the order required that executive-branch agencies certify that they had assessed the inflationary impact of major legislative proposals, regulations, and rules. Although the OMB sought to delegate review responsibilities to the agencies themselves, COWPS and the OMB shared responsibility for reviewing the statements, with council economists playing the major role with respect to regulations. The council's formal economic analyses of proposed rules were placed in the public record as part of the rule-making process. Pursuant to this executive order, the OMB circulated a memorandum specifying how to comply with the inflationary impact review. The OMB recommended a quantified comparison of the costs and benefits of any proposed regulation that would result in costs in excess of $100 million and/or have a specified effect on productivity, employment levels, energy consumption, or the supplies of important inputs to the production process.[27]

Although the executive review process may have increased regulators' recognition of costs and resulted in the elimination of regulatory proposals that could not be justified economically, the program was plagued by several problems. The first was that compliance was once again voluntary: COWPS had to rely on the agencies themselves to determine whether their activities met the OMB's criteria and were subject to review as part of the Inflationary Impact Statement Program. The second problem was that the quality of the analyses was at times quite limited. James C. Miller III, assistant director of the council, noted in a 1977 essay: "Altogether too many [impact statements] are unduly brief, fail to address the relevant issues, and contain grossly defective analysis . . . While some [agencies] have given [the program] strong support, others have been hostile to it or, at best, have viewed it as a necessary hurdle." Miller suggested that the resistance of agency attorneys and key constituencies had been critical in affecting the quality of the impact statements. However, the statements' quality was also affected by the third problem: the position of the impact statement in the regulatory process meant that impact analysis was not integrated into the decision-making process. Miller explained that the impact statements were "prepared after a proposal has been drawn up and thus the analyst's task becomes one of justifying the approach taken."[28]

The fourth problem was tied to COWPS's limited authority. Because the council lacked the formal power to reject regulations that failed to meet the cost-benefit test, its power was limited to that of persuasion. Indeed, in August 1976 the Department of Agriculture unilaterally refused to comply with the review process despite the costliness of USDA price supports.[29] In addition, because the review program had been established by executive order, it extended only to agencies within the executive branch, and the independent regulatory commissions were thus beyond its reach.

Regulatory Review in the Carter Administration

The Carter administration's regulatory review initiatives were a continuation of those of the Nixon and Ford administrations. The inflationary impact statement and COWPS remained in place, tainted by the history of the previous two years, during which they had been used, albeit unsuccessfully, to restrain the EPA. In January 1977, acting EPA administrator John Quarles announced that the agency would no longer comply with the review process or be bound by the OMB's directives. The OMB did not attempt to reassert its authority in this matter. However, the next few years brought a renewal of regulatory review, albeit within a new institutional context and with a new set of procedures. Perhaps because Carter was more sympathetic to regulation (particularly social regulation) than his predecessors, the reform initiatives gained greater legitimacy.

In January 1978, Carter established the Regulatory Analysis and Review Group. The group consisted of representatives of several executive agencies, including the Council of Economic Advisers; the OMB; the Departments of Agriculture, Commerce, Education, Energy, Health and Human Services, Housing and Urban Development, the Interior, Justice, Labor, Transportation, and the Treasury; and the EPA. Unlike COWPS, RARG was to engage in the oversight of a very limited number of select rules and regulations deemed to have a potentially significant impact on inflation (i.e., having an annual cost to industry of at least $100 million).[30] There were a number of sharp disagreements surrounding the creation of RARG. The EPA's Douglas Costle was concerned that RARG would focus on the EPA, much as its predecessor had, in hopes of reining in the agency. These fears were relieved when RARG was limited to reviewing annually no more than four rules per agency, and no more than ten to twenty rules in all. Similarly, there were concerns about the composition of RARG's executive committee, initially designed to represent major economic policy-making agencies such as the CEA and the OMB, and not the regulators. It was feared that a review group dominated by economists would place undue weight on the economic effects of social regulations. As a result, the executive committee was reshaped to provide greater balance between the CEA and OMB economists and representatives of the social regulatory agencies.[31]

Even more significant than the creation of RARG was Carter's Executive Order No. 12044, issued in March 1978. The order explained: "Regulations shall be as simple and clear as possible. They shall achieve legislative goals effectively and efficiently. They shall not impose unnecessary burdens on the economy, on individuals, on public or private organizations, or on State and local governments." Pursuant to these policy goals, the order established guidelines for the review of significant rules. Building on earlier efforts, Carter required agencies to accompany each major significant rule with a regulatory analysis containing a statement of the problem, a discussion of alternative responses, an analysis of the economic impact of each of the alternatives, and a detailed justification for the agency's decision. The executive order did not require cost-benefit analysis but required that options be compared on the basis of cost-effectiveness. Because cost-benefit analysis is one of the criteria used in deciding whether a policy is justified, the imposition of cost-benefit analysis is considered a threat. Cost-effectiveness analysis, in contrast, accepts the goals of the policy as justified. The objective is to determine the most efficient means to reach them.[32]

The executive order went beyond earlier efforts in that it established guidelines for the development of regulations and mandated the evaluation of existing regulations. Each agency was required to publish a semiannual agenda of regulations in the *Federal Register*. The agenda was to list the agency's proposed regulations, and the need for and the legal basis of the proposed actions. Agencies were required to give the public early and meaningful opportunities to participate in the development of new regulations. This was to be facilitated by publishing advance notice of proposed rule-making, publicizing and holding open hearings, and providing at least sixty days for public comment. Agency executives were required to approve each significant rule before its publication in the *Federal Register*, basing their decision on numerous criteria, including the consideration of multiple alternatives, the selection of the least burdensome alternative, and the development of an evaluation plan to assess the continued effectiveness of all new regulations.[33]

Executive Order No. 12044 required the review not only of proposed rules but also of existing regulations, and it mandated the periodic determination of whether the regulations were achieving the policy goals (i.e., simplicity, clarity, efficiency) established in the executive order. In deciding whether an existing regulation was to be reviewed, an agency had to consider a number of factors, including the need for the regulation; the type and number of complaints received by the agency; the compliance costs entailed by the regulation; the clarity of the regulation's language; the length of time since the last review; and the question of whether economic or technological changes had affected the need for the regulation. In each case, the review of existing regulations was to follow the procedure established for the review of proposed regulations, thus focusing attention on the question of cost-effectiveness.[34]

In July 1978, Carter called for a review of RARG. In October 1978, as a result of this review, he created the Regulatory Council. Unlike RARG, the council was composed of representatives of regulatory agencies, both executive and independent. In all, thirty-five agencies were represented. It was chaired by EPA administrator Douglas Costle and funded out of the EPA's budget. As George Eads and Michael Fix suggest, it "was seen as a counterweight to RARG and a regulator's lobby"—a body that represented the regulatory agencies rather than those within the administration who sought to limit the economic impact of regulatory policies. The Regulatory Council thus executed a different mandate then RARG did. Critics of regulation had often complained that the decentralization of regulatory agencies resulted in policies that were either redundant or in conflict. In the former instance, the costs of compliance were far greater than necessary because the regulated parties had to maintain relationships with multiple agencies; in the latter, compliance was impossible. The council was directed to prevent regulatory duplication by publishing semiannual regulatory calendars and by providing a context in which regulators could consider the need for, and the compatibility and cost-effectiveness of, their actions.[35]

The regulatory review process established by Carter suffered from a number of problems, some of which could have been anticipated given the experiences of the Ford administration. Notably, agencies were once again responsible for determining which of their proposed rules had a significant impact on the economy. In addition, RARG's impact was necessarily limited by its mandate and its lack of legal sanctions. As noted above, it was forced to concentrate its efforts on ten to twenty regulations per year, a number that seemed meager in light of the explosion of rules during the 1970s. Even when agencies were "RARGed," the group had no authority to force recalcitrant agencies to comply with its recommendations. Because the group's efforts were largely confined to the public-comment period, it could not even force change by delaying rulemaking. Moreover, a highly publicized controversy over OSHA's cotton dust standard led the president, under pressure from the AFL-CIO and prominent members of Congress, to reject RARG's recommendation and to side with OSHA. This incident reduced RARG's credibility and led agencies to suspect that Carter would not actively intervene in regulatory decision-making.[36]

Despite RARG's lack of formal powers, the regulatory review process was significant because it introduced new norms and criteria into the regulatory process. First, as in the previous administration, there was an explicit application of economic analysis to determine whether new regulations were justified. Susan and Martin Tolchin refer to RARG as "another turning point in presidential management of regulation," characterized by "the ascendancy of economists over lawyers." They continue: "Shaped by their own discipline, White House economists did not even bother to conceal their disdain for what they considered rigid, legalistic approaches adopted by many of the agencies, especially when they encountered opposition."[37] While economic criteria were employed in White House review processes, it is perhaps more significant that they were internalized in the agencies subject to review—a point that will be explored in greater detail below.

Second, the RARG review process laid the foundations for the activities of the Reagan administration with respect to both the growing role of executive review in the postcomment period and the expansion of the review process to rules already on the books. In an important decision, *Sierra Club v. Costle* (1981), the D.C. District Court of Appeals reaffirmed the president's authority to monitor the activities of executive-branch agencies to determine whether they are in keeping with the administration's policy. Moreover, it affirmed White House intervention during the postcomment period as exercised under the provisions of the guidelines used by the Carter administration.[38] Although Reagan's regulatory review activities were presented by contemporary critics as quite revolutionary, they were an extension or continuation of the approach established during the Carter administration and even earlier. It is to the activities of the Reagan and Bush administrations that we now turn our attention.

Regulatory Review in the Reagan and Bush Administrations

Ronald Reagan assumed the presidency with a firm commitment to reducing regulation. On the campaign trail, he freely linked regulation to the economic decline of the past decade. As he said in a 1980 speech, "When the real take-home pay of the average American worker is declining steadily and eight million Americans are out of work, we must carefully re-examine our regulatory structure to assess to what degree regulations have contributed to this situation."[39] David Stockman, Reagan's OMB director, made the connection more strikingly in his "Economic Dunkirk" memorandum, an early statement of the Reagan administration's economic policy. In this memo, he warned of "a ticking regulatory timebomb" and predicted that the regulations of the 1970s would "sweep through the industrial economy with near gale force" unless there was "a series of unilateral administrative actions to reduce the regulatory burden.[40] The administration promised regulatory relief and reform, expanding regulatory review and establishing stringent criteria for the justification of new policies.

In January 1981, Reagan created the Presidential Task Force on Regulatory Relief, chaired by Vice-President George Bush. The task force was charged with reviewing proposed rules and existing regulations to determine whether they yielded net social benefits. It was to recommend changes and compile a list of those regulations that were most burdensome for business. By means of an executive order, the president placed a freeze on pending executive-branch regulations and called on regulatory agencies to cease issuing final rules for the next sixty days as the task force examined the impact of the pending regulations. In the end, the vast majority of the regulations were put into effect. However, from January 1981 to August 1983, when the task force was disbanded, it identified 119 regulations for review. Of this number, 76 were revised or vacated.[41]

Less than a month after the creation of the Task Force on Regulatory Relief, Reagan issued Executive Order No. 12291, the centerpiece of the administration's regulatory reform effort. James C. Miller III, a member of the task force who had had extensive experience with the Inflationary Impact Statement Program during the Ford administration, shaped the Reagan executive order to remedy some of the chief defects of earlier approaches. The executive order proclaimed that "regulatory action shall not be taken unless the potential benefits to society for the regulation outweigh the potential costs to society." Pursuant to this policy, the executive order required that all executive-branch agencies prepare a regulatory impact analysis to accompany each major rule. (Major rules were defined much as they had been under Carter's Executive Order No. 12044.) However, the new executive order authorized the OMB to identify any rule as a major rule subject to review. An agency, unless it received an OMB waiver, was required to conduct a cost-benefit analysis to determine "the potential net benefits of [each major] rule, including an evaluation of effects that cannot be quantified in monetary terms." Sixty days before the publication of the proposed rule, the RIA was to be presented, along with the proposed rule-making package, to the OMB. A final RIA and a draft of the final rule were to be submitted thirty days before the publication of the final rule in the *Federal Register*. Murray Weidenbaum, then chairman of the Council of Economic Advisers, identified the significance of the cost-benefit requirement, noting, "No longer will we tolerate the view that economic issues are necessarily on a lower rung of the ethical ladder than some regulatory issues."[42]

As noted above, earlier review efforts had been plagued by a lack of enforcement powers. Executive Order No. 12291 addressed this problem by giving the OMB the power to delay the rule-making process. Upon filing the initial RIA, an agency could be forced to refrain from publishing the notice of proposed rule-making until the review and necessary consultation were completed. The order also forbade an agency's publishing a final RIA or rule before it had responded to the OMB's comments and amended the rule-making file accordingly. In essence, the agency could be prevented from proceeding until it had met the conditions established by the OMB. Any conflicts arising under the executive order would be referred to the task force. To strengthen agencies' review processes, the OMB released guidelines recommending that all costs and benefits be monetized and expressed in constant-dollar terms, and that agencies apply a 10-percent discount rate in their calculations. The OMB promptly made the new review procedures mandatory. In 1981, ninety-five regulations were returned by the OMB or with-drawn by the agencies under OMB pressure for failure to meet the criteria. An additional eighty-seven were returned or withdrawn the next year, and there were similar rates of rejection for the remainder of the Reagan presidency.[43]

The obligation to conduct an RIA and the technical demands of cost-benefit analysis often strained agencies' resources and forced a greater reliance on outside contractors. According to one estimate by Paul Port-ney, the costs paid to outside contractors could range from $100,000 to several million dollars, depending on the structure of the industry being regulated (i.e., the heterogeneity of the sector), the complexity of the regulation, and the kinds of primary research required to determine the magnitude of the benefits (these research costs can be particularly high in the case of various health regulations). Portney estimated that if the cost of the agency personnel required to conduct in-house analyses and to monitor analyses conducted outside the agency was included, the direct costs of conducting the regulatory analyses required under Execu-tive Order No. 12291 would be in the range of $17 million to $25 mil-lion per year.[44]

The cost of conducting the analyses was a heavy burden to agencies that were laboring under significant budget cuts. Between 1981 and 1984, agencies' budgets underwent a 14-percent reduction (in inflation-adjusted figures). The reductions were reflected, in part, in a reduction in the number of regulatory personnel. By 1984, the number of full-time positions in the major regulatory agencies had declined by 16 percent from the 1980 figure. This contrasts sharply with the changes in the regulatory work force during the 1970s. Between 1970 and 1975, the staffing at the major agencies had increased by 168 percent; when taken as a whole, the 1970s saw a 328-percent increase in the number of reg-ulators.[45] The combination of budget cuts and new procedural require-ments, it was feared, would greatly reduce the regulatory agencies' ability to regulate. Indeed, the annual number of new rules was about 25 percent less than it had been during the Carter administration. New rules tended to place a greater emphasis on compliance costs and on the use of market mechanisms rather than on the much-vilified "command and control" approaches to regulation.[46]

The executive review process quickly became embroiled in contro-versy. Although Executive Order No. 12291 conveyed the image of a highly rational regulatory review process predicated on the use of cost-benefit analysis, it gave the OMB a tremendous amount of discretion. The OMB had the power to classify any regulation as requiring an RIA or to waive the RIA requirement (as was commonly done for changes that weakened or eliminated existing regulations). Moreover, there were concerns that the OMB had become a de facto court of appeals for interests that had been unsuccessful at the agency level. Critics argued that White House directives to the OMB and ex parte communications from business groups were not placed in the public record despite the fact that they might have influenced regulatory clearance. In essence, these critics portrayed the review system as a means of circumventing the safeguards of the Administrative Procedure Act. The Reagan administration responded to these allegations on a number of occasions by asserting that the "factual materials" submitted to the OMB regarding proposed regulations were subsequently sent to the relevant agencies to be inserted into the record.[47]

After Reagan's reelection, the administration deemphasized regulatory reform. A series of scandals at the EPA and in the Department of the Interior made further regulatory change politically expensive. Moreover, by 1987 Congress was once again under unified Democratic control. Further reform initiatives effectively ceased for the remainder of the Reagan presidency. Despite George Bush's former service as head of the Task Force on Regulatory Relief, the Bush presidency was responsible for significant increases in regulation. By fiscal year 1991, the amount of money (adjusted for inflation) devoted to regulation was 22 percent greater than that spent in the last year of the Carter administration. President Bush supported no significant deregulatory legislation. Moreover, he did not veto or threaten to veto new regulatory legislation. As a result, major new initiatives such as the Clean Air Act of 1990, the Americans with Disabilities Act, and the Nutrition Labeling and Education Act were passed and signed into law, promising growing expenditures for regulation for decades to come.[48]

With respect to regulatory reform, the Bush administration encountered immediate difficulties when the appointee to the directorship of the OMB's Office of Information and Regulatory Affairs failed to survive the confirmation process. Following the failed confirmation, the office played a reduced role in regulatory review, and the gap left by the OMB was filled, in part, by the President's Council on Competitiveness, chaired by Vice-President Dan Quayle. The council actively promoted the use of cost-benefit analysis, pursuant to Reagan's Executive Order No. 12291. Moreover, a number of high-profile actions raised a great deal of concern about the council's role in regulatory politics. Rather than blocking new regulations, the council focused on promoting revisions that would make new regulations more cost-beneficial. Moreover, it promoted the streamlining of the regulatory process in some important instances (e.g., Food and Drug Administration drug approval) in hopes of reducing the costs of compliance. The growing activism of the President's Council on Competitiveness, when combined with a moratorium on new regulations announced in the 1992 State of the Union Address, suggested that President Bush had begun to follow more closely the path of his predecessor.[49]

DEREGULATION AND THE ADMINISTRATIVE RESPONSE TO REFORM

The reforms described above caused an increasing centralization of regulatory authority in the White House and the OMB. These changes were accompanied by deregulatory initiatives in the regulatory agencies and Congress. The executive review processes had an impact on the administration of policy and on the kinds of alternatives considered by regulators. Policy choices at the agency level stimulated, in many cases, a legislative response. Indeed, most of the significant deregulatory initiatives of the 1970s and 80s were preceded by policy innovations within the regulatory agencies.

As suggested earlier, agencies that found themselves subject to executive review commonly responded by creating their own professional policy analysis and evaluation offices in order to comply with the review requirements and develop independent data bases that could be used to counter the challenges posed by other agencies and interests. For example, during the Nixon administration EPA administrator Ruckelshaus created an Office of Policy and Evaluation as a result of his experiences with the Quality of Life review process. The EPA's proposals were commonly challenged by the Department of Commerce, which had an economics staff and access to industry data and analyses. As Alfred Marcus explains, Ruckelshaus "needed EPA economists to gather information and run a regulatory review process that would internalize the debate taking place outside the agency. By trying to internalize this debate, Ruckelshaus hoped to recapture the autonomy the EPA was losing to the White House and the Commerce Department."[50] The policy and evaluation office continued to expand during the 1970s.

The EPA was not alone. Indeed, during the 1970s most major regulatory agencies created or expanded policy and evaluation offices. The Justice Department's Antitrust Division created an Economic Policy Office in 1973, which grew in importance over the decade; and during the same period the Federal Trade Commission professionalized and expanded its Bureau of Economics and created an Office of Policy Planning and Evaluation and a number of planning and screening committees. Under the direction of Chairman Charles Ferris, the Federal Communication Commission's Office of Plans and Policy was expanded in the late 1970s and placed under the control of an economist. By 1979, all professional positions in the office were occupied by economists. The

Civil Aeronautics Board's Office of Economic Analysis was created in 1977, under the direction of Alfred Kahn. Staffed with highly qualified economists, it was given a broad mandate to oversee and identify problems in CAB policies and processes. At the same time, Daniel O'Neal, chairman of the Interstate Commerce Commission, created an Office of Policy and Analysis, staffed by economists and given an expansive mandate.[51]

Although there was an unmistakable trend toward the creation of policy offices staffed with economists, two points should be borne in mind. The first is that the regulatory reform efforts were not the only factors at work. As noted earlier, the policy debates of the late 1970s and the 1980s focused on the excesses of regulation and on the need to subject regulatory action to economic analysis. These debates undoubtedly forced some regulators to be more self-critical when examining their agencies' actions. Moreover, as shown in chapter 7, numerous court decisions forced agencies to be more sensitive to the economic effects of their decisions. Particularly in the independent agencies (those formally immune from executive orders), reform-minded executives made changes in their agencies' organizational structure to create the analytic capacity needed to redirect the policy process.

The second point to bear in mind is that some agencies did not undergo fundamental changes until the 1980s, when Reagan administration appointees pursued the president's reform agenda. Take the example of OSHA. The Occupational Safety and Health Act partially insulated OSHA's policies from economic review by establishing feasibility as the proper criterion for health regulations. Despite ongoing concerns about the costs of select OSHA policies, the agency's administrators resisted creating an economics staff during the 1970s. Instead, the agency hired outside contractors to do economic analysis. Although it had a Policy Office, OSHA did not hire full-time economists until 1979. It was Thorne Auchter, Reagan's appointee to OSHA, who ultimately forced change by incorporating cost-effectiveness and cost-benefit tests into the process for promulgating new standards.[52]

Regardless of their causes, economic professionalization and the growing reliance on planning and evaluation offices had important consequences. Most obviously, these changes promoted the application of economic analysis in the policy process. As suggested above, this was often a defensive measure. To avoid conflicts during executive review, agencies sought to consider the cost-benefit justification (or, where appropriate, the cost-effectiveness) of new rules and enforcement actions at an earlier stage in the policy process. On other occasions, reform-minded executives were concerned with the economic foundations of agencies' decisions and tried to introduce deregulation by administrative means. Fighting against well-entrenched programs, they looked to the agency economists as natural allies. Finally, in some instances economists gradually assumed a greater role in the policy process when attorneys realized the benefits of considering the economic dimensions of agencies' actions. As economists became more prominent in the activities of particular regulatory agencies, the executive review processes became redundant. The same analyses that would be conducted by the OMB as part of the review process were now being conducted quite early in the regulatory process.

The assertion that bureaucrats promoted deregulation seems, at first glance, to be counterintuitive. Bureaucrats have a reputation for vigorously protecting their organizational mandates and resources; and their activities are, in the words of William Niskanen, "budget-maximizing."[53] This characterization of bureaucratic behavior fails to take into account the power of disciplinary norms and ideas. Economists working within the agencies were familiar with the economic critique of regulation. Moreover, policies that prevented market competition and promoted high prices and inefficiency were antithetical to the norms of their profession. Thus, as economists gained a greater role within the agencies, their hostility toward many of the policies they were charged with implementing became evident, and they promoted deregulatory experimentation, especially when such experimentation was supported by sympathetic agency executives.

The reliance on economic analysis and the integration of economic criteria into the regulatory process naturally resulted in many innovations that had deregulatory effects. This occurred in three different ways. First, in some cases the growing reliance on economic analysis forced changes in an agency's enforcement actions. Regulations lacking economic rationale were simply left unenforced by economically minded regulatory staffs. Second, the application of economic approaches to the solution of implementation problems resulted in a number of significant administrative innovations. In these cases deregulation did not occur, but regulations were designed to promote greater efficiency and flexibility, removing some of the regulatory burden and reducing the economic impact of regulation. Third, economic analysis was used by regulatory staffs and reform-minded administrators to promote deregulation by administrative means. These initiatives provided the basis for deregulatory legislation that formalized the administrative changes and often went beyond what would have been possible in the absence of new statutory authority.

Antitrust policy provides the best example of the role that economic analysis can play in redefining enforcement actions without reference to an imposed reform agenda. In 1973, at the Justice Department's Antitrust Division, Assistant Attorney General Thomas Kauper created an economic policy office. Over the course of the next few years, the office was expanded and staffed with economists recruited from the nation's best economics programs. Economists were assigned to each investigation to work with attorneys in determining whether there was a sufficient basis for prosecutions. The growing judicial concern with the economic rationale for antitrust policy forced attorneys to be sensitive to the positions of the economists. In this capacity, economists routinely refused to support cases that they thought were lacking in economic merits, even if these cases could be prosecuted under existing precedents. As a result, the Antitrust Division's case load was redefined to focus almost exclusively on horizontal restraints (e.g., price-fixing), thus ending for all practical purposes many of the standards established under the antitrust laws. These changes occurred without the direction of Kauper's successors during the Carter administration, who continued to stress the importance of active enforcement. A similar sequence of events took place at the Federal Trade Commission, where the policy priorities as shown by the pattern of the commission's enforcement actions stood in stark contrast to the populist rhetoric of Michael Pertschuk, Carter's FTC Chairman and a strong consumer advocate.[54]

The changes in antitrust policy provide a first model of how economic analysis, once integrated into the policy process, can produce deregulatory results. A second model can be found in the activities of the EPA. During the second half of the 1970s, as noted in chapter 7, above, EPA administrators Train and Costle discovered that the air pollution deadlines were unachievable. In hopes of allowing for new industrial investment in nonattainment areas and continued improvement in air quality, the EPA began to experiment with a number of administrative innovations, including offsets, the bubble, and emissions banking. These innovations drew on economic arguments regarding the role of incentives in regulatory design. In essence, it was argued that a market for pollution would create incentives to reduce emissions where this could be done most cost-effectively, both within the firm and within the economy as a whole. Although certain corporations actively advocated the new position, there was much controversy surrounding the proposals. Ultimately, they gained support within the agency because they were promoted by economists and policy analysts in the EPA's policy office and the state agencies responsible for administering state implementation plans.[55] These innovations, which mark the ascendancy of economic norms within the environmental regulatory system, a system traditionally dominated by environmental scientists and advocacy groups, imply "that pollution decision-making is an economic problem to be worked out by business firms rather than a moral or political problem to be worked out by political institutions."[56]

The EPA innovations closely paralleled the other regulatory reform efforts of the period. They were designed to promote more efficient means of realizing regulatory objectives without questioning the status of the objectives themselves. Similar experimentation took place in other agencies, such as the Securities and Exchange Commission. The SEC progressively simplified and integrated its securities registration requirements in response to debates in the economics discipline regarding the economics of information. In essence, the simplification of regulatory requirements was justified on the basis of the "efficient market" hypothesis, which suggests that all relevant information about a corporation is reflected in the market prices of its existing securities. Market actors (especially large institutional investors) scrutinize all public information on a corporate issue and make their investment decisions on this basis. The disclosure requirements of the New Deal securities regulations were based on the desire to eliminate fraudulent securities issues and thus provide greater stability in investment finance. However, the economic arguments regarding market efficiency became ever more influential as SEC economists evaluated the performance of existing regulations. Similar considerations resulted in the elimination of fixed brokerage fees in the early 1970s and the introduction of competition in securities underwriting through simplified registration (i.e., shelf registration) a decade later.[57]

The activities at the Antitrust Division, the EPA, and the SEC were shaped, in large part, by agency economists. In the case of the Antitrust Division, economic criteria were integrated into the policy process; the changing mix of professional norms had an influence on enforcement decisions. In the case of the EPA as in the case of the SEC, bureaucrats appealed to contemporary economics debates when seeking to adjust regulations to meet new challenges. In each case, the staff of a highly professionalized agency applied its particular expertise to address important regulatory problems.

It is somewhat more challenging to explain the deregulatory legislation because of the diverse set of elected officials, interest groups, and institutions involved. During the late 1960s and the early 1970s, as noted in chapter 6, above, a number of new advocacy groups were formed. For reasons beyond the scope of this study, the consumer movement began to lose its force by the middle of the decade. Many consumer advocates supported deregulation, at least in its initial manifestation during the 1970s. But they no longer had as much political influence as they had had but a few years earlier.[58] Although it is true that business groups expanded and became more active, they were divided over deregulation when it was considered on a policy-by-policy basis. For obvious reasons, the regulated firms commonly opposed deregulation. As David Vogel correctly concludes, the deregulatory efforts of the period "meant neither a defeat for business nor a victory for consumer lobbyists: business was divided and consumer groups were largely indifferent."[59]

When examining the deregulatory legislation of the period, one must acknowledge the advocacy of key political entrepreneurs in Congress and the White House who were critical in shaping the policy agenda. Moreover, a number of well-publicized hearings provided a forum in which parties could address notable cases of regulatory failure and present the arguments for deregulation to a much wider audience. In many cases, however, elected officials supported deregulation because it seemed attractive, if somewhat ambiguous. Moreover, their initiatives commonly followed rather than led the activities within the regulatory agencies. Many of the basic deregulatory statutes accepted and extended the deregulatory actions introduced at the agency level. Perhaps no better examples exist than the deregulation of air and surface transportation.

As explained in chapter 5, the Civil Aeronautics Board was created as a result of the Civil Aeronautics Act of 1938. The act established a regulatory system largely analogous to that created for regulating surface transportation. Over time, CAB's regulations maintained airline profitability by establishing rates that bore little relationship to the underlying costs of service. Long flights were typically priced well in excess of the average cost of service, allowing carriers to use these excess profits to subsidize shorter runs. There could be little doubt that CAB had created and maintained significant barriers to entry into the industry. During the first forty years of the agency's existence, it had refused to allow new trunk airlines to enter, despite the incredible increases in air travel. Because it prohibited price competition between air carriers, they commonly tried to attract customers by offering more flights. As a consequence, air carriers functioned with much excess capacity. The increased costs led the carriers to request rate increases. The agency's regulation of airline transportation appeared to be an area ripe for deregulation.[60]

In 1975, the Senate Judiciary Committee began investigations into the deregulation of air transportation. The hearings, directed by Senator Edward Kennedy, publicized a significant amount of evidence against existing CAB regulations and revealed that deregulation had the support of a broad coalition, including some businesses and consumer groups and a number of government agencies, including the Council of Economic Advisers, the Council on Wage and Price Stability, the Department of Transportation, the Antitrust Division, and the Federal Trade

Commission. The attention focused on airline regulations led President Ford to recommend deregulatory legislation. Likewise, President Carter advocated airline deregulation both in his presidential campaign and after assuming office.[61]

Although the hearings facilitated the passage of major legislation, the activities at the agency level resulted in more immediate deregulatory efforts, which shaped the final legislation. In 1975, CAB economists conducted an agency self-study. The final report concluded that the agency should put an end to price regulation and eliminate barriers to entry and exit. In response, CAB initiated its own deregulatory actions in 1976, lowering barriers to entry and opening the door to price competition. In that year, it relaxed regulations on charter flights, thus allowing them to offer lower prices than established carriers. In 1977, responding to concerns about the new competition, CAB authorized established carriers to provide discount fares under a limited set of restrictions. In the next year, CAB continued its administrative deregulation of the industry by granting requests to award markets to multiple carriers at fares far below those charged by the established carriers. With the introduction of price competition and the reduction (and proposed elimination) of barriers to entry, major strides had been made toward deregulating the industry.[62]

Many of CAB's efforts toward deregulating the industry reflected the influence of Alfred Kahn, an academic economist and advocate of competitive deregulation appointed to be Carter's CAB chairman in 1977. Together with Elizabeth Bailey, another economist and Carter appointee, Kahn reorganized the agency. He created and staffed a new Office of Economic Analysis. This office provided a base for CAB economists who had been strong proponents of deregulation under previous administrations, and it increased the number of economists in the agency. Working with these economists and with a number of newly recruited bureau chiefs who shared the economists' commitment to deregulation, Kahn quickly eliminated most of the price and entry restrictions imposed on the airline industry. Indeed, within one year of his arrival nearly half of all coach-class passenger miles were being flown at discount rates. This had the immediate effect of increasing the number of passengers by 10 percent and almost doubling the industry's profitability within a single year.[63]

In October 1978, Congress passed the Airline Deregulation Act, essentially authorizing and extending CAB's deregulatory actions. Support for the legislation was strong, largely because of three factors: (1) the Kennedy hearings had popularized the critique of CAB regulations and promoted the formulation of a broad coalition; (2) Kahn had lobbied effectively on behalf of deregulation; and (3) the example of successful deregulatory actions at CAB had done much to limit the opposition to, and the uncertainly about, the effects of deregulation. The events at CAB played a critical role in shaping the legislation. The act authorized airlines to enter one new route per year until 1981, when CAB would cease to exercise control over entry. It also extended CAB's flexible approach to fares, eliminating fare regulations in 1982, and it eliminated CAB in 1984, transferring its duties to the Department of Transportation.[64]

Deregulatory activities at the Interstate Commerce Commission were even more striking than those at CAB.[65] Although administrative decisions initiated the deregulation of both trucking and railroads, trucking is more interesting because of the extraordinary activism of the ICC, and the motor carriers' strong opposition to deregulation. The Motor Carrier Act of 1935 had extended ICC regulations to trucking. Under the provisions of the act, the ICC issued operating licenses to motor carriers, creating significant barriers to entry. Carriers had to file proposed rate changes with the commission. If a proposed rate was protested by other carriers, the ICC investigated it and usually suspended it. Indeed, rates were essentially set by carriers in rate bureaus, functioning under an antitrust exemption granted in the Reed-Bulwinkle Act of 1948. The ICC's regulations dramatically increased motor carriers' rates, as well as their profits, forcing the economy to absorb billions of dollars of excess costs per year. Trucking regulation was difficult to justify. Given the structure of the industry (i.e., the lack of economies of scale and the large market), competition would, in the absence of regulation, maintain prices that reflected costs.[66] Although the costs and competitive restraints forced many to question the wisdom of regulation, regulation received the strong support of truckers and the Teamster's Union, thus making deregulation politically untouchable.

The ICC began deregulation in 1975, when it issued a rule forbidding rate bureaus to challenge the rate filings of their members, essentially allowing carriers to defect from the regulatory cartel. Six months later, the ICC expanded the commercial zones around major cities which fell outside the boundaries of ICC rate regulations. This act completely deregulated a significant portion of the previously regulated markets. Deregulation accelerated under the direction of Carter's ICC chairman Daniel O'Neal and three subsequent commission appointees, Thomas Trantum, Darius Gaskins, Jr., and Marcus Alexis. During the Carter administration, the ICC approved an increasing proportion of the applicants for new route authority. Moreover, the ICC continued to promote competition by expanding the zones exempt from regulation, allowing private carriers to engage in activities that had been regulated in the past, and deregulating all shipments being made under government contract. The ICC also reduced the barriers to entry by refusing to consider the effect of a new entrant on the business of existing carriers, and by ending the policy of requiring new carriers to prove that their services could not be provided by existing firms. The effects of the ICC's deregulatory initiatives were immediate and, quite predictably, raised concerns on the part of the trucking industry and the teamsters.[67]

Congress got involved in the movement toward motor carrier deregulation when Senator Kennedy's Antitrust and Monopoly Subcommittee held hearings in October 1977. As in the case of the airlines, the hearings allowed for a public discussion of the negative impact of regulation. However, motor carrier deregulation differed from airline deregulation in that Congress was forced to restrain the deregulatory actions of the regulators. In 1979 the chairman of the Senate Commerce Committee, Howard Cannon, instructed the ICC not to continue in its deregulatory efforts for fear that it could preempt the passage of deregulatory legislation. The Senate Appropriations Committee gave the ICC similar instructions. Finally, Congress passed the Motor Carriers Act of 1980, which authorized and extended many of the ICC initiatives. It reduced barriers to entry by allowing only the carriers authorized to provide a given service to raise objections to new firms' entry into the market for that service, and by forcing those who raised such objections to bear the burden of proof when protesting the authorization of new applicants. It also eliminated barriers to price-competition, loosened territorial and operating restrictions, and limited the antitrust exemption for collective rate-making.[68]

As these examples suggest, the agencies, once they had been professionalized and placed under the direction of reform-minded administrators, were responsible for significant deregulatory initiatives. My argument is neither that the professional economics staffs within the agencies were solely responsible for the changes in regulatory policy nor even that they were chiefly responsible, though in some instances (e.g., the case of antitrust) this was the case. Rather, the professionalization of the agencies created within them a crucial constituency for deregulation and reform, a constituency that facilitated policy change. The regulatory agencies, in short, developed in such a fashion as to have a distinct deregulatory bias.

The 1970s was a peculiar decade with respect to regulation. It began with a new wave of regulations based on the commitment to promoting public health, as well as on a strong suspicion that corporations, if left to their own devices, would adopt practices that threatened workers, consumers, and the environment. The initiatives of the societal regime quickly proved to be the most expensive regulations in U.S. history.

As the decade progressed, policy-makers' concern shifted from public health to compliance costs and the regulatory burden. Thus, the decade ended with regulatory reform and reversal. I have argued that during this period a new efficiency regime emerged. The administrative reforms of the 1970s and 80s were not driven by the desire to create neutral competence or to integrate interest groups more effectively into the regulatory process. Rather, reform consisted of a centralization of decision-making and the application of economic analysis as a means of determining whether regulations were justified in terms of their costs and benefits. Regulations were subjected to strict scrutiny because it was believed that market forces were sufficient to limit many of the problems addressed by regulation. There were new goals as well. The efficiency regime reflects an overwhelming concern with corporate efficiency and profitability, and it differs from the earlier regulatory regimes in that its popular roots are difficult to identify. Indeed, the initiatives addressed in this chapter appear to have their origins in elite politics and in institutional change.

The reforms and deregulatory initiatives of the late 1970s and the 1980s stimulated changes in the some of the social regulatory agencies. As noted earlier, the EPA responded to growing concerns about compliance costs by inaugurating incentive-based approaches to the implementation of the Clear Air Act. Innovations such as the bubble, the offset, and emissions banking were efforts to accommodate the critiques of "command and control" regulation. Improvements in macroeconomic performance or a reassertion of quality-of-life concerns may limit the vitality of the efficiency regime. Alternatively, the basic principles of this emerging regime may be incorporated into the regulatory system as a whole, fundamentally altering the goals of regulatory policies, the nature of regulatory politics, and the texture of state-corporate relations. To the extent that this takes place, the notion of an analytically distinct efficiency regime may prove superfluous. The basic principles of the new regime may become defining principles in all of the regulatory agencies, regardless of their origins.

Conclusion

THE HISTORY OF REGULATION IS THE HISTORY OF STATE-economy relations and institutional change. By using a regime framework and examining regulatory change over time, one can gain an appreciation for the continuity of goals and administrative models across regulatory policy areas. One can also identify the interpretations of regulatory policy that have prevailed at various times in the past hundred years. This historical knowledge is useful in understanding the sources of the contemporary policy debates. As noted in chapter 8, above, the regulatory debates of the 1970s and 80s have highlighted the costs of regulation and the effects of compliance on corporate profitability and competitiveness. Increasingly, it was assumed that the justification for a proposed or existing regulatory policy could be determined by examining its costs and benefits. This perspective on regulation and this concentration on economic performance are in many ways natural. The economic stagnation of the past two decades and the growing challenge posed by foreign-based competitors have introduced great uncertainty into the life of the nation.

A historical focus can also reveal the limitations of the contemporary portrayal of regulation. Compare the regulatory critique presented in chapter 8 with the debates about railroad regulation which took place in the first decade of this century. Speaking for the House Interstate Commerce Committee during the debates preceding the passage of the Hepburn Act in 1906, Congressman Charles Townsend situated railroad regulation in the following context: "When the railroads were assuming to say how the country was to be developed, what men should prosper, and who should fail, which cities should grow and which should not, then the people affected by such conditions—and who were not?—insisted that the servant should not be the master and that the Congress should pass a law to enforce their rights under the contract between the carriers and the public; the right to impartial treatment and to just and reasonable rates and regulations."[1] Townsend went on to present the proposed regulatory legislation as providing the basis for "an era of equal rights and opportunities under just and impartial law." He urged immediate passage, declaring: "Temporizing will bring nothing but disaster. Already we hear the rumbling of discontent, and socialism smiles in satisfaction with every delay. Regulation of a public servant is not a departure from the principles of popular government; but disregard of a righteous law and indifference to legal restrictions imposed to protect the people's rights are more than socialism—they are anarchy."[2] As Townsend's statements suggest, the legislative debates were not devoted to the technical features of the regulation of natural monopolies. To be certain, legislators debated the practical utility of various provisions and the specialized demands of implementation. However, there was also an acute recognition that the new policies would redefine the relationship between the national state and the economy and would affect the political and property rights of multiple parties.

One of the goals of this book has been to emphasize the economic, political, and intellectual forces that combined to shape major regulatory initiatives. The regulatory-regime framework has facilitated the realization of this goal. The history of regulation is, in many ways, a history of democratic politics. Unorganized citizens and a variety of social and economic groups mobilize in response to economic change. Their demands, once synthesized with political-economic and administrative reform doctrines, find an expression in the policies and institutions that constitute new regulatory regimes. As suggested above, the goals of regulation have changed significantly over time, reflecting differences in the economic context, the demands for change, and the dominant conceptions of the political economy. Thus, the Progressive Era's market regime was linked explicitly to the goal of revitalizing markets or compensating for their absence. For many of that regime's proponents, the goal was much simpler. They promoted regulation out of a desire for self-preservation and the security of the past. Corporations actively integrated formerly separate markets. They acquired or eliminated their rivals and exercised economic power on a scale previously unknown. Many advocates of regulation were simply seeking to defend themselves from the more threatening aspects of economic change and its political repercussions. One cannot ignore the economic rationale for the policies of the market regime, but markets had a significance that transcended their economic utility. Many interpreted the rise of the large-scale corporate economy as a threat to individual autonomy, political accountability, and a decentralized social structure. Regulation was one means of preserving many of the traditional values that were incompatible with the momentous economic-structural changes of the period.

The New Deal initiatives can also be presented in strictly economic terms. Rather than seeking a return to the market or the creation of marketlike outcomes, policy-makers promoted the goal of economic stability to prevent further deflation and unemployment. This often entailed using policies to render markets irrelevant. Once again, the events of the Great Depression and prevailing political-economic theories gave regulation broader significance. For all their virtues, markets placed certain groups at a permanent disadvantage. Farmers and laborers, for example, found it exceptionally difficult to maintain their incomes during the period owing to the surplus of labor and agricultural commodities, the sharp decline in aggregate demand, and the lack of effective organization. Regulatory policies allowed policy-makers to redistribute income toward the regulated, thus replacing a market-based distribution of wealth with a politically defined distribution of wealth. This system had another advantage. Integrating the regulated interests into the regulatory process by means of a system of government-supervised self-regulation could give these interests a greater role in defining the content of policy. Such an arrangement allowed economic interests to replace conflict and competition with a new cooperative ethos. Drawing on institutional economics and the New Nationalist strands of Progressive thought, policy-makers saw such efforts as contributing to a new economic order.

Almost four decades after the election of Franklin Roosevelt, the nation experienced another burst of regulatory policy-making. The new regulations, like the earlier ones, could be justified in narrowly economic terms. Environmental protection and occupational safety and health regulations can be interpreted as means of making corporations internalize those costs of production which they would otherwise thrust upon society. Rather than forcing workers to accept the risks of workplace exposure to toxic chemicals, policy required corporations to restrict workers' exposure and internalize the costs in the pricing mechanism. As suggested in chapter 6, however, the societal regime was more than an attempt to manage negative externalities. Its key initiatives expressed a new vision of the political economy, a vision that construed regulation as a means of forcing corporations to be accountable and compensating for the more oppressive aspects of the capitalist production process. Policy-makers and advocates of regulation combined economic justifications and political arguments. They derived regulatory policy initiatives from a larger political philosophy.

It is useful in regulatory studies to employ a wide lens, one that moves beyond the economic to focus on the political origins and aspirations of policy. It is particularly important if one is to arrive at a balanced assessment of policy. When evaluating public policies, one must consider a wide range of factors. Economic costs are unquestionably important. It is imperative to understand the costs of administration, the expenses incurred by the regulated, and the effects of policy on economic performance. However, an exclusive focus on the economic factors can be misleading. When analyzing regulatory policy, or any public policy, one must be concerned, above all, with the goals of policy both as articulated by policy-makers and as expressed in implementation actions. It may be the case, for example, that certain OSHA regulations carry significant costs and protect the health of a limited number of workers. However, OSHA did not design its regulations with the goal of maximizing net social benefits or enhancing economic efficiency. Rather, standards were created to force corporations to take responsibility for the welfare of workers. Policies are often demanded not because they are efficient but because inactivity would undermine important political values. To refuse to guarantee a safe workplace, for example, could impose costs that cannot be monetized but are nonetheless real. When regulation is viewed as a response to democratically articulated demands, the cost-benefit performance of specific policies becomes of secondary importance. Administrative and economic efficiency are of instrumental value. They allow the public to get more of what it values, be that environmental quality, workplace safety, or consumer protection.

The history of regulation reveals several patterns of state-economy relations. It also displays a record of institutional change. Policy-makers link administrative reform doctrines to policy initiatives in hopes of creating the administrative capacities needed to implement policy and meet the demands of mobilized interests. Although there were significant variations in the administrative doctrines integrated into each of the regulatory regimes, there has also been a significant degree of continuity. Progressive reformers promoted an expanded role for expert administrators as part of a broader program of advancing administrative neutrality and creating the capacity to address the complexities of regulatory policy. They justified these efforts, in part, through a belief in the separation of politics and administration and a new-found faith in the role of scientific and social-scientific knowledge in addressing problems of public policy. Administrative neutrality also held the promise of limiting the influence of the regulated. Members of Congress and a series of presidents supported independent regulatory commissions such as the Interstate Commerce Commission and the Federal Trade Commission, in part because they believed that these commissions would prove capable of withstanding the pressures of partisan politics and the demands of the regulated, and would have the procedural flexibility and technical competence to regulate effectively.

The New Deal reveals its continuity with the Progressive Era both in its faith in policy expertise and in its reliance on independent agencies. The two eras differed, however, with respect to the role of economic interests in the administrative process. In keeping with the associationalism of the 1920s, New Deal policy-makers sought to create quasi-corporatist arrangements as a basis for defining and administering regulatory policies. As explained in chapters 4 and 5, regulated interests were integrated into the policy process by means of a system of government-supervised self-regulation. Legislation delegated authority to the regulatory agencies, which, in turn, vested considerable authority in the regulated interests. Thus, regulators gave agricultural commodity groups, securities associations, and securities exchanges a central role in regulating their own affairs within a framework established by the agencies.

With the emergence of the societal regime, public-interest advocates and congressional policy entrepreneurs joined in creating some rather remarkable institutional innovations, many of which enhanced group participation in the policy process. Fearful of excessive delegation and the loss of control it entailed, they incorporated action-forcing provisions into regulatory legislation, and expanded access to the courts and the administrative process. Thus, legislation required extended rule-making processes or public funding for interveners. The expanded access to the courts provided an additional means of entering the policy process. Advocacy groups seeking to force agencies into action or to contest permissive regulatory standards used litigation-based strategies with ever-greater frequency during the 1970s and 80s. At the same time, the new regulatory focus forced an ever-greater reliance on scientific and social-scientific experts within the agencies. Complex regulatory problems such as workplace exposure to toxic chemicals and environmental degradation cannot be addressed without the necessary technical resources. Both the integration of analysis into the policy process and expanded opportunities for group participation limited the agencies' discretion.

During the 1970s and 80s, new initiatives increased the role of expert analysis and centralized regulatory review in agency evaluation offices and the Office of Management and Budget. Under the efficiency regime, new regulations were deemed appropriate only if they yielded net social benefits, as determined through the economic analysis of regulations. Although the new opportunities for group participation realized under the societal regime remained largely in place, the open administrative decision-making process discussed in chapter 6 faced a formidable barrier in the new review requirements. To be certain, agency compliance and OMB review has varied from agency to agency. However, many important agencies, such as the Environmental Protection Agency, have been forced to devote greater resources to addressing the costs and benefits of their actions. Because the new analytical requirements can effectively stop the regulatory process, the innovations of the efficiency regime may have effects that extend to the agencies established as part of earlier regimes. Carried to its logical conclusion, the application of cost-benefit methodologies could rationalize the actions of agencies in an otherwise fragmented and uncoordinated regulatory system.

As suggested throughout the later chapters of this book, the professionalization of regulatory agencies and the administrative reliance on social-scientific and scientific knowledge comprise a significant trend that is seen in all the regimes I have discussed here. The growing reliance on expert administrators is, in many respects, a positive trend, for it allows agencies to base regulatory rule-making on contemporary scientific research. This is a necessity given the focus of contemporary regulatory policies. Moreover, professionalization can enhance the capacity to plan and evaluate implementation actions. However, there is a negative side to agency professionalization. Regulatory complexity forces administrators to rely on highly professionalized scientific and social-scientific staffs. When these professionals bring their disciplinary norms and methodologies to bear on the policy process, they translate policy deliberations into a highly specialized language specific to their area of expertise, and the highly technical discourse surrounding many regulatory policies may make the debates impenetrable to those lacking the requisite training. Laymen and specialists from other professions may simply lack the expertise necessary to communicate in policy discourse. Complexity, in short, creates formidable barriers to participation in regulatory politics.[3]

Professionalization insulates both policies and agencies' decision-making from popular politics. It also enhances agencies' responsiveness to debates within the disciplines and within the specialized policy communities surrounding most policy arenas. The consensus within these communities regarding the justification for certain policies and enforcement priorities may have little relation to an agency's mandate or to the political consensus. Nevertheless, academic debates about the positive and negative aspects of a given policy may, through their influence on an agency's professional staffs, affect implementation. This may force a redefinition of an agency's priorities. In extreme cases, administrators may question whether sufficient justification exists for the continued implementation of the policy in question.

This was, of course, part of the explanation of regulatory reform and deregulation presented in chapter 8. The regulatory changes of the 1970s and 80s were driven, in large part, by an economic discourse that united agency economists, executive review offices, and businesses that were willing to fund supportive research and to appeal regulations that forced corporations to absorb large compliance costs. As economics-based review processes were put into place, the critical question was not whether a given regulation was supported by the public or whether it was a faithful interpretation of the enabling legislation. Rather, concern focused on whether the economic benefits exceeded the costs. A highly specialized discourse focusing narrowly on the economic effects of regulation was raised above competing discourses that may have been more directly related to the goals of the policies in question. The efficiency regime adopted as a fundamental principle the assertion that the justification of all regulatory activity must depend on that activity's economic impact, as determined by cost-benefit analysis. This single decision rule effectively limits the relevance of popular political demands. It also turns attention away from the public interest as assessed by the public, and focuses attention on the costs borne by the regulated interests.

The core assumption adopted in the efficiency regime's regulatory oversight is that regulations should not detract significantly from economic growth and corporate profitability. Given the regime's political-economic context and lack of popular origins, this should not be surprising. The core principals of the efficiency regime are being rapidly incorporated into all regulatory agencies and into the executive regulatory review process. Because it is far easier to calculate compliance costs than social benefits, the reliance on cost-benefit-based evaluation methodologies and the centralization of regulatory authority threaten to redefine the nature of regulatory politics. The evolution of regulatory institutions and the new focus of regulatory policy-making may, in the end, limit the impact of the popular forces that have played such a critical role in the history of regulation.

Notes

Introduction

1. This definition is drawn, in part, from James E. Anderson, *Public Policy-Making*, 3d ed. (New York: Holt, Rinehart & Winston, 1984), p. 3.

2. The term *regime* is used here, as it is commonly used in international relations, to describe a configuration of institutions and that allows for the resolution of conflicts among a number of parties. See the discussion of regimes and regime change in Stephen D. Krasner, "Structural Causes and Regime Consequences: Regimes as Intervening Variables," in *International Regimes*, ed. Stephen D. Krasner (Ithaca, N.Y.: Cornell University Press, 1983), pp. 1–5. For a recent application of a regime framework to regulatory policy, see Richard A. Harris and Sidney M. Milkis, *The Politics of Regulatory Change: A Tale of Two Agencies* (New York: Oxford University Press, 1989). Harris and Milkis provide a somewhat different definition of a regulatory regime: "a constellation of (1) new ideas justifying governmental control over business activity, (2) new institutions that structure regulatory politics, and (3) a new set of policies impinging on business" (p. 25).

1 A Regulatory-Regime Framework: Understanding Regulatory Change

1. See Michael Cohen, James March, and Johan Olsen, "A Garbage Can Model of Organizational Choice," *Administrative Science Quarterly* 17 (March 1972): 1–25; and John W. Kingdon, *Agendas, Alternatives, and Public Policies* (Glenview, Ill.: Scott, Foresman, 1984).

2. See the discussion of the role of state institutions in constraining policy options in Margaret Weir and Theda Skocpol, "State Structures and the Possibili-

ties for 'Keynesian' Responses to the Great Depression in Sweden, Britain, and the United States," in *Bringing the State Back In*, ed. Peter B. Evans, Dietrich Rueschemeyer, and Theda Skocpol (Cambridge: Cambridge University Press, 1985), pp. 107–63.

3. Throughout this book, regimes will be labeled to reflect a defining characteristic rather than the political period in question. This is done for two reasons. First, the regimes are embedded in institutions, and these outlive the periods of origin. Elements of the market regime, for example, continue to exist some seventy-five years after the end of the Progressive Era. Second, some periods (e.g., the late 1960s and the 1970s, which originated many social regulatory initiatives) simply lack useful labels.

4. See Donald R. Brand, *Corporatism and the Rule of Law: A Study of the National Recovery Administration* (Ithaca, N.Y.: Cornell University Press, 1988).

5. Dietrich Rueschemeyer and Peter B. Evans, "The State and Economic Transformation: Toward an Analysis of the Conditions Underlying Effective Intervention," in Evans, Rueschemeyer, and Skocpol, *Bringing the State Back In*, p. 52; and Stephen Skowronek, *Building a New American State: The Expansion of National Administrative Capacities, 1877–1920* (Cambridge: Cambridge University Press, 1982).

6. See George J. Stigler, "The Theory of Economic Regulation," *Bell Journal of Economics and Management Science* 2, no. 1 (1971): 3–21; and Richard A. Posner, "Theories of Economic Regulation," ibid. 5, no. 2 (1974): 337–52.

7. James G. March and Johan P. Olsen, *Rediscovering Institutions: The Organizational Basis of Politics* (New York: Free Press, 1989), pp. 160–61.

8. See Richard E. Neustadt, *Presidential Power: The Politics of Leadership from FDR to Carter* (New York: John Wiley & Sons, 1980); and Theodore Lowi, *The Personal President: Power Invested, Promise Unfulfilled* (Ithaca, N.Y.: Cornell University Press, 1985).

9. See Archibald Cox, *The Court and the Constitution* (Boston: Houghton Mifflin, 1987), pp. 117–44; and Lawrence Baum, *The Supreme Court*, 3d ed. (Washington, D.C.: Congressional Quarterly Press, 1989), p. 21.

10. See Robert A. Solo, *The Political Authority and the Market System* (Cincinnati: South-Western Publishing, 1974).

11. See Richard B. Stewart, "The Reformation of American Administrative Law," *Harvard Law Review* 88, no. 8 (1975): 1667–1813; and R. Shep Melnick, *Regulation and the Courts: The Case of the Clean Air Act* (Washington, D.C.: Brookings Institution, 1983).

12. Morris P. Fiorina, "Flagellating the Federal Bureaucracy," *Society* 20, no. 3 (1983): 66–74.

13. See Michael Pertschuk, *Revolt against Regulation: The Rise and Pause of the Consumer Movement* (Berkeley: University of California Press, 1982). Pertschuk discusses the mobilization of business in response to the activities of the Federal Trade Commission, and the congressional response to this mobilization.

14. See Elizabeth Sanders, "The Regulatory Surge of the 1970s in Historical Perspective," in *Public Regulation: New Perspectives on Institutions and Policies*, ed. Elizabeth E. Bailey (Cambridge: MIT Press, 1987). For a broad over-

view of the conflicts between distinct regional economies, and the effects of these conflicts on public policy, see Richard Franklin Bensel, *Sectionalism and American Political Development, 1880–1980* (Madison: University of Wisconsin Press, 1984).

15. See Eugene Nelson White, *The Regulation and Reform of the American Banking System, 1900–1929* (Princeton: Princeton University Press, 1983), chap. 1.

16. See Michael D. Reagan, *Regulation: The Politics of Policy* (Boston: Little, Brown, 1987), pp. 178–207.

17. Kenneth J. Meier, *Regulation: Politics, Bureaucracy, and Economics* (New York: St. Martin's Press, 1985), pp. 139–74; and Alfred A. Marcus, *The Adversary Economy: Business Responses to Changing Government Requirements* (Westport, Conn.: Quorum Books, 1984), p. 42.

18. James E. Anderson, *Public Policy-Making*, 3d ed. (New York: Holt, Rinehart & Winston, 1984), p. 3.

19. On the importance of bureaucratic expertise, see Francis E. Rourke, *Bureaucracy, Politics, and Public Policy* (Boston: Little, Brown, 1984).

20. William T. Gormley, Jr., *The Politics of Public Utility Regulation* (Pittsburgh: University of Pittsburgh Press, 1983), p. 29.

21. See Marc Allen Eisner, *Antitrust and the Triumph of Economics: Institutions, Expertise, and Policy Change* (Chapel Hill: University of North Carolina Press, 1991), for a discussion of the changes in antitrust policy stimulated by the adoption of new economic ideas.

22. See Marver Bernstein, *Regulating Business by Independent Commission* (Princeton: Princeton University Press, 1955).

23. For a discussion of intervener funding, see Barry B. Boyer, "Funding Public Participation in Agency Proceedings: The Federal Trade Commission Experience," *Georgetown Law Review* 70 (1981): 51–172.

24. A large literature has conceptualized the relationship through the application of agency theory. For a review, see Terry M. Moe, "The New Economics of Organization," *American Journal of Political Science* 28, no. 4 (1984): 739–77; and Tharáinn Eggertsson, *Economic Behavior and Institutions* (Cambridge: Cambridge University Press, 1990), pp. 39–55.

25. Stewart, "Reformation of American Administrative Law," p. 1676.

26. See Emmette S. Redford, *Democracy in the Administrative State* (New York: Oxford University Press, 1969).

27. See Barry R. Weingast and Mark J. Moran, "Bureaucratic Discretion or Congressional Control: Regulatory Policy Making by the Federal Trade Commission," *Journal of Political Economy* 91 (October 1983): 765–800; and Barry R. Weingast and Mark J. Moran, "The Myth of the Runaway Bureaucracy: The Case of the FTC," *Regulation* 6, no. 3 (1982): 22–28. For a critical assessment of this position, see Terry Moe, "An Assessment of the Positive Theory of Congressional Dominance," *Legislative Studies Quarterly* 12 (November 1987): 475–500. Moe departs from the political control thesis in his belief that legislators and bureaucrats show a great capacity for strategic behavior.

28. David Mayhew, *Congress: The Electoral Connection* (New Haven: Yale University Press, 1973).

29. See Morris S. Ogul, *Congress Oversees the Bureaucracy* (Pittsburgh: University of Pittsburgh Press, 1976).

30. Joel D. Aberbach, *Keeping a Watchful Eye: The Politics of Congressional Oversight* (Washington, D.C.: Brookings Institution, 1990), pp. 38, 41.

31. Ibid., p. 79.

32. Ibid., p. 81.

33. See Mathew D. McCubbins and Thomas Schwartz, "Congressional Oversight Overlooked: Police Patrols versus Fire Alarms," *American Journal of Political Science* 28, no. 1 (1984): 165–79.

34. James Willard Hurst, *Law and the Conditions of Freedom in the Nineteenth Century United States* (Madison: University of Wisconsin Press, 1956), p. 9.

35. Alexis de Tocqueville, *Democracy in America,* ed. Richard D. Heffner (New York: New American Library, 1956), p. 215.

36. See Jonathan R. T. Hughes, *The Governmental Habit: Economic Controls from Colonial Times to Present* (New York: Basic Books, 1977).

37. See Jack H. Knott and Gary J. Miller, *Reforming Bureaucracy: The Politics of Institutional Choice* (Englewood Cliffs, N.J.: Prentice-Hall, 1987).

38. See Hugh Heclo, "Issue Networks and the Executive Establishment," in *The New American Political System,* ed. Anthony King (Washington, D.C.: American Enterprise Institute, 1977); John Kingdon, *Agendas, Alternatives, and Public Policies* (Boston: Little, Brown, 1984); Paul A. Sabatier, "Knowledge, Policy-Oriented Learning, and Policy Change: An Advocacy Coalition Framework," *Knowledge: Creation, Diffusion, Utilization* 8, no. 4 (1987): 649–92; and Jeff Worsham, "The Political Economy of Financial Regulation: Subgovernments, Subtypes, and the Congressional Connection" (Ph.D diss., University of Wisconsin, Madison, 1991).

39. See Frederick C. Mosher, *Democracy in the Public Service* (New York: Oxford University Press, 1968).

40. Douglas Yates, *Bureaucratic Democracy: The Search for Democracy and Efficiency in American Government* (Cambridge: Harvard University Press, 1982), p. 72.

41. Figures taken from Kay Schlozman and John T. Tierney, *Organized Interests and American Democracy* (New York: Harper & Row, 1986), p. 67.

42. Robert Salisbury, "Interest Representation—The Dominance of Institutions," *American Political Science Review* 78, no. 1 (1984): 64–76.

43. This paragraph draws heavily on Schlozman and Tierney, *Organized Interests and American Democracy,* pp. 70–73. On this subject, see Claus Offe, "Two Logics of Collective Action," in *Disorganized Capitalism: Contemporary Transformation of Work and Politics,* ed. John Keane (Cambridge: MIT Press, 1985).

44. See Graham K. Wilson, *Business and Politics,* 2d ed. (Chatham, N.J.: Chatham House, 1990), pp. 39–66. Also see David Vogel, *Fluctuating Fortunes: The Political Power of Business in America* (New York: Basic Books, 1989), chap. 1.

45. Stephen Krasner, "Approaches to the State: Alternative Conceptions and Historical Dynamics," *Comparative Politics* 16 (January 1984): 225.

2   Progressivism and the Creation of National Regulatory Authority

1. Robert Higgs, *Crisis and Leviathan: Critical Episodes in the Growth of American Government* (New York: Oxford University Press, 1987), pp. 79–80.

2. See Alfred D. Chandler, Jr., "United States: Seedbed of Managerial Capitalism," in *Managerial Hierarchies: Comparative Perspectives on the Rise of the Modern Industrial Enterprise*, ed. Alfred D. Chandler, Jr., and Herman Daems (Cambridge: Harvard University Press, 1980).

3. See Thomas K. McCraw, "Rethinking the Trust Question," in *Regulation in Perspective: Historical Essays*, ed. Thomas K. McCraw (Cambridge: Harvard University Press, 1981), p. 32; and Lewis L. Gould, "The Progressive Era," in *The Progressive Era*, ed. Lewis L. Gould (Syracuse, N.Y.: Syracuse University Press, 1974), p. 2.

4. These figures are taken from Stanley Lebergott, *The Americans: An Economic Record* (New York: W. W. Norton, 1984), p. 340; and Richard Hofstadter, *The Age of Reform: From Bryan to F.D.R.* (New York: Random House, 1955), p. 174.

5. Higgs, *Crisis and Leviathan*, pp. 84–85.

6. See Jane Addams, *Twenty Years at Hull House* (New York: Macmillan, 1910).

7. Hofstadter, *Age of Reform*, pp. 174–86.

8. See Vincent P. Carosso, *Investment Banking in America: A History* (Cambridge: Harvard University Press, 1970), pp. 29–50, for a detailed discussion of the relationship between investment houses and the railroads.

9. Samuel P. Hays, *The Response to Industrialism, 1885–1914* (Chicago: University of Chicago Press, 1957), pp. 54–57.

10. Foster Rhea Dulles and Melvyn Dubofsky, *Labor in American History*, 4th ed. (Arlington Heights, Ill.: Harlan Davidson, 1984), pp. 121–41, 196.

11. Christopher L. Tomlins, *The State and the Unions: Labor Relations, Law, and the Organized Labor Movement in America, 1880–1960* (Cambridge: Cambridge University Press, 1985), pp. 60–95.

12. See Hays, *Response to Industrialism*, pp. 27–32. Also see Solon Buck, *The Granger Movement: A Study of Agricultural Organization and Its Political, Economic, and Social Manifestations, 1870–1880* (Cambridge: Harvard University Press, 1913); and John D. Hicks, *The Populist Revolt* (Lincoln: University of Nebraska Press, 1961).

13. Walter Dean Burnham, *Critical Elections and the Mainsprings of American Politics* (New York: W. W. Norton, 1965), pp. 71–90.

14. Hays, *Response to Industrialism*, pp. 58–63.

15. For a compelling discussion of this strand of Progressivism, see David B. Danbom, *The World of Hope: Progressives and the Struggle for an Ethical Public Life* (Philadelphia: Temple University Press, 1987).

16. See Stephen Skowronek, *Building a New American State: The Expansion of National Administrative Capacities, 1877–1920* (Cambridge: Cambridge University Press, 1982), pp. 168–69.

17. Higgs, *Crisis and Leviathan*, p. 115.

18. This paragraph draws on Stanley P. Caine, "The Origins of Progressiv-

ism," in Gould, *Progressive Era*. Also see Samuel P. Huntington, *American Politics: The Promise of Disharmony* (Cambridge: Harvard University Press, 1981).

19. Quoted in Richard T. Ely, *Ground under Our Feet* (New York: Macmillan, 1938), p. 135.

20. Caine, "Origins of Progressivism," p. 17.

21. Herbert Croly, *The Promise of American Life*, ed. Arthur M. Schlesinger, Jr. (Cambridge: Harvard University Press, 1965), p. 400.

22. "People's Platform of 1892," in *National Party Platforms, 1840–1960*, ed. Kirk H. Porter and Donald Bruce Johnson (Urbana: University of Illinois Press, 1961), p. 90.

23. *Wabash, St. Louis & Pacific Railway Co. v. Illinois*, 118 U.S. 557 (1886).

24. See Thurman W. Arnold, *The Folklore of Capitalism* (New Haven: Yale University Press, 1937), pp. 185–206.

25. *Congressional Record*, 51st Congress, 1st sess., March 21, 1890, 21:2457, reprinted in *The Legislative History of the Federal Antitrust Laws and Related Statutes*, ed. Earl W. Kintner (New York: Chelsea House, 1978), 1: 117.

26. Louis D. Brandeis, *Business—A Profession* (Boston: Small, Maynard, 1914), p. 260.

27. Theodore Roosevelt, "The Big Stick and the Square Deal," *The Progressives*, ed. Carl Resek (Indianapolis, Ind.: Bobbs-Merrill, 1967), p. 190.

28. Theodore Roosevelt, *The New Nationalism* (Englewood Cliffs, N.J.: Prentice-Hall, 1961), p. 24, emphasis added.

29. Ibid., p. 192.

30. "Progressive Party Platform of 1912," in Porter and Johnson, *National Party Platforms*, p. 178.

31. Woodrow Wilson, *The New Freedom: A Call for the Emancipation of the Generous Energies of a People* (New York: Doubleday, Page, 1913), p. 197.

32. Ibid., p. 202.

33. Ibid., p. 222.

34. See Gabriel Kolko, *The Triumph of Conservatism: A Reinterpretation of American History, 1900–1916* (New York: Free Press, 1963). Kolko argues, "National progressivism was able to short-circuit state progressivism, to hold nascent radicalism in check by feeding the illusions of its leaders—leaders who could not tell the difference between federal regulation *of* business and federal regulation *for* business" (p. 285). Also see James Weinstein, *The Corporate Ideal in the Liberal State, 1900–1918* (Boston: Beacon Press, 1968).

35. See the perceptive account of Progressive reforms in Leon Epstein, *Parties in the American Mold* (Madison: University of Wisconsin Press, 1987). Also see Walter Dean Burnham, "The Appearance and Disappearance of the American Voter," in *The Political Economy: Readings in the Politics and Economics of American Public Policy* (Armonk, N.Y.: M. E. Sharpe, 1984).

36. Frank J. Goodnow, *Politics and Administration* (New York: Macmillan, 1900), pp. 10–11.

37. Woodrow Wilson, "The Study of Administration," in *The Administrative Process and Democratic Theory*, ed. Louis C. Gawthrop (New York: Houghton Mifflin, 1970), pp. 79, 80.

38. Ibid., p. 84.

39. See R. Jeffrey Lustig, *Corporate Liberalism: The Origins of Modern American Political Theory, 1890–1920* (Berkeley: University of California Press, 1982), pp. 183–92; and David F. Noble, *America by Design: Science, Technology, and the Rise of Corporate Capitalism* (Oxford: Oxford University Press, 1977), chap. 10.

40. Jack H. Knott and Gary J. Miller, *Reforming Bureaucracy: The Politics of Structural Choice* (Englewood Cliffs, N.J.: Prentice-Hall, 1987), pp. 40–43.

41. See *Humphrey's Executor v. United States*, 295 U.S. 602 (1935).

42. Quoted in Marver H. Bernstein, *Regulating Business by Independent Commission* (Princeton: Princeton University Press, 1955), p. 38.

43. Skowronek, *Building a New American State*, chap. 2.

44. See the discussion of the state during this period in ibid., pp. 39–84.

45. See Murray Edelman, *The Symbolic Uses of Politics* (Urbana: University of Illinois Press, 1964), chap. 2.

3 Regulating Railroads and Corporate Conduct: The Political Economy of the Market Regime

1. See Robert E. Cushman, *The Independent Regulatory Commissions* (New York: Oxford University Press, 1941), pp. 61–62.

2. See the discussion in Marver H. Bernstein, *Regulating Business by Independent Commission* (Princeton: Princeton University Press, 1955), pp. 23–25.

3. Cushman, *Independent Regulatory Commissions*, p. 41. This section draws, in part, on Cushman's summary of the legislative debates.

4. See Gabriel Kolko, *Railroads and Regulation, 1877–1916* (New York: W. W. Norton, 1976), in which the railroads' position on national regulation is explored in some detail. See the Senate debates, reprinted in *The Economic Regulation of Business and Industry: A Legislative History of U.S. Regulatory Agencies*, ed. Bernard Schwartz (New York: Chelsea House, 1973), 1: 90–254.

5. *The Cullom Report, January 18, 1886*, in Schwartz, *Economic Regulation of Business and Industry*, 1: 86.

6. *Munn v. Illinois*, 94 U.S. 113 (1877).

7. *Wabash, St. Louis & Pacific Railway Co. v. Illinois*, 118 U.S. 557 (1886).

8. Competing explanations of the origins of railroad regulation can be found in Solon Buck, *The Granger Movement: A Study of Agricultural Organization and Its Political, Economic, and Social Manifestations, 1870–1880* (Cambridge: Harvard University Press, 1913), and Kolko, *Railroads and Regulation*.

9. Of course, the rational response to a prohibition of pooling would be consolidation. Railroads could merge to internalize the functions fulfilled by a pooling arrangement. Indeed, this was the eventual response. Railroad consolidation reduced the number of independent lines, thus eliminating competition in many regions.

10. See the account of Reagan's proposals and the discussion of how competing explanations are best reconciled in Stephen Skowronek, *Building a New American State: The Expansion of National Administrative Capacities, 1877–1920* (Cambridge: Cambridge University Press, 1982), pp. 138–50.

11. Ibid., pp. 138–39.

12. This rest of this section draws on a number of secondary sources, including Merle Fainsod, Lincoln Gordon, and Joseph C. Palamountain, Jr., *Government and the American Economy*, 3d ed. (New York: W. W. Norton, 1959); and Carl McFarland, *Judicial Control of the Federal Trade Commission and the Interstate Commerce Commission, 1920–1930* (Cambridge: Harvard University Press, 1933).

13. Figures from *Third Annual Report of the Interstate Commerce Commission* (Washington, D.C.: Government Printing Office, 1889), pp. 3–7, app. 1.

14. *Counselman v. Hitchcock*, 142 U.S. 547 (1892).

15. The rate-making process is described in great detail, along with the history of the commission's rate-making, in *Eleventh Annual Report of the Interstate Commerce Commission, December 6, 1897* (Washington, D.C.: Government Printing Office, 1897), pp. 9–37.

16. In *Cincinnati, New Orleans, and Texas Pacific Railway Co. v. Interstate Commerce Commission* 162 U.S. 184 (1896), the majority decision questioned, albeit in an obiter dictum, whether the Interstate Commerce Act conveyed rate-making powers. This question became central to the Court's decision in *Interstate Commerce Commission v. Cincinnati, New Orleans, and Texas Pacific Railway Co.*, 167 U.S. 479 (1897).

17. The Maximum Rate Case, reprinted in Schwartz, *Economic Regulation of Business and Industry*, 1: 580, 581.

18. *Eleventh Annual Report of the Interstate Commerce Commission*, p. 15.

19. *Texas and Pacific Railway Co. v. Interstate Commerce Commission*, 162 U.S. 197 (1896).

20. *Interstate Commerce Commission v. Alabama Midland Railway Co.*, 168 U.S. 144 (1897), reprinted in Schwartz, *Economic Regulation of Business and Industry*, 1: 587.

21. *Eleventh Annual Report of the Interstate Commerce Commission*, p. 42.

22. Quoted in ibid., pp. 50–51.

23. Ibid., p. 51.

24. In *United States v. Trans-Missouri Freight Association*, 166 U.S. 290 (1897), and *United States v. Joint Traffic Association*, 171 U.S. 505 (1898), the Supreme Court determined that traffic associations—the organizational response to the antipooling provision of the Interstate Commerce Act—were in violation of the Sherman Antitrust Act. As a response, railroads abandoned efforts to regulate rates and traffic via association and turned to corporate consolidation. The effects of industry competition made the ICC's lack of authority all the more distinct.

25. See Cushman, *Independent Regulatory Commissions*, p. 68.

26. *Northern Securities Co. v. United States*, 193 U.S. 197 (1904).

27. Theodore Roosevelt, "Annual Message, December 5, 1905," in Schwartz, *Economic Regulation of Business and Industry*, 1: 613.

28. Joshua Bernhardt, *The Interstate Commerce Commission: Its History, Activities, and Organization* (Baltimore: Johns Hopkins Press, 1923), pp. 20–21.

29. Ibid., pp. 26–28. After the passage of the Hepburn and Mann-Elkins acts, additional legislation continued to expand the ICC's jurisdiction and increase its duties. In 1911 Congress passed legislation increasing the commission's respon-

sibility in the enforcement of safety requirements. The next year, the Panama Canal Act required that the ICC enforce a provision prohibiting the joint ownership of railroads and of the competing ships using the canal. In 1913 Congress passed the Valuation Act, assigning the ICC the difficult task of determining the value of all railroad property in accordance with a rather complex set of procedures. Valuation was of critical importance, given the role of rate-making in establishing rates of return on railroad investment.

30. See Cushman, *Independent Regulatory Commissions*, p. 103; Bernhardt, *Interstate Commerce Commission*, pp. 27–28.

31. See Skowronek, *Building a New American State*, pp. 271–83.

32. Ibid.

33. Fainsod, Gordon, and Palamountain, *Government in the American Economy*, pp. 269–70.

34. See the discussion of the legislative debates in Hans Thorelli, *The Federal Antitrust Policy: The Origination of an American Tradition* (Baltimore: Johns Hopkins Press, 1954).

35. See Thomas K. McCraw, "Mercantilism and the Market: Antecedents of American Industrial Policy," in *The Politics of Industrial Policy*, ed. Claude E. Barfield and William A. Schambra (Washington, D.C.: American Enterprise Institute, 1986).

36. See *Standard Oil of New Jersey v. United States*, 221 U.S. 1 (1911).

37. See the discussion in Cushman, *Independent Regulatory Commissions*, pp. 179–81; and Marc Allen Eisner, *Antitrust and the Triumph of Economics* (Chapel Hill: University of North Carolina Press, 1991).

38. See the discussion of the Wilson-Roosevelt debates in John Morton Blum, *The Republican Roosevelt* (Cambridge: Harvard University Press, 1954). Also see Woodrow Wilson, *The New Freedom* (New York: Doubleday, Page, 1913).

39. Davies's account of his role in recommending new legislation and designing a new agency is reproduced in Cushman, *Independent Regulatory Commissions*, pp. 184–85.

40. Woodrow Wilson, "Special Message to Congress, January 20, 1914," in Schwartz, *Economic Regulation of Business and Industry*, 3: 1732.

41. Senate debates, 63d Congress, 2d sess., June 25–August 4, 1914, in Schwartz, *Economic Regulation of Business and Industry*, 3: 1765.

42. The debates are summarized in Cushman, *Independent Regulatory Commissions*, pp. 177–213.

43. Senate debates, 63d Congress, 2d sess., June 25–August 4, 1914, in Schwartz, *Economic Regulation of Business and Industry*, 3: 1765.

44. Ibid., p. 1765.

45. Ibid., pp. 1753, 1760.

46. Ibid., pp. 1774, 1769.

47. Ibid., pp. 1760, 1763.

48. Ibid., p. 1803.

49. Ibid., p. 1807.

50. *Annual Report of the Federal Trade Commission* (Washington, D.C.: Government Printing Office, 1916), p. 6.

51. The figures are compiled in *Annual Report of the Federal Trade Commission* (Washington, D.C.: Government Printing Office, 1926), pp. 25, 79.

52. *Annual Report of the Federal Trade Commission* (Washington, D.C.: Government Printing Office, 1922), p. 16.

53. Gerard C. Henderson, *The Federal Trade Commission: A Study in Administrative Law and Procedure* (New Haven: Yale University Press), pp. 332–37; Eisner, *Antitrust and the Triumph of Economics*, p. 60.

54. Stanley E. Boyle, "Economic Reports and the Federal Trade Commission: Fifty Years' Experience," *Federal Bar Journal* 24 (Fall 1964): 489–509.

55. The report is summarized in *Annual Report of the Federal Trade Commission* (Washington, D.C.: Government Printing Office, 1918), pp. 22–25.

56. See Cushman, *Independent Regulatory Commissions*, pp. 214–15; and Thomas C. Blaisdell, *The Federal Trade Commission: An Experiment in the Control of Business* (New York: Columbia University Press, 1932), pp. 186–87.

57. See Robert Solo, *The Political Authority and the Market System* (Cincinnati, Ohio: South-Western Publishing, 1974).

58. The history of decisions restricting the authority of the FTC is presented in greater detail in Eisner, *Antitrust and the Triumph of Economics*, pp. 59–75.

59. *Federal Trade Commission v. Gratz*, 253 U.S. 421, 427–28 (1920).

60. *Federal Trade Commission v. Western Meat Co.*, 272 U.S. 554 (1926); *Federal Trade Commission v. Eastman Kodak Co.*, 274 U.S. 619 (1927).

61. *Claire Furnace Co. v. Federal Trade Commission*, 285 F. 936 (D.C. Cir. 1923).

62. *Federal Trade Commission v. American Tobacco Co.*, 264 U.S. 298 (1924).

63. See the discussion in Blaisdell, *Federal Trade Commission*, pp. 37–74.

64. This discussion draws on Samuel P. Huntington, "The Marasmus of the ICC: The Commission, the Railroads, and the Public Interest," in *The Politics of American Economic Policy Making*, ed. Paul Peretz (Armonk, N.Y.: M. E. Sharpe, 1987), pp. 80–97.

65. Senate debates, 66th Congress, 2d sess., December 4–20, 1919, in Schwartz, *Economic Regulation of Business and Industry*, 3: 1600.

66. Huntington, "Marasmus of the ICC," p. 82.

67. Ibid., pp. 85–89. Also see the discussion of the ICC in Bernstein, *Regulating Business by Independent Commission*.

68. See *Annual Report of the Federal Trade Commission* (Washington, D.C.: Government Printing Office, 1930); and the discussion in Eisner, *Antitrust and the Triumph of Economics*, pp. 64–67.

69. See Mark J. Green, Beverly C. Moore, and Bruce Wasserstein, *The Closed Enterprise System* (New York: Grossman, 1972), p. 324; and William E. Kovacic, "The Federal Trade Commission and Congressional Oversight of Antitrust Enforcement: A Historical Perspective," in *Public Choice and Regulation: A View from Inside the Federal Trade Commission*, ed. Robert J. MacKay, James C. Miller III, and Bruce Yandle (Stanford, Calif.: Hoover Institution Press, 1987).

70. See Ellis W. Hawley, "Herbert Hoover, the Commerce Secretariat, and the Vision of an 'Associative State,' 1921–1928," *Journal of American History* 61 (June 1974): 116–40.

4   The New Deal: Relief, Recovery, and Regulatory Change

1. Figures taken from Susan Previant Lee and Peter Passell, *A New Economic View of American History* (New York: W. W. Norton, 1979), chap. 16; and Robert Higgs, *Crisis and Leviathan: Critical Episodes in the Growth of American Government* (New York: Oxford University Press, 1987), p. 161.

2. Lee and Passell, *New Economic View of American History*, pp. 363–64.

3. See Robert D. Cuff, *The War Industries Board: Business-Government Relations during World War I* (Baltimore: Johns Hopkins University Press, 1973).

4. See David F. Noble, *America by Design: Science, Technology, and the Rise of Corporate Capitalism* (New York: Oxford University Press, 1977), pp. 76–83; and Ellis W. Hawley, "Three Facets of Hoover Associationalism: Lumber, Aviation, and Movies, 1921–1930," in *Regulation in Perspective: Historical Essays*, ed. Thomas K. McCraw (Cambridge: Harvard University Press, 1981). For a discussion of the relationship between the 1920s and the New Deal, see Robert F. Himmelberg, *The Origins of the National Recovery Administration: Business, Government, and the Trade Association Issue, 1921–1933* (New York: Fordham University Press, 1976).

5. See Marc Allen Eisner, *Antitrust and the Triumph of Economics: Institutions, Expertise, and Policy Change* (Chapel Hill: University of North Carolina Press, 1991), pp. 64–66.

6. Higgs, *Crisis and Leviathan*, pp. 163–64.

7. William J. Barber, *From New Era to New Deal: Herbert Hoover, the Economists, and American Economic Policy, 1921–1933* (Cambridge: Cambridge University Press, 1985), pp. 104–45.

8. See Thomas Ferguson, "Industrial Conflict and the Coming of the New Deal: The Triumph of Multinational Liberalism in America," in *The Rise and Fall of the New Deal Order, 1930–1980*, ed. Steve Fraser and Gary Gerstle (Princeton: Princeton University Press, 1989).

9. Robert M. Collins, *The Business Response to Keynes, 1929–1964* (New York: Columbia University Press, 1981), pp. 23–28.

10. Barber, *From New Era to New Deal*, pp. 121–22.

11. Quoted in ibid., p. 122.

12. Kim McQuaid, *Big Business and Presidential Power: From FDR to Reagan* (New York: William Morrow, 1982), p. 24.

13. The seminal work on realignments is Walter Dean Burnham, *Critical Elections and the Mainsprings of American Politics* (New York: W .W. Norton, 1970). On the limitations of the notion of realignment and an alternative conceptualization, see Thomas Ferguson and Joel Rogers, *Right Turn: The Decline of the Democrats and the Future of American Politics* (New York: Hill & Wang, 1986).

14. See "Democratic Platform of 1932," in *National Party Platforms, 1840–1960*, comp. Kirk H. Porter and Donald Bruce Johnson (Urbana: University of Illinois Press, 1961), pp. 331–33.

15. Franklin D. Roosevelt, "Everyman Has a Right to Live," campaign speech delivered September 23, 1932, reprinted in *New Deal Thought*, ed. Howard Zinn (Indianapolis, Ind.: Bobbs-Merrill, 1966), pp. 49–50, 52.

16. Franklin D. Roosevelt, "Bold, Persistent Experimentation," campaign Speech delivered May 22, 1932, reprinted in Zinn, *New Deal Thought*, p. 81.

17. Rexford G. Tugwell, *In Search of Roosevelt* (Cambridge: Harvard University Press, 1972), pp. 116–17.

18. Raymond Moley, *After Seven Years* (New York: Harper & Row, 1939), pp. 189–90.

19. Tugwell, *In Search of Roosevelt*, pp. 281, 282.

20. Higgs, *Crisis and Leviathan*, pp. 172–73.

21. This is the argument made in Ellis W. Hawley, *The New Deal and the Problem of Monopoly: A Study in Economic Ambivalence* (Princeton: Princeton University Press, 1966). For a competing argument, see Donald R. Brand, *Corporatism and the Rule of Law: A Study of the National Recovery Administration* (Ithaca, N.Y.: Cornell University Press, 1988). Brand presents the New Deal as a relatively coherent corporatist experiment.

22. Felix Frankfurter's draft of the 1936 Democratic party platform, reprinted in *Roosevelt and Frankfurter: Their Correspondence, 1928–1945*, annotated by Max Freedman (Boston: Little, Brown, 1967), pp. 351–52.

23. Rexford G. Tugwell, *The Battle for Democracy* (New York: Columbia University Press, 1935), p. 94.

24. Ibid., p. 259.

25. Rexford G. Tugwell, Thomas Munro, and Roy E. Stryker, *American Economic Life and the Means of Improvement*, 3d ed. (New York: Harcourt, Brace, 1930), pp. 387, 388.

26. Ibid., p. 726.

27. Rexford G. Tugwell and Howard C. Hill, *Our Economic Society and Its Problems: A Study of American Levels of Living and How to Improve Them* (New York: Harcourt, Brace, 1934), p. 544.

28. Ibid., p. 499.

29. See ibid., pp. 497–544; and more generally, Rexford G. Tugwell, *The Industrial Discipline and the Governmental Arts* (New York: Columbia University Press, 1933).

30. James M. Landis, *The Administrative Process* (New Haven: Yale University Press, 1938), p. 24.

31. This is a tremendous simplification of the complicated discussions leading up to the passage of the National Industrial Recovery Act. For a more complete exploration, see Himmelberg, *Origins of the National Recovery Administration*, pp. 181–212.

32. "Statement by the President of the United States of America Outlining Policies of the National Recovery Administration, June 16, 1933," in Hugh S. Johnson, *The Blue Eagle from Egg to Earth* (New York: Doubleday, Doran, 1935), pp. 440, 441.

33. Hawley, *New Deal and the Problem of Monopoly*, p. 33.

34. See Brand, *Corporatism and the Rule of Law*, pp. 90–91.

35. Quoted in Foster Rhea Dulles and Melvyn Dubofsky, *Labor in America: A History*, 4th ed. (Arlington Heights, Ill.: Harlan Davidson, 1984), p. 258.

36. Ibid., p. 259.

37. Quoted in Collins, *Business Response to Keynes*, p. 29.

38. Ibid., p. 30.

39. See McQuaid, *Big Business and Presidential Power*, pp. 29–34; Collins, *Business Response to Keynes*, pp. 57–58; and Hawley, *New Deal and the Problem of Monopoly*, pp. 61–62.

40. Higgs, *Crisis and Leviathan*, p. 180.

41. Otis L. Graham, Jr., *Toward a Planned Economy: From Roosevelt to Nixon* (New York: Oxford University Press, 1976), p. 30.

42. Quoted in Merle Fainsod, Lincoln Gordon, and Joseph C. Palamountain, Jr., *Government in the American Economy*, 3d ed. (New York: W. W. Norton, 1959), p. 537.

43. See Gerald Swope, "Planning and Economic Organization," *Proceedings of the Academy of Political Science* 15, no. 4 (1934): 452–57.

44. Anthony J. Badger, *The New Deal: The Depression Years, 1933–1940* (New York: Hill & Wang, 1989), pp. 88–92.

45. *Schechter v. United States*, 295 U.S. 495 (1935).

46. Eisner, *Antitrust and the Triumph of Economics*, pp. 76–83.

47. See William E. Leuchtenburg, *Franklin D. Roosevelt and the New Deal, 1932–1940* (New York: Harper & Row, 1963), pp. 84–90.

5   Regulating Land, Labor, and Capital: The Political Economy of the Associational Regime

1. Ellis W. Hawley, *The New Deal and the Problem of Monopoly: A Study in Economic Ambivalence* (Princeton: Princeton University Press, 1966), p. 189.

2. Merle Fainsod, Lincoln Gordon, and Joseph C. Palamountain, Jr., *Government and the American Economy*, 3d ed. (New York: W. W. Norton, 1959), chap. 6.

3. See Richard S. Kirkendall, "The New Deal and Agriculture," in *The New Deal: The National Level*, ed. John Braeman, Robert H. Bremner, and David Brody (Columbus: Ohio State University Press, 1975), 1: 85.

4. Ibid.

5. See the discussion in Anthony J. Badger, *The New Deal: The Depression Years, 1933–1940* (New York: Hill & Wang, 1989), pp. 157–58. See the discussion of the American Farm Bureau Federation in Luther Tweeten, *The Foundations of Farm Policy* (Lincoln: University of Nebraska Press, 1979). For a clear discussion of agricultural interests' role in the regulatory subsystem, see Kenneth J. Meier, *Regulation: Politics, Bureaucracy, and Economics* (New York: St. Martin's Press, 1985), chap. 5.

6. Badger, *New Deal*, pp. 49–52.

7. Kirkendall, "New Deal and Agriculture," p. 88.

8. See William E. Leuchtenburg, *Franklin D. Roosevelt and the New Deal, 1932–1940* (New York: Harper & Row, 1963), pp. 49–52, 75–76. Also see the discussion in Theda Skocpol and Kenneth Finegold, "State Capacity and Economic Intervention in the Early New Deal," *Political Science Quarterly* 97, no. 2 (1982): 255–78.

9. Badger, *New Deal*, p. 159.

10. See Leuchtenburg, *Franklin D. Roosevelt and the New Deal*, pp. 75–76;

and Albert U. Romasco, *The Politics of Recovery: Roosevelt's New Deal* (New York: Oxford University Press, 1983), pp. 165–67.

11. Fainsod, Gordon, and Palamountain, *Government and the American Economy*, p. 135.

12. *United States v. Butler*, 297 U.S. 1 (1936).

13. Romasco, *Politics of Recovery*, pp. 173–74.

14. Fainsod, Gordon, and Palamountain, *Government and the American Economy*, pp. 136–38.

15. See Meier, *Regulation*, p. 130.

16. See the discussion of the USDA in ibid., pp. 123–26.

17. See Skocpol and Finegold, "State Capacity and Economic Intervention in the Early New Deal," for a similar interpretation of agricultural regulation.

18. Charles L. Schultze, *The Distribution of Farm Subsidies: Who Gets the Benefits?* (Washington, D.C.: Brookings Institution, 1971), p. 29.

19. Foster Rhea Dulles and Melvyn Dubofsky, *Labor in America: A History*, 4th ed. (Arlington Heights, Ill.: Harlan-Davidson, 1984), pp. 241–42, 253–54.

20. Christopher L. Tomlins, *The State and the Unions: Labor Relations, Law, and the Organized Labor Movement in America, 1880–1960* (Cambridge: Cambridge University Press, 1985), pp. 105–7.

21. Hawley, *New Deal and the Problem of Monopoly*, pp. 75–79, 89–90.

22. Tomlins, *State and the Unions*, pp. 109–14.

23. See Donald R. Brand, *Corporatism and the Rule of Law: A Study of the National Recovery Administration* (Ithaca, N.Y.: Cornell University Press, 1988), pp. 243–54.

24. Dulles and Dubofsky, *Labor in America*, pp. 262–63.

25. Brand, *Corporatism and the Rule of Law*, pp. 243–54.

26. *Schechter v. United States*, 295 U.S. 495 (1935).

27. See Fainsod, Gordon, and Palamountain, *Government and the American Economy*, pp. 190–91.

28. Peter H. Irons, *The New Deal Lawyers* (Princeton: Princeton University Press, 1982), p. 236.

29. Ibid., pp. 237–40; and J. Warren Madden, "The Birth of the Board," in *The Wagner Act after Ten Years*, ed. Louis G. Silverberg (Washington, D.C.: Bureau of National Affairs, 1945).

30. James A. Gross, *The Making of the National Labor Relations Board: A Study in Economics, Politics, and the Law* (Albany: State University of New York Press, 1974), pp. 159–67, 234–36.

31. Tomlins, *State and the Unions*, p. 154.

32. "House Commerce Committee Minority Report," in *The Economic Regulation of Business and Industry: A Legislative History of U.S. Regulatory Agencies*, ed. Bernard Schwartz (New York: Chelsea House, 1973), 4: 2969.

33. See Terry M. Moe, "Interests, Institutions, and Positive Theory: The Politics of the NLRB," *Studies in American Political Development* 2 (1987): 236–99.

34. *National Labor Relations Board v. Jones and Laughlin Steel Corp.*, 301 U.S. 1 (1937).

35. Tomlins, *State and the Unions*, p. 156.

36. Dulles and Dubofsky, *Labor in America*, p. 288; Tomlins, *State and the Unions*, p. 148.

37. Badger, *New Deal*, pp. 118–19.

38. Robert Sobel, *Inside Wall Street: Continuity and Change in the Financial District* (New York: W. W. Norton, 1982), pp. 102–6, 194–95; and Susan Previant Lee and Peter Passell, *A New Economic View of American History* (New York: W. W. Norton, 1979), pp. 363–68.

39. Joel Seligman, *The Transformation of Wall Street: A History of the Securities and Exchange Commission and Modern Corporate Finance* (Boston: Houghton Mifflin, 1982), pp. 1–11.

40. Lee and Passell, *New Economic View of American History*, p. 369.

41. William J. Shultz and M. R. Caine, *Financial Development of the United States* (New York: Prentice-Hall, 1937), pp. 646–47, 667–70.

42. See Seligman, *Transformation of Wall Street*, pp. 20–38; and Vincent P. Carosso, *Investment Banking in America: A History* (Cambridge: Harvard University Press, 1970), pp. 332–51.

43. John E. Owens, "The State Regulation and Deregulation of Financial Institutions and Services in the United States," in *The State, Finance, and Industry*, ed. Andrew Cox (New York: St. Martin's Press, 1986), pp. 172–77. See Helen M. Burns, *The American Banking Community and New Deal Banking Reforms, 1933–1935* (Westport, Conn.: Greenwood Press, 1974).

44. See Seligman, *Transformation of Wall Street*, pp. 70–71.

45. Ibid., p. 76.

46. Ralph F. De Bedts, *The New Deal's SEC: The Formative Years* (New York: Columbia University Press, 1964), pp. 56–66.

47. Ibid., pp. 73–85; Carosso, *Investment Banking in America*, pp. 375–79. See the discussion of the legislative debates in Robert E. Cushman, *The Independent Regulatory Commissions* (New York: Oxford University Press, 1941), pp. 341–45.

48. Louis D. Brandeis, *Other People's Money* (New York: Frederick A. Stokes, 1914).

49. William O. Douglas, "Protecting the Investor," *Yale Review* 23 (Spring 1934): 523.

50. The following discussion draws, in part, on Thomas K. McCraw, "With the Consent of the Governed: SEC's Formative Years," *Journal of Policy Analysis and Management* 1, no. 3 (1982): 346–70.

51. De Bedts, *New Deal's SEC*, pp. 144–50.

52. Quoted in Thomas K. McCraw, *Prophets of Regulation* (Cambridge: Harvard University Press, 1984), p. 192.

53. Ibid.

54. De Bedts, *New Deal's SEC*, pp. 149–50.

55. Quoted in ibid., p. 163.

56. Carosso, *Investment Banking in America*, p. 409; Seligman, *Transformation of Wall Street*, pp. 167–74.

57. Michael E. Parrish, *Securities Regulation and the New Deal* (New Ha-

ven: Yale University Press, 1970), pp. 216–19; McCraw, *Prophets of Regulation*, pp. 195–96; De Bedts, *New Deal's SEC*, pp. 163–66; Seligman, *Transformation of Wall Street*, pp. 164–67.

58. A 1936 amendment to the Securities Exchange Act required that brokers and dealers not associated with the exchanges register with the SEC or lose their use of interstate communications and transportation to execute their transactions. Carosso, *Investment Banking in America*, pp. 385–91; Parrish, *Securities Regulation and the New Deal*, pp. 214–16.

59. Quoted in Parrish, *Securities Regulation and the New Deal*, p. 214.

60. Quoted in Seligman, *Transformation of Wall Street*, p. 186.

61. Willard E. Atkins, George W. Edwards, and Harold G. Moulton, *The Regulation of the Securities Markets* (Washington, D.C.: Brookings Institution, 1946), pp. 72–73.

62. McCraw, "With the Consent of the Governed," p. 359.

63. See Seligman, *Transformation of Wall Street*, pp. 123–38; Carosso, *Investment Banking in America*, pp. 295–99.

64. Hawley, *New Deal and the Problem of Monopoly*, pp. 330, 332; De Bedts, *New Deal's SEC*, pp. 112–26.

65. Atkins, Edwards, and Moulton, *Regulation of Securities Markets*, pp. 75–83; Hawley, *New Deal and the Problem of Monopoly*, pp. 232–36; De Bedts, *New Deal's SEC*, pp. 126–43.

66. *Electric Bond and Share Co. v. Securities and Exchange Commission*, 303 U.S. 419 (1938).

67. See De Bedts, *New Deal's SEC*, pp. 173–83.

68. Seligman, *Transformation of Wall Street*, p. 247; see also pp. 247–67.

69. On the regulation of the airlines industry and the history of the Civil Aeronautics Board, see Emmette S. Redford, *The Regulatory Process* (Austin: University of Texas Press, 1969).

70. Cushman, *Independent Regulatory Commissions*, pp. 389–91.

71. Ibid., pp. 391–401.

72. Hawley, *New Deal and the Problem of Monopoly*, pp. 243–44.

73. "Lea Report on the Civil Aeronautics Bill," April 28, 1938, in Schwartz, *Economic Regulation of Business and Industry*, 4: 3066.

74. See the Civil Aeronautics Act of 1938, in Schwartz, *Economic Regulation of Business and Industry*, 4: 2987–3061.

75. Civil Aeronautics Authority, *Annual Report* (Washington, D.C.: Government Printing Office, 1939), p. 2.

76. Daniel P. Kaplan, "The Changing Airline Industry," in *Regulatory Reform: What Actually Happened?* ed. Leonard W. Weiss and Michael K. Glass (Boston: Little, Brown, 1986), pp. 41–42.

6   Compensating for Capitalism: The New Social Regulation

1. Alfred A. Marcus, *The Adversary Economy* (Westport, Conn.: Quorum Books, 1984), pp. 39–43.

2. Figures taken from David Vogel, "The 'New' Social Regulation in Historical and Comparative Perspective," in *Regulation in Perspective: Historical*

Essays, ed. Thomas K. McCraw (Cambridge: Harvard University Press, 1981), p. 162.

3. See the argument presented in Richard A. Harris and Sidney M. Milkis, *The Politics of Regulatory Change: A Tale of Two Agencies* (New York: Oxford University Press, 1989).

4. See Marver H. Bernstein, *Regulating Business by Independent Commission* (Princeton: Princeton University Press, 1955); and Samuel P. Huntington, "The Marasmus of the ICC," *Yale Law Journal* 61 (April 1952): 467–509.

5. See James Q. Wilson, *Political Organizations* (New York: Basic Books, 1973).

6. See David Vogel, *Fluctuating Fortunes: The Political Power of Business in America* (New York: Basic Books, 1989), pp. 38–42.

7. On the emergence of postmaterialist values, see Ronald Inglehart, *The Silent Revolution: Changing Values and Political Styles among Western Publics* (Princeton: Princeton University Press, 1977).

8. Kay Lehman Schlozman and John T. Tierney, *Organized Interests in American Democracy* (New York: Harper & Row, 1986), p. 76.

9. Information on dates of founding is from Foundation for Public Affairs, *Public Interest Profiles, 1988–1989* (Washington, D.C.: Congressional Quarterly Press, 1988).

10. See Jeffrey M. Berry, *The Interest Group Society* (Boston: Little, Brown, 1984), pp. 16–45.

11. See Harris and Milkis, *Politics of Regulatory Change*, pp. 62–75. For an earlier statement of this position, see Richard A. Harris, *Coal Firms under the New Social Regulation* (Durham, N.C.: Duke University Press, 1985).

12. G. William Domhoff, *Who Rules America?* (Englewood Cliffs, N.J.: Prentice-Hall, 1967), p. 5. See C. Wright Mills, *The Power Elite* (New York: Oxford University Press, 1956), for an earlier statement of this position.

13. G. William Domhoff, *The Higher Circles: The Governing Class in America* (New York: Random House, 1970), p. 250.

14. See Herbert Marcuse, *One Dimensional Man: Studies in the Ideology of Advanced Industrial Society* (Boston: Beacon Press, 1964).

15. Charles A. Reich, *The Greening of America* (New York: Random House, 1970), pp. 350–51.

16. Herbert Marcuse, *An Essay on Liberation* (Boston: Beacon Press, 1969), p. 89.

17. See Assar Lindbeck, *The Political Economy of the New Left: An Outsider's View*, 2d ed. (New York: Harper & Row, 1977).

18. Bernstein, *Regulating Business by Independent Commission*, p. 87.

19. Ibid., p. 92.

20. The capture theory is also presented effectively in Huntington, "Marasmus of the ICC." By the early 1970s, economists increasingly addressed the question of regulatory capture, albeit without the historical and institutional context provided in earlier analyses. See, e.g., George J. Stigler, "The Theory of Economic Regulation," *Bell Journal of Economics and Management Science*, 2, no. 1 (1971): 3–21.

21. Theodore J. Lowi, *The End of Liberalism: The Second Republic of the United States*, 2d ed. (New York: W. W. Norton, 1979), p. 51.

22. Ibid., p. 297. Also see Kenneth Culp Davis, *Discretionary Justice: A Preliminary Inquiry* (Baton Rouge: Louisiana State University Press, 1969).

23. Richard B. Stewart, "The Reformation of American Administrative Law," *Harvard Law Review* 88, no. 8 (1975): 1712.

24. Ibid., p. 1809.

25. See R. Shep Melnick, *Regulation and the Courts: The Case of the Clean Air Act* (Washington, D.C.: Brookings Institution, 1983), pp. 9–13.

26. See the discussion in Terry M. Moe, "The Politics of Bureaucratic Structure," in *Can the Government Govern?* ed. John E. Chubb and Paul E. Peterson (Washington, D.C.: Brookings Institution, 1989).

27. This discussion was shaped, in part, by William Gormley's comments on an earlier version of this argument presented to the annual meeting of the Midwest Political Science Association in 1991.

28. Gary C. Bryner, *Bureaucratic Discretion: Law and Policy in Federal Regulatory Agencies* (New York: Pergamon Press, 1987).

29. Andrew Shonfield, *Modern Capitalism: The Changing Balance of Public and Private Power* (London: Oxford University Press, 1965), p. 298.

30. This point is made in Graham K. Wilson, *Business and Politics: A Comparative Introduction*, 2d ed. (Chatham, N.J.: Chatham House, 1990), pp. 39–66.

31. See the discussion in Howard Ball, *Controlling Regulatory Sprawl: Presidential Strategies from Nixon to Reagan* (Westport, Conn.: Greenwood Press, 1984); and Chap. 8 below.

32. See Martha Derthick and Paul J. Quirk, *The Politics of Deregulation* (Washington, D.C.: Brookings Institution, 1985).

7   Regulating Risk: The Political Economy of the Societal Regime

1. Mark E. Rushefsky, "Elites and Environmental Policy," in *Environmental Politics and Policy: Theories and Evidence*, ed. James P. Lester (Durham, N.C.: Duke University Press, 1989), p. 262.

2. Walter A. Rosenbaum, "The Bureaucracy and Environmental Policy," in Lester, *Environmental Politics and Policy*, pp. 213–14.

3. For a review of the National Environmental Policy Act and its impact on administration, see Rosenbaum, "Bureaucracy and Environmental Policy." For a more detailed analysis, see Serge Taylor, *Making Bureaucracies Think: The Environmental Impact Statement Strategy of Administrative Reform* (Stanford, Calif.: Stanford University Press, 1984).

4. See Kenneth J. Meier, *Regulation: Politics, Bureaucracy, and Economics* (New York: St. Martin's Press, 1985), p. 143; John C. Esposito, *Vanishing Air: Ralph Nader's Study Group Report on Air Pollution* (New York: Grossman, 1970); and Charles O. Jones, *Clean Air: The Policies and Politics of Pollution Control* (Pittsburgh: University of Pittsburgh Press, 1975), pp. 175–210. On the politics surrounding the creation of the EPA and the wave of environmental legislation, see Richard A. Harris and Sidney M. Milkis, *The Politics of Regulatory Change: A Tale of Two Agencies* (New York: Oxford University Press, 1989).

5. Meier, *Regulation*, pp. 146–51; Paul R. Portney, "Air Pollution Policy," in *Public Policies for Environmental Protection*, ed. Paul R. Portney (Washington, D.C.: Resources for the Future, 1990).

6. R. Shep Melnick, *Regulation and the Courts: The Case of the Clean Air Act* (Washington D.C.: Brookings Institution, 1983), pp. 25–31.

7. Ibid., pp. 142–43.

8. Alfred Marcus, *Promise and Performance: Choosing and Implementing an Environmental Policy* (Westport, Conn.: Greenwood Press, 1980), pp. 141–49.

9. Arthur J. Magida, "EPA to Ask Congress to Relax Deadlines on Water Plan," *National Journal* 6, no. 51 (1974): 1903; Marcus, *Promise and Performance*, pp. 149–60, 168.

10. Quoted in Richard Corrigan, "EPA Ending Year-Long Shakedown Cruise; Ruckelshaus Cast as Embattled Spokesman," *National Journal* 3, no. 41 (1971): 2042. This section draws on Marcus, *Promise and Performance*, pp. 31–52; and Harris and Milkis, *Politics of Regulatory Change*, pp. 225–33.

11. See Marcus, *Promise and Performance*, pp. 44–45; and Richard Corrigan, "Success of New Agency Depends upon Ruckelshaus' Direction," *National Journal* 2, no. 47 (1970): 2591–95.

12. Corrigan, "Success of New Agency Depends upon Ruckelshaus' Direction," p. 2592. See the discussion of the EPA in Terry M. Moe, "The Politics of Bureaucratic Structure," in *Can the Government Govern?* ed. John E. Chubb and Paul E. Peterson (Washington, D.C.: Brookings Institution, 1989).

13. Marc K. Landy, Marc J. Roberts, and Stephen R. Thomas, *The Environmental Protection Agency: Asking the Wrong Questions* (New York: Oxford University Press, 1990), pp. 34–36.

14. Melnick, *Regulation and the Courts*, pp. 38–43; Gary C. Bryner, *Bureaucratic Discretion: Law and Policy in Federal Regulatory Agencies* (New York: Pergamon Press, 1987), pp. 98–100.

15. Corrigan, "EPA Ending Year-Long Shakedown Cruise," p. 2042; Landy, Roberts, and Thomas, *Environmental Protection Agency*, p. 34; Christopher J. Bosso, *Pesticides and Politics: The Life Cycle of a Public Issue* (Pittsburgh: University of Pittsburgh Press, 1987), pp. 152–54.

16. Marcus, *Promise and Performance*, p. 110.

17. Ibid., pp. 110–14.

18. This discussion of the rule-making process draws heavily on Bryner, *Bureaucratic Discretion*, pp. 94–105.

19. See Alfred A. Marcus, "Environmental Protection Agency," in *The Politics of Regulation*, ed. James Q. Wilson (New York: Basic Books, 1980).

20. See the argument in Moe, "Politics of Bureaucratic Structure."

21. Marcus, *Promise and Performance*, pp. 87–88.

22. This discussion of the courts relies on Melnick, *Regulation and the Courts*; and Lettie McSpadden Wenner, "The Courts and Environmental Policy," in Lester, *Environmental Politics and Policy*, pp. 238–60.

23. Melnick, *Regulation and the Courts*, pp. 343–60.

24. Ibid., pp. 71–80. See *Sierra Club v. Ruckelshaus*, 344 F. Supp. 253 (D. D.C. 1972); and James A. Noone, "Doubts about 'Clean' Fuels Fail to Deter

EPA, States, on Air Pollution Battle Plans," *National Journal* 4, no. 26 (1972): 1052.

25. *Kennecott Copper Corp. v. Environmental Protection Agency*, 462 F.2d 846 (D.C. Cir. 1972); Bryner, *Bureaucratic Discretion*, p. 96.

26. *Portland Cement Association v. Ruckelshaus*, 486 F.2d 375 (D.C. Cir. 1973). The expanded rule-making process was incorporated in the 1977 amendments to the Clean Air Act and are reviewed above.

27. Melnick, *Regulation and the Courts*, pp. 240–43. See Carlisle Ford Runge, "Economic Criteria and 'Net Social Risk' in the Analysis of Environmental Regulation," in *Environmental Policy under Reagan's Executive Order: The Role of Benefit-Cost Analysis*, ed. V. Kerry Smith (Chapel Hill: University of North Carolina Press, 1984), pp. 187–202.

28. *Lead Industries Association v. Environmental Protection Agency*, 647 F.2d 1130, 1149 (D.C. Cir. 1980).

29. *Ethyl Corp. v. Environmental Protection Agency*, 541 F.2d 1 (D.C. Cir. 1976). See Marcus, "Environmental Protection Agency."

30. *Buckeye Power Co. v. Environmental Protection Agency*, 481 F.2d 162 (6th Cir. 1973); *Appalachian Power Co. v. Environmental Protection Agency*, 477 F.2d 495 (4th Cir. 1973); *Duquesne Light Co. v. Environmental Protection Agency*, 481 F.2d 1 (3d Cir. 1973); *Union Electric Co. v. Environmental Protection Agency*, 427 U.S. 246 (1976). See Melnick, *Regulation and the Courts*, pp. 193–238.

31. Quoted in Corrigan, "EPA Ending Year-Long Shakedown Cruise," p. 2040.

32. Quoted in ibid., p. 2041.

33. See John Quarles, *Cleaning Up America* (Boston: Houghton Mifflin, 1976), pp. 30–36; Meier, *Regulation*, p. 146; and Richard S. Frank, "EPA and Justice Department Clash over Antipollution Enforcement," *National Journal* 3, no. 41 (1971): 2048–53.

34. See Marcus, *Promise and Performance*, pp. 90–94. Ruckelshaus is quoted in Noone, "Doubts about 'Clean' Fuels Fail to Deter EPA, States," p. 1051.

35. *Kennecott Copper Corp. v. Environmental Protection Agency*, 462 F.2d 846 (D.C. Cir. 1972).

36. See Corrigan, "EPA Ending Year-Long Shakedown Cruise," p. 2040; John F. Burby, "EPA Alive and Well, but Meeting Stiffer Resistance," *National Journal* 6, no. 12 (1974): 431–38; and Marcus, "Environmental Protection Agency," p. 289.

37. John F. Burby, "EPA's New Team Girds for Stubborn Fight to Fulfill Mandate," *National Journal* 6, no. 15 (1974): 533–43; and Landy, Roberts, and Thomas, *Environmental Protection Agency*, pp. 38–39.

38. Melnick, *Regulation and the Courts*, pp. 50–51. See Bruce Yandle, "The Emerging Market in Air Pollution Rights," *Regulation* 2, no. 4 (1978): 21–29.

39. J. Dicken Kirschten, "Environmentalists Come in from the Cold in Carter Administration," *National Journal* 9, no. 11 (1977): 382–84.

40. Melnick, *Regulation and the Courts*, p. 51.

41. Costle is quoted in Landy, Roberts, and Thomas, *Environmental Protec-*

tion Agency, pp. 40–42; see also J. Dicken Kirschten, "EPA: A Winner in the Annual Budget Battles," *National Journal* 10, no. 4 (1978): 140–41.

42. See Yandle, "Emerging Market in Air Pollution Rights"; M. T. Maloney and Bruce Yandle, "Bubbles and Efficiency: Cleaner Air at Lower Costs," *Regulation* 4, no. 3 (1980): 49–52; and T. H. Tietenberg, "Uncommon Sense: The Program to Reform Pollution Control Policy," in *Regulatory Reform: What Actually Happened?* ed. Leonard W. Weiss and Michael W. Klass (Boston: Little, Brown, 1986).

43. *ASARCO Inc. v. Environmental Protection Agency*, 578 F.2d 319 (D.C. Cir. 1978).

44. See the theoretical justification in Charles L. Schultze, *The Public Use of Private Interest* (Washington, D.C.: Brookings Institution, 1977).

45. Landy, Roberts, and Thomas, *Environmental Protection Agency*, pp. 247–50; Richard N. L. Andrews, "Deregulation: The Failure at EPA," in *Environmental Policy in the 1980s: Reagan's New Agenda*, ed. Norman J. Vig and Michael E. Kraft (Washington, D.C.: Congressional Quarterly, 1984), pp. 161–80; Lawrence Mosher, "Move over, Jim Watt, Ann Gorsuch Is the Latest Target of Environmentalists," *National Journal* 13, no. 43 (1981): 1900.

46. Mosher, "Move over, Jim Watt," pp. 1899, 1902; Lawrence Mosher, "Environmentalists Sue to Put an End to 'Regulatory Mass Resistance,'" *National Journal* 13, no. 51 (1981): 2233–34; and idem, "EPA Critics Agree Agency under Gorsuch Hasn't Changed Its Spots," ibid. 14, no. 46 (1982): 1941–44.

47. Landy, Roberts, and Thomas, *Environmental Protection Agency*, pp. 247–50; Meier, *Regulation*, pp. 163–68; Dick Kirschten, "Ruckelshaus May Find EPA's Problems Are Budgetary as Much as Political," *National Journal* 15, no. 13 (1983): 659–60.

48. Kirschten, "Ruckelshaus May Find EPA's Problems Are Budgetary"; Lawrence Mosher, "Ruckelshaus's First March on EPA—Another $165.5 Million for Its Budget," *National Journal* 15, no. 26 (1983): 1344–45; Landy, Roberts, and Thomas, *Environmental Protection Agency*, pp. 247–50; Lawrence Mosher, "'Acceptable' Risk—Can Government Decide Whether to Be Safe or Sorry?" *National Journal* 15, no. 49 (1983): 2529–32; and Rochelle L. Stanfield, "Global Guardian," ibid. 19, no. 50 (1987): 3138–42.

49. See the discussion of the origins of the Occupational Safety and Health Act in Charles Noble, *Liberalism at Work: The Rise and Fall of OSHA* (Philadelphia: Temple University Press, 1986), chap. 3. For a discussion of the debates about whether to locate OSHA in the executive branch, see Moe, "Politics of Bureaucratic Structure."

50. See the discussion in Noble, *Liberalism at Work*, pp. 68–98; and Meier, *Regulation*, pp. 202–10.

51. See W. Kip Viscusi, "Reforming OSHA Regulation of Workplace Risks," in Weiss and Klass, *Regulatory Reform*.

52. Steven Kelman, *Regulating America, Regulating Sweden* (Cambridge: MIT Press, 1981), p. 89.

53. Ibid.

54. James W. Singer, "New OSHA Head May Signal Change in Agency's Ap-

proach," *National Journal* 7, no. 51 (1975): 1725–34. See the discussion in Larry N. Gerston, Cynthia Fraleigh, and Robert Schwab, *The Deregulated Society* (Pacific Grove, Calif.: Brooks/Cole, 1988), pp. 177–78.

55. See the discussion of risk assessment in Mark E. Rushefsky, *Making Cancer Policy* (Albany: State University of New York Press, 1986), pp. 21–58.

56. See Steven Kelman, "Occupational Safety and Health Administration," in Wilson, *Politics of Regulation*.

57. This discussion of the OSHA policy process draws heavily on Bryner, *Bureaucratic Discretion*, pp. 121–33.

58. Ibid.

59. Graham K. Wilson, *The Politics of Safety and Health: Occupational Safety and Health in the United States and Great Britain* (Oxford: Oxford University Press, 1985), pp. 36–43.

60. Ibid., p. 105.

61. See *Industrial Union Department v. American Petroleum Institute*, 448 U.S. 607.

62. See the discussion of the origins of the asbestos standard in John Mendeloff, *Regulatory Safety: An Economic and Political Analysis of Occupational Safety and Health Policy* (Cambridge, Mass.: MIT Press, 1979), pp. 58–64.

63. *Industrial Union Department v. Hodgson*, 499 F.2d 467, 477–78 (D.C. Cir. 1974).

64. See the discussion of the cotton dust standard in W. Kip Viscusi, "Cotton Dust Regulation: An OSHA Success Story?" *Journal of Policy Analysis and Management* 4, no. 3 (1985): 325–43.

65. Ibid., quotation is from *American Textile Manufacturers Institute v. Donovan*, 452 U.S. 490 (1981).

66. For a more detailed overview of OSHA's relationship to the courts, see Wilson, *Politics of Safety and Health*, pp. 83–111.

67. See Timothy B. Clark, "What's All the Uproar over OSHA's 'Nit-Picking' Rules?" *National Journal* 10, no. 40 (1978): 1594–96.

68. See Charles Culhane, "Administration Works to Shift Safety, Health Programs to States Despite Labor Criticism," *National Journal* 4, no. 26 (1972): 1041–49; and idem, "Labor, Business Press Administration to Change Safety and Health Programs," ibid. 4, no. 27 (1972): 1093–1102.

69. See Linda E. Demkovich, "OSHA Launches Dual Effort to Reduce Job Health Hazards," *National Journal* 6, no. 49 (1974): 1831–39.

70. Quoted in James E. Singer, "New OSHA Head May Signal Change in Agency's Approach," *National Journal* 7, no. 51 (1975): 1727.

71. See James W. Singer, "New OSHA Task Force—Political Payoff or False Alarm?" *National Journal* 8, no. 28 (1976): 973–75; and Gerston, Fraleigh, and Schwab, *Deregulated Society*, pp. 178–79.

72. See James W. Singer, "A New OSHA Tries to Put Its Pieces Back Together Again," *National Journal* 9, no. 27 (1977): 1046–49; Philip J. Harter, "In Search of OSHA," *Regulation* 1, no. 5 (1977): 33–39; and Meier, *Regulation*, pp. 213–17.

73. Demkovich, "OSHA Launches Dual Effort," p. 1831.

74. See Meier, *Regulation*, pp. 215–16; and Rushefsky, *Making Cancer Policy*, pp. 88–94.

75. See Timothy B. Clark, "The 'Facts' about OSHA's 1,100 Revoked Regulations," *National Journal* 10, no. 28 (1978): 1298–99; and idem, "What's All the Uproar Over OSHA's 'Nit-picking' Rules?"

76. Quoted in Michael Wines, "They're Still Telling OSHA Horror Stories, but the 'Victims' Are New," *National Journal* 13, no. 45 (1981): 1985. See the discussion of the Reagan administration and OSHA in Noble, *Liberalism at Work*; Meier, *Regulation*, pp. 218–21; and Gerston, Fraleigh, and Schwab, *Deregulated Society*, pp. 184–93.

77. Figures drawn from Wines, "They're Still Telling OSHA Horror Stories," pp. 1985–86.

78. Gerston, Fraleigh, and Schwab, *Deregulated Society*, pp. 186–91.

79. Quoted in Kenneth Noble, "More Jeers by Critics and Cheers by Businessmen," *New York Times*, May 6, 1985; and Michael Wines, "Auchter's Record at OSHA Leaves Labor Outraged, Business Satisfied," *National Journal* 15, no. 40 (1983): 2008.

80. Gerston, Fraleigh, and Schwab, *Deregulated Society*, p. 190.

81. Wilson, *Politics of Safety and Health*, p. 64.

82. See "Environmental Protection Agency: A Clean Sweep," *National Journal* 17, no. 29 (1986): 1167–69; and Kirk Victor, "OSHA's Turnabout," ibid. 21, no. 47 (1991): 2889–92.

83. See Jonathan Rauch, "The Regulatory President," *National Journal* 23, no. 48 (1991): 2902–6.

84. Quoted in Lawrence Mosher, "Costle: The Reaganites Can't Erase the Environment's 'Real' Problems," *National Journal* 13, no. 2 (1981): 65.

85. *International Harvester Co. v. Ruckelshaus*, 478 F.2d 615, 650–51 (D.C. Cir. 1973), quoted in Melnick, *Regulation and the Courts*, p. 60.

8 Regulatory Reform and the Emergence of a New Regime

1. Richard A. Harris and Sidney M. Milkis, *The Politics of Regulatory Change: A Tale of Two Agencies* (New York: Oxford University Press, 1989), p. 293.

2. See the argument in Thomas Ferguson and Joel Rogers, *Right Turn: The Decline of the Democrats and the Future of American Politics* (New York: Hill & Wang, 1986).

3. The results of numerous opinion polls addressing regulation are reproduced in Robert Y. Shapiro and John M. Gillroy, "The Polls: Regulation—Part I," *Public Opinion Quarterly* 48 (1984): 531–42; and Robert Y. Shapiro and John M. Gillroy, "The Polls: Regulation—Part II," ibid. 48 (1984): 666–67. The Opinion Research Corporation conducted the polls, beginning in 1946 in one case, and in 1965 in the other. Both polls revealed growing concerns about profitability and growing demands for government regulation of business profits. The data from the years prior to the 1970s have been excluded from the discussion because of the subject matter addressed in this chapter.

4. Shapiro and Gillroy, "Polls: Regulation—Part I," pp. 535, 537.

5. Shapiro and Gillroy, "Polls: Regulation—Part II," p. 668.

6. Ibid., pp. 669, 671.

7. See the discussion in Graham K. Wilson, *Business and Politics*, 2d ed. (Chatham, N.J.: Chatham House, 1990), pp. 48–50; and Thomas Byrne Edsall, *The New Politics of Inequality* (New York: W. W. Norton, 1984), p. 113. See Vogel's argument regarding the resurgence of business during this critical period in David Vogel, *Fluctuating Fortunes: The Political Power of Business in America* (New York: Basic Books, 1989), p. 146.

8. Kay Lehman Schlozman and John T. Tierney, *Organized Interests and American Democracy* (New York: Harper & Row, 1986), pp. 76–77.

9. Ferguson and Rogers, *Right Turn*, pp. 86–88; Edsall, *New Politics of Inequality*, pp. 117–20.

10. Schlozman and Tierney, *Organized Interests and American Democracy*, pp. 222, 224, 249; Vogel, *Fluctuating Fortunes*, pp. 210–13.

11. James E. Alt and K. Alec Chrystal, *Political Economics* (Berkeley: University of California Press, 1983), pp. 103–25; and Douglas A. Hibbs, Jr., *The American Political Economy: Macroeconomics and Electoral Politics* (Cambridge: Harvard University Press, 1987), pp. 128, 176, 200–208.

12. *Economic Report of the President* (Washington, D.C.: Government Printing Office, 1979), pp. 87, 91.

13. See Marc Allen Eisner and Kenneth J. Meier, "Presidential Control versus Bureaucratic Power: Explaining the Reagan Revolution in Antitrust," *American Journal of Political Science* 34, no. 1 (1990): 269–87.

14. See George J. Stigler, "The Theory of Economic Regulation," *Bell Journal of Economics and Management Science* 2, no. 1 (1971): 3–21. See the discussion of Stigler in Kenneth J. Meier, *The Political Economy of Regulation: The Case of Insurance* (Albany: State University of New York Press, 1988).

15. See Richard A. Posner, "Theories of Economic Regulation," *Bell Journal of Economics and Management Science* 5, no. 3 (1974): 337–52; Sam Peltzman, "Toward a More General Theory of Regulation," *Journal of Law and Economics* 19 (August 1976): 211–40; and Thomas Romer and Howard Rosenthal, "Modern Political Economy and the Study of Regulation," in *Public Regulation: New Perspectives on Institutions and Policies*, ed. Elizabeth E. Bailey (Cambridge: MIT Press, 1987).

16. Robert C. Fellmeth, ed., *The Interstate Commerce Omission: The Public Interest and the ICC* (New York: Grossman, 1970), p. 37.

17. Mark J. Green, "Uncle Sam the Monopoly Man," in *The Monopoly Makers: Ralph Nader's Study Group Report on Regulation and Competition*, ed. Mark J. Green (New York: Grossman, 1973), pp. 4, 27.

18. Fellmeth, *Interstate Commerce Omission*, p. 190.

19. *Economic Report of the President, February 1975* (Washington, D.C.: Government Printing Office, 1975), p. 159.

20. Murray L. Weidenbaum, "On Estimating Regulatory Costs," *Regulation* 2, no. 3 (1978): 14–17.

21. Charles Noble, *Liberalism at Work: The Rise and Fall of OSHA* (Philadelphia: Temple University Press, 1986), p. 116.

22. See the discussion of cost-benefit analysis in James T. Campen, *Benefit, Cost, and Beyond: The Political Economy of Benefit-Cost Analysis* (Cambridge: Ballinger, 1986), pp. 58–60; and Steven Kellman, "Cost-Benefit Analysis: An Ethical Critique," *Regulation* 5, no. 1 (1981): 33–40.

23. See the discussion of the causes of inflation in Leon N. Lindberg, "Models of the Inflation-Disinflation Process," in *The Politics of Inflation and Economic Stagnation*, ed. Leon N. Lindberg and Charles S. Maier (Washington, D.C.: Brookings Institution, 1985).

24. George C. Eads and Michael Fix, *Relief or Reform? Reagan's Regulatory Dilemma* (Washington, D.C.: Urban Institute Press, 1984), pp. 46–48; Larry N. Gerston, Cynthia Fraleigh, and Robert Schwab, *The Deregulated Society* (Pacific Grove, Calif.: Brooks/Cole, 1988), pp. 42–43.

25. The process is reviewed in Eads and Fix, *Relief or Reform*, p. 48.

26. Ibid., pp. 49–50; Alfred A. Marcus, *Promise and Performance: Choosing and Implementing an Environmental Policy* (Westport, Conn.: Greenwood Press, 1980), pp. 125–27.

27. This discussion of COWPS draws on Howard Ball, *Controlling Regulatory Sprawl: Presidential Strategies from Nixon to Reagan* (Westport, Conn.: Greenwood Press, 1984), pp. 51–54; Eads and Fix, *Relief or Reform*, pp. 50–54; Gerston, Fraleigh, and Schwab, *Deregulated Society*, pp. 43–44; and Thomas O. McGarity, *Reinventing Rationality: The Role of Regulatory Analysis in the Federal Bureaucracy* (Cambridge: Cambridge University Press, 1991), pp. 18–19.

28. James C. Miller III, "Lessons of the Economic Impact Statement Program," *Regulation* 1, no. 4 (1977): 16, 18.

29. This is discussed in ibid., p. 17.

30. See the discussion of the Carter initiatives in Gerston, Fraleigh, and Schwab, *Deregulated Society*, pp. 44–48.

31. Eads and Fix, *Relief or Reform*, pp. 55–56.

32. McGarity, *Reinventing Rationality*, p. 19.

33. Gerston, Fraleigh, and Schwab, *Deregulated Society*, pp. 46–47.

34. Ibid.; Christopher DeMuth, "The White House Review Programs," *Regulation* 4, no. 1 (1980): 13–26.

35. Eads and Fix, *Relief or Reform*, pp. 61–62.

36. Ball, *Controlling Regulatory Sprawl*, pp. 58–60; Susan Tolchin, "Presidential Power and the Politics of RARG," *Regulation* 3, no. 4 (1979): 44–49; Gary C. Bryner, *Bureaucratic Discretion: Law and Policy in Federal Regulatory Agencies* (New York: Pergamon Press, 1987), pp. 134–40.

37. Susan J. Tolchin and Martin Tolchin, *Dismantling America: The Rush to Deregulate* (Boston: Houghton Mifflin, 1983), p. 49.

38. Eads and Fix, *Relief or Reform*, pp. 63–65.

39. Quoted in Dick Kirschten, "President Reagan after Two Years—Bold Actions but Uncertain Results," *National Journal* 15, no. 1 (1983): 7.

40. Quoted in Timothy B. Clark, "OMB to Keep Its Regulatory Powers in Reserve in Case Agencies Lag," *National Journal* 13, no. 11 (1981): 426.

41. Richard N. L. Andrews, "Economics and Environmental Decisions, Past and Present," in *Environmental Policy under Reagan's Executive Order: The Role of Benefit-Cost Analysis*, ed. V. Kerry Smith (Chapel Hill: University of

North Carolina Press, 1984), pp. 73–74; Ball, *Controlling Regulatory Sprawl*, pp. 66–68; and Timothy B. Clark, "If Reagan Wants to Trump the Regulators, Here's OMB's Target List for Openers," *National Journal* 13, no. 3 (1981): 94–98.

42. Quoted in Timothy B. Clark, "Do the Benefits Justify the Costs? Prove It, Says the Administration," *National Journal* 13, no. 31 (1981): 1382.

43. Office of Management and Budget, "Interim Regulatory Impact Analysis Guidance, June 12, 1981," in E. W. Kelley, *Policy and Politics in the United States: The Limits of Localism* (Philadelphia: Temple University Press, 1987), pp. 284–87; McGarity, *Reinventing Rationality*, p. 22.

44. Paul R. Portney, "The Benefits and Costs of Regulatory Analysis," in Smith, *Environmental Policy under Reagan's Executive Order*, pp. 229, 231.

45. Murray L. Weidenbaum, "Regulatory Reform under the Reagan Administration," in *The Reagan Regulatory Strategy: An Assessment*, ed. George C. Eads and Michael Fix (Washington, D.C.: Urban Institute Press, 1984), pp. 32, 34–35.

46. See Lawrence Mosher, "Will EPA's Budget Make It More Efficient or Less Effective," *National Journal* 13, no. 33 (1981): 1466–69; and William A. Niskanen, *Reaganomics: An Insider's Account of the Policies and the People* (New York: Oxford University Press, 1988), p. 131.

47. Ball, *Controlling Regulatory Sprawl*, pp. 93–97.

48. Jonathan Rauch, "The Regulatory President," *National Journal* 23, no. 48 (1991): 2902–6.

49. Kirk Victor, "Quayle's Quiet Coup," *National Journal* 23, no. 27 (1991): 1676–80.

50. Alfred Marcus, "Environmental Protection Agency," in *The Politics of Regulation*, ed. James Q. Wilson (New York: Basic Books, 1980), p. 289. Also see Eads and Fix, *Relief or Reform*, pp. 49–50.

51. Marc Allen Eisner, *Antitrust and the Triumph of Economics: Institutions, Expertise, and Policy Change* (Chapel Hill: University of North Carolina Press, 1991); Jeremy Tunstall, *Communications Deregulation: The Unleashing of America's Communications Industry* (Oxford: Basil Blackwell, 1986), p. 248; Martha Derthick and Paul J. Quirk, *The Politics of Deregulation* (Washington, D.C.: Brookings Institution, 1985), pp. 79–82; and Thomas K. McCraw, *Prophets of Regulation* (Cambridge: Harvard University Press, 1984), pp. 274–75.

52. Noble, *Liberalism at Work*, p. 191; Thomas F. Walton and James Langenfeld, "Regulatory Reform under Reagan—The Right Way and the Wrong Way," in *Regulation and the Reagan Era: Politics, Bureaucracy, and the Public Interest*, ed. Roger E. Meiners and Bruce Yandle (New York: Holmes & Meier, 1989), pp. 50–55.

53. See William Niskanen, *Bureaucracy and Representative Democracy* (Chicago: Aldine Atherton, 1971).

54. See Marc Allen Eisner, "Institutional History and Policy Change: Exploring the Origins of the New Antitrust," *Journal of Policy History* 2, no. 3 (1990): 262–89; and Thomas E. Kauper, "The Role of Economic Analysis in the Antitrust Division before and after the Establishment of the Economic Policy Office: A Lawyer's View," *Antitrust Bulletin* 29, no. 1 (1984): 111–32.

55. Marc K. Landy, Marc J. Roberts, and Stephen R. Thomas, *The Environ-*

mental Protection Agency: Asking the Wrong Questions (New York: Oxford University Press, 1990), pp. 214–22; and Errol Meidinger, "The Development of Emissions Trading in U.S. Air Pollution Regulation," in *Making Regulatory Policy*, ed. Keith Hawkins and John M. Thomas (Pittsburgh: University of Pittsburgh Press, 1989).

56. Meidinger, "Development of Emissions Trading," p. 183.

57. Joseph Auerbach and Samuel L. Hayes III, *Investment Banking and Diligence: What Price Deregulation?* (Boston: Harvard Business School Press, 1986), pp. 108–19; Joel Seligman, *The SEC and the Future of Finance* (New York: Praeger, 1985), pp. 195–280.

58. See Michael Pertschuk, *Revolt against Regulation: The Rise and Pause of the Consumer Movement* (Berkeley: University of California Press, 1982).

59. Vogel, *Fluctuating Fortunes*, p. 169.

60. Daniel P. Kaplan, "The Changing Airline Industry," in *Regulatory Reform: What Actually Happened*, ed. Leonard W. Weiss and Michael W. Klass (Boston: Little, Brown, 1986), pp. 42–44.

61. Stephen Breyer, *Regulation and Its Reform* (Cambridge: Harvard University Press, 1982), pp. 317–40.

62. Ibid., pp. 44–45; and Derthick and Quirk, *Politics of Deregulation*, pp. 76–77.

63. McCraw, *Prophets of Regulation*, pp. 274–77.

64. Kaplan, "The Changing Airline Industry," p. 45.

65. This discussion of the ICC draws on Thomas Gale Moore, "Rail and Trucking Deregulation," in Weiss and Klass, *Regulatory Reform*, pp. 14–39; and Derthick and Quirk, *Politics of Deregulation*.

66. Breyer, *Regulation and Its Reform*, p. 224.

67. Moore, "Rail and Trucking Deregulation," pp. 17–22.

68. Ibid., pp. 26–27; Derthick and Quirk, *Politics of Deregulation*, pp. 73–74, 97–98.

Conclusion

1. House Debates, 59th Congress, 1st sess., January 30–February 7, 1906, in *The Economic Regulation of Business and Industry: A Legislative History of U.S. Regulatory Agencies*, ed. Bernard Schwartz (New York: Chelsea House, 1973), 1: 626.

2. Ibid., p. 636.

3. See William T. Gormley, "Regulatory Issue Networks in a Federal System," *Polity* 18, no. 4 (1986): 595–620.

Index